ABOUT BEING NORMAL: MY LIFE IN ABNORMAL CIRCUMSTANCES

ALSO BY DESMOND FENNELL

Mainly in Wonder (1959)

The Changing Face of Catholic Ireland (1968)

The State of the Nation: Ireland since the 60s (1983)

Beyond Nationalism: The Struggle against Provincialism in the Modern World (1985)

Nice People and Rednecks: Ireland in the 1980s (1986)

A Connacht Journey (1987)

The Revision of Irish Nationalism (1989)

Bloomsway: A Day in the Life of Dublin (1990)

Heresy: The Battle of Ideas in Modern Ireland (1993)

Dreams of Oranges: An Eyewitness Account of the Fall of Communist East Germany (1996)

Uncertain Dawn: Hiroshima and the Beginning of Postwestern Civilisation (1996)

The Postwestern Condition: Between Chaos and Civilisation (1999)

The Turning Point: My Sweden Year and After (2001)

The Revision of European History (2003)

Cutting to the Point: Essays and Objections 1994–2003 (2003)

About Behaving Normally in Abnormal Circumstances (2007)

Ireland After the End of Western Civilisation (2009)

Third Stroke Did It: The Staggered End of European Civilisation (2012)

www.desmondfennell.com

ABOUT BEING NORMAL

MY LIFE IN ABNORMAL CIRCUMSTANCES

Desmond Fennell

SOMERVILLE PRESS

Somerville Press Ltd,
Dromore, Bantry,
Co. Cork, Ireland

First published 2017

Designed by Maurice Sweeney
Typeset in Bembo
maurice.sweeney@gmail.com

ISBN: 978 0 9955239 20

Printed and bound in Spain
by GraphyCems, Villatuerta, Navarra

*For my family who have
nourished me with their love*

CONTENTS

FOREWORD

ONE WRITES AN autobiography in order to tell the story of one's life to others. But what if throughout one's adult life one has already, at successive stages, written revelatory essays or passages that portray one's circumstances and observations, and one's simultaneous or near-simultaneous thoughts?

Being a writer and thinker I have done this repeatedly, and those successive circumstances and observations, and my thoughts about them and about my country or the world, form the evolving core of my long life story. Rather than attempting to recall and reconstruct in words from the present point in time the successive stages of that evolving core, I prefer to present such writings in a roughly chronological order, with occasional linking narrative. It will make, I believe, for a more accurate, immediate and 'live' way of telling my life-story.

Increasingly from page 17 onwards, it becomes obvious that my central preoccupations have been man and the instance of mankind that is called Ireland.

Desmond Fennell
Dublin 2017

PART 1:
FROM OBSERVATION
TO IDEALISM, 1929-1980

CHILDHOOD CHRISTMAS *

WHEN MY TWELVE-YEAR-OLD sister Rosemary writes a letter to Santa Claus and looks forward eagerly to his coming, I often wonder is she very shrewd or merely very innocent. I like to think that the angel who guards the magic of childhood has given her a more than ordinary wisdom—a blessed reluctance to tear that veil of spider-silk which bears no patching. For Santa Claus is surely the focal point of the enchanted adventure which Christmas meant for all of us children, and when we ceased to believe in him we ceased to be children.

I must have been very young when I listened in amazement while the Santa Claus in a Dublin shop told me of his trip from the North Pole and greatest of thrills pointed out to me the actual balloon suspended from the ceiling by which he had travelled. I still remember the feeling of reverence with which I reached up to receive a present from the very hands of Santa as he smiled from the chimney of his cottage in Woolworths of Belfast. But my loss of faith in the 'shop Santa Clauses' in no way weakened my belief in the true one. I did not even regard them as imposters but rather they took the place in the ritual of my Santa religion that Catholics give to statues of the saints. They 'excited my devotion', reminding me of and prefiguring the real and true, the venerable Santa Claus.

By the time I had become a sceptic, people were not so anxious that I go to bed early and the really significant change occurred. At first I was allowed to help in putting up the decorations; later I was given the job as my very own. I had been taken from the pit where all was a world of fantasy and put in charge of the props and the scenery. Child no longer and not yet adult, I was left standing in the wings, and from there I watched the make-believe go on for the benefit of my young sisters.

But if I became an infidel at least I refused to turn blasphemer. There had always been something holy about my feeling for Santa Claus and I was grateful to him. I felt no inclination now to join in mockery of those who still believed and in a vague way I felt there was something wrong, something sacrilegious almost, about

* From *The Leader,* Dublin, Christmas 1950.

my father's attempt to capture Santa by smearing glue around the fireplace.

My childhood Christmases were spent in Belfast and that city of necessity clings to all my Christmas memories. The Belvue Tram had a very special place in creating that enchanted atmosphere which seems to me now to have swirled around and transformed those days at the end of December. This was a tram all lit with rows of lights which used to pass our house at a particular time each night for a number of nights before Christmas. Its purpose was to advertise the Carnival at Belvue. But in my imagination it was much more than a tram with rows of lights; I knew it was a tram, of course, but that was a troublesome detail best forgotten. It was associated in my mind with all that was wonderful and magical, with the sparkling treasure-chambers of the Arabian Nights and the jewelled gateway of heaven.

While those mental associations come to me vaguely now as from a distant world there is one very concrete incident which will never allow me forget the Belvue Tram. I was getting ready for bed one Christmas Eve in the room on the very top of our three-storey house. I had on my pyjama-trousers but nothing else when I was tempted to look out and see if the tram were coming. The lower part of the window was up, and leaning out as far as I could I looked up the road. Just then the window-sash fell gently onto my back, pinning me. I could neither move backwards nor raise the window. I began to call 'Granny' at the top of my voice. Again and again I called, piteously and at length desperately. Nothing happened. I noticed vaguely a small group of passers-by gathered on the footpath across the road looking up at me. At last there was a noise of doors downstairs, a rush of feet on the stairs behind me, and then my mother was in the room and lifting the window. The dentist's wife next door had seen the crowd collecting and, not knowing what the cause was, had come round to give the alarm. Not even she had heard my shouts. I think everyone was quite amused but all I remember is my mother's remark that she was sorry she hadn't taken advantage of the position in which I was pinned to give me a good 'skelping'.

Of course, the journey to Belfast whether by train or car was the gateway to the magic world and was full of anticipation and excitement. The arrival was an adventure—the specially installed miniature church in the railway station emitting hymn after hymn through its gleaming gold windows, the old familiar whine of the trams pregnant with memories, the great Christmas tree at the City Hall being decorated for its Christmas Eve illumination. Then, at the house which was veritable home for me, joyful welcomings and showers of kisses and my grandmother's arms wide open for her 'dear big son'.

It was, as I said, only when I became an infidel and banished myself from the Eden of childhood that I had to work by the sweat-of-my-brow and take a share in the preparations for Christmas. There was one task, however, which I cannot remember ever having been too young to perform. I mean the grating of breadcrumbs for the stuffing of the turkey. I enjoyed this work. It was a delight to demolish those formidable loaves into great heaps of fleecy crumbs. It gave me a sense of achievement when I saw the white mass mount up inside the great enamelled bread-bin which was the receptacle we used on this occasion. I suppose too that amid the fuss and bustle it gave me that feeling of being needed, of 'belonging' somewhere, which every child yearns for.

Midnight Mass was an experience of my adolescence. Before that I used always go to early Mass on Christmas morning, usually with my grandfather. How I loved those mornings! Just as in my childhood superstition Sundays always turned out fine and Good Friday always rained in torrents, Christmas morning too had its peculiar quality. Sometimes there was a light coating of snow, but it never rained and the air was always indescribably fresh. I think this dry freshness and the peace of the morning in contrast with the hectic bustle of the days before gave it its atmosphere of exhilaration. I loved when we met people and I could chime in my 'Happy Christmas' in accompaniment to my grandfather's greeting. Perhaps the joy and freshness that appeared to reign in the streets and in the church at Mass came only from my own heart—but I think it was more than that. I believe that in some way people who are together have a power without speaking to, or even knowing each other, of communicating a sentiment, creating an atmosphere.

As for the beauties of the Christmas liturgy, I am afraid they had to wait for later years for appreciation for 'where your treasure is...' and my treasures of the moment were at home stuffed in a grey stocking and scattered at the foot of the Christmas tree. The Crib, of course, was a delight, but it could hardly have been otherwise and I have never ceased to find it so.

Christmas morning passed with much excitement and a furore of cooking, and the dining-room table put on its Christmas clothes. The magic of the Christmas table was due to my aunt's never-failing ingenuity. The paper-napkins and table-mats with their holly branches and reindeer and sleds full of Santa and toys and cheering children, the strips of coloured ribbon, the little clay figures of 'fellows' all muffled up in Santa-red suits lying on the snow of the table-cloth or caught frozen, with one foot in the air, while scampering over it; the square of frozen water remarkably like a piece of mirror glass amid scintillating frost and cotton wool snow with more little fellows tumbling and sliding. These things and more unusual inventions used to set the fibres of my imagination a-tingle. For years now when I look at the Christmas table and see merely pretty decorations, I am amazed at my own prosaic mind and I wonder to what place above or beneath the earth has fled that other vision.

In the late afternoon some of us would rouse ourselves—the grown-ups from their books and the fire or their postprandial nap, and I from my dreamland of toys—and take a walk in the thickening twilight. At that hour in those Belfast suburbs there hung a great quiet, and the whine of a tram or the rumble of a bus was rare and lonely. The shuttling intercourse of the city was, for the moment, no more and its life had disintegrated into thousands of little groups gathered around Christmas trees. You could see the tree in every window, whether of houses right on the footpath's edge—as so many are in Belfast —or in windows of houses standing back behind gardens, with shrubs or a shadowy tree thickening the darkness and showing up the fairy lights with greater brilliance. Almost every tree had its fairy-lights and in few houses (till the war came) were blinds drawn, so that to walk along a road was a thrilling experience. The warm glow of light in the room, or if the tree were the only source of light, the dancing shadows of a fire on the wallpaper and pictures—these in contrast to the sharp clear air and the gathering darkness outside produced an effect of homeliness and warmth, of intimate family atmosphere, that told me I was looking at the soul of Christmas. And then we would arrive back home and find it all around our own Christmas tree and by the great coal fire which was the pride of my grandfather.

Adolescence was to bring other joys to Christmas of a different and sometimes a deeper kind. An *Adeste Fideles* would move me to tears, there would be nights of 'Consequences' and 'Postman's Knock' and Dublin's Moore Street on a foggy December evening with its stalls and crowds, its lights and its whole gamut of the calls of Christmas would hold me spellbound. But the magic of childhood which gave its own strange thrills to Christmas and which our adult language is unable to express, that magic went with that other 'me' into the fairy hills and like the lost children of Hamelin has not been heard of since.

My father, Tom Fennell, a Sligoman, had met my mother, Julia Carolan, when as a tea salesman he visited her father's grocery shop in Belfast. After marrying in Belfast, they left for America where my father got a good job with the Bay State Fishing Company. When my mother was pregnant with me, they returned to Belfast for the birth, staying with the Carolan family: my grandfather Francis Carolan, his wife Jenny—both from Co. Tyrone—my uncle Bonnie and aunt Geraldine. (Another uncle, Edmund, had settled in New York.)

After my birth in 1929 my parents returned to America, leaving me in the care of grandparents, uncle and aunt until I was nearly four. In 1933, after my father had lost his job due to the American Depression, they returned to Belfast with a sister Geraldine for me and shortly after left again, this time for Dublin, taking me with them. There we spent a few months on the Hill of Howth in what I think was a wooden house before moving to a house-cum-grocery-shop in East Wall, Dublin. After a year or two we moved to a house with front and back garden in Clontarf, where I grew up. After attending the local Holy Faith Convent school for a couple of years, I was sent to the Christian Brothers' O'Connell School. When my primary education was finished I cycled daily to the Jesuits' Belvedere College (where, I later learned, James Joyce had been a pupil).

The parental regime, with my father at the helm, was strict and oppressive, especially for me as the eldest. He did two cruel things to me and some sneaky things. But I adapted with stoic fortitude to, among other things, not being allowed consort with the local boys, let alone girls. My father, a good businessman, established a prosperous wholesale grocery business in the city centre. Some nights he read Dickens to the assembled family. A second sister, Rosemary, was born in 1938. During the war years 1939-45 I learned to enjoy vegetable gardening in our back garden. For some weeks of my summer holidays from school, my father had me work for his business, cycling around Dublin taking orders from his shopkeeper customers. In my later teens I found freedom and pleasure in two ways: by getting up early, going to the nearby park of Clontarf Castle and, with the help of two little Oxford books of British birds and trees, identifying some of both, and then going to 7 o'clock Mass in the local church; alternatively, by going on all-day cycling trips with Mark Downes, a boy from the local Big House who was a good companion.

I experienced no love from my parents, rather a hope (especially by my mother) that I, by going on to university—the first in my extended family to do so— could become the Irish Ambassador to Paris or some such glamorous public person. (Later I came to sympathise with my parents as unconnected immigrants in Dublin striving to move up socially by whatever means they had.) The love in my life came from my Belfast family. Uncle Bonnie and Aunt Geraldine visited us occasionally (Bonnie, like his sister a schoolteacher, told me he thought the parental regime too strict). On Christmas visits to Belfast my grandfather and grannie made me feel cherished. One summer after her death, when uncle and aunt were on holiday, I was sent to Belfast to look after grandad. I cooked for him and spoke a little Irish with him that he recalled haltingly from his youth in Glenelly, Co. Tyrone, in the later nineteenth century.

At the Christian Brothers' O'Connell School I learned Irish, at the Jesuits' Belvedere College Latin, Greek, French and German; the first two

leading to an entrance scholarship to University College Dublin (UCD),
where I studied History and Economics; the latter two to first places in
Ireland in the Leaving Certificate Examination. A Belvedere school report
to my parents said that Desmond should play rugby to learn team spirit.
For a year I took part in rugby practice and disliked that it often rained
and that the rules allowed players to knock me down. I preferred the school
debating societies in Irish and English.

At university, the Catholic lay apostolate Opus Dei, founded in Spain,
had begun recruiting. I joined its male section. They had a house in Dublin
which I visited occasionally. When I was 21, I left my parents' house and
moved in with my Opus Dei colleagues to the great anger of my father.

VOCAL AT UCD ⋆

IN THE BEGINNING, nationality was a fact; in the beginning, that is, of
the modern world, when a fluid Europe was settling into its moulds.
It was a fact but it was nothing more. It had not yet been kindled
into a vital idea by friction with the mind of man. The reality was
the independently growing traditions of government, the particular
views of life reflected in institutions and usages. When men sensed
the binding ties, they sensed also the dividing differences. Nationality from being an ignored fact became a conception in the mind
of man. Nationality, the living idea, was generated and born. The
cultivation of that idea and its use as a motive force and a source of
inspiration in every field of activity is nationalism. If the concept of
nationalism is a whole code of ideas and principles based on a central idea; nationality was based on a fundamental reality, nationalism
is the creative product of that fact.

It is worthwhile to have our terms clear before turning to Ireland.

⋆ From 'The State of the Nation' in *The National Student*, UCD, Feb. 1949. A 19-year-old
student of history is trying to identify the components of his world and his stance with regard to them. Our history professor, Robin Dudley Edwards, recommended it to the class
as 'worth reading'. Later in a book I would change my definition of a nation and accept
that the Irish still formed one, but an abnormal one. From that first publication onwards I
was fated to be a close scrutiniser and frequent challenger of the conventional naming and
descriptions of things.

The inhabitants of this island from a very early time had every claim to nationhood. Distinctive methods of government, distinctive laws and language, distinctive social habits made up the necessary basic reality. Our insularity and the fact that we were uncontaminated by the 'one world, one Empire' tradition of Roman government helped to bring about the early awareness of nationality which developed in Ireland. If, however, the Irish anticipated Europe by hundreds of years in the conception of nationality, it was from Europe that the later creed of nationalism came to us. It gave us another spiritual justification of our struggle for survival. We mingled it with our religion, assimilated it into our very nature. The Irish anticipated Europe by hundreds of years in the conception of nationality; it was from Europe that the later creed of nationalism came to us. It gave us another spiritual justification of our struggle for survival. We mingled it with our religion, assimilated it into our very nature.

Obviously nationalism had a purpose in Ireland. It raised the people to a pitch of national effort which had its culmination in 1921. The greatness of the effort brought exhaustion, the greatness of the gain of freedom made a people used to failure believe they had won everything.

The elation and relief of the moment caused the incompleteness of the gain to be ignored. The civil war obscured the national cause and drained the nation's heart to apathy. Nationalism, for the ordinary man, seemed to have gained its purpose. And even if nationalism had not lost its purpose, the people wishfully hoped it had done so.

But all the time, as the nationalistic tempo had been rising to a crescendo, the basic reality of nationality was disappearing. Nationality was changing from an idea based on fact to a myth based on a vivid imagination and memory. Perhaps it was a sense of urgency springing from a subconscious awareness of the vanishing foundations which gave impetus to the final nationalist effort.

Ideas of government and legal justice had been among the first of the nation's hallmarks to fade and change. Dress, etiquette, notions of culture and education, language—all the many things which make up a people's tradition and right to nationhood—followed. It was not merely that they changed—that was happening everywhere—

but they became alienated, separated from the stream of national thought and tradition. In all these things what was distinctively Irish gradually ceased to exist. In all these things the standards and ideas of the English-speaking world came to be our ideas and standards.

Our parliament modelled on Westminster, our laws largely English, our etiquette and social usage English, English the language of almost the entire country, what claim have we to nationhood? Race? But purity of race is not essential to nationhood, and anyhow our Danish, Norman, Scots and English elements would be something of a stumbling-block. Tradition and history? But we have separated ourselves from our traditions and our present ideas have their roots elsewhere. Exiled from our national heritage, our history is merely the story of our biological antecedents.

We have coins of our own and stamps and a tricolour and a national anthem, and our letter-boxes are painted emerald green, but the basic fact of nationality—distinctive national institutions and culture and way of life—are non-existent. Our nationality is a myth of imagination. Those things which make up a nation we just have not got.

It is these hard facts which give urgency to our efforts to regain the Six Counties. Our real motives are a sense of duty to our co-religionists and a hope of economic advantage. But our greatest impetus must be nationalism, and the apathy of the ordinary people concerning partition is evidence of how weak that force is. People will not be nationalistic without a sufficient purpose, and just now the people refuse to realise that regaining the Six Counties is a sufficient purpose. But underlying it all is the natural difficulty of being nationalistic when there is no nation to begin with. If we are ever to get back the Six Counties it must be before the last vestiges of nationalism follow the last traces of nationality into the realm of non-existence.

The disappearance of our nation (apart from its effects on nationalism and partition) should not in reality alarm us. Nations are not indispensable to human life or to the full self-realisation of the individual. They are not primordial. We were created not into nations but into the general world of men. The modern nations are no better a foundation for our serious ideas and thought than were the city-states which Aristotle believed eternal. And the much talked-of disappearance of the Irish nation does not mean the disappearance of you and me or of any of us. The proof of that is that the Irish nation is no longer a fact—we are a people certainly but not a nation—while you and I are still very much facts. The most it can mean will be a change of outlook, a shift of ideals, a certain amount of revaluation.

The nationalist dream, built around a living idea of nationality with its roots in solid fact, had a good chance of accomplishment. The sooner we realise that the basic reality has gone, the better for ourselves. The persistence of half Europe in its persuasion that the Roman Empire was still in existence centuries after it had ceased to be caused a great deal of trouble and did little good. Hegel, speaking of greatness in men who have made history, said: 'They were thinking men who had an insight into the requirements of the time— what was ripe for development. This was the very Truth for their age, for their world, the species next in order so to speak which was already formed in the womb of time. It was theirs to know this nascent principle.' The greatness of a people also, if it is to be great, lies in the timely perception of the part it is called upon to play.

When we cease to be a national entity, of what larger comity will we become a part? Will it be a new medieval commonwealth with the English language and the British tradition taking the place of Latin and Rome, or a union of Europe and America around an Atlantic Mediterranean sea or a revived Catholic Christendom? These are pressing questions.

The nationalism of the old European world is undergoing a general weakening. No nation has been so completely denationalised as Ireland. Neither has any European country a population so far-flung. Irish radiation has formed a vast kinship which by its very lack of the impediments of nationality is eminently pliable and adaptable. In it exists the nucleus of an extended fatherland.

This is the case whether we perceive it or not, but if these facts are to have life and creative power, we must grasp them with our minds, kindle and nourish them with our understanding.

❖

My two sisters won parental approval. While piano lessons (The Hungar-

ian Rhapsody!) had bored me, Geraldine became adept on the traditional Irish harp. While she too disapproved of me, Rosemary and I were, despite the disparity of ages, pals. Both of them did a degree in Economics, Roman Law, Jurisprudence and Political Science at UCD and went on to get MAs. Rosemary pursued a professional career that had to do mainly with agricultural policy, particularly in the EU. First she worked in An Foras Talúntais (The Agricultural Institute), then in the British Ministry of Agriculture; later, as a lecturer for four years at Wye College, London University, while taking a PhD; and finally for many years at Oxford University into a still flourishing retirement. In her free time she published four books on the Best Street Markets in France and visited much of the world. Geraldine first worked as a curator in the National Museum in Dublin, then spent a stint in an economics institute in Switzerland. She finally opted for marketing psychology which she pursued academically mainly in the US, later transatlantically from Belfast, where Aunt Geraldine and Uncle Bonnie still lived. Aggrieved over her inherited share of the modest parental estate, she had separated from the rest of the family and did not report to us the deaths of those two loved persons. She died at age 82 in Belfast. Neither of my sisters married.

TO SISTER GERALDINE ON HER BIRTHDAY★

Geraldine, Geraldine,
You're seventeen today.
Listen to the chaffinch chirping,
Seagull crying, blackbird whistling.
I can tell you what they say –
'Geraldine, Geraldine,
You're seventeen today.'
Once a cooing baby,
Now you're seventeen,
Think of all the joys and sadness,
All the good sense, all the madness,
That have come and gone between.

★ Written at age 20.

Geraldine, Geraldine,
You're seventeen today.
Churchbells clanging all the morning,
Flinging out a ringing warning
For the city to be gay.
'Geraldine, Geraldine,
Is seventeen today.'

Think of all the long years,
That have still to come.
May your springtime see the flowering
Of your heart's desires, while showering
Almond-blossoms on your way.

Geraldine, Geraldine,
Today you're seventeen.
One thing at the end I ask you—
When the years are flitting past you.
Rubbing off the summer sheen,
Geraldine, Geraldine,
Be always seventeen.

Having got my BA in History and Economics in 1950, I wanted an MA in Modern History. I wrote to the Rector of Bonn University asking him to grant me a scholarship for a semester and almost by return of post got it. Prof Desmond Williams was my MA supervisor. At 29 he was the youngest professor ever appointed in UCD. With a German wife he had returned from Germany where he had been working in Berlin for British Intelligence on the German war archives. An inspiring lecturer, he combined wisdom about the human condition with the historical narrative. The subject he gave me for my MA thesis was 'The Catholic workers' movement in the Rhineland in 1848'.

His three pieces of advice to me prior to departure were: Note how German children retain a sense of wonder longer than Irish children; note the outstanding human qualities of German women schoolteachers (he had married one!); read the German Romantic writers (of the early nineteenth century).

In Bonn I found lodgings with a Silesian family who had fled before the advancing Russian army. Bonn was then the political capital of West Germany and that country was flourishing amid its remaining ruins under the impetus of Ludwig Erhard's Social Market Economy. A few days after my arrival in early November for the start of the Winter semester came St Martin's feastday, a big day in the Catholic Rhineland, especially for children. Aedan O'Beirne was the Irish diplomatic representative in Bonn. At twilight on that day I stood with him on a hotel balcony and, as all the city's churchbells tolled, watched ten thousand children in ordered rows, each child bearing a Chinese lantern, walk singing through the darkening city centre.

I got down to my research in the university library and joined the non-duelling student fraternity Rheinfels which involved much formal beer-drinking with lads who had fought in Russia. When the sixth of December, the feast of St Nicholas, arrived, it was a matter of sitting with adults and children around a table and, while the menacing figure of Knecht Ruprecht stood ready with his broom to whack misbehaving children, sing 'Nicholas ist ein guter Mann, den man nicht genug loben kann' *and so on. There remained only a couple of weeks to Christmas with its Midnight Mass hymns, and darkness followed by bright light, followed by presents for everyone from the* Christkind *(Child Jesus). I was falling in love with Germany and understood why German, or at least Rhineland, children retain their sense of wonder longer than Irish children.*

A friend who had a connection with the trade union movement put in a word for me in that quarter, and because the subject of my thesis had to do with German working-class history, the trade union federation, the Gewerkschaftsbund, paid for a second semester at the university on condition that I present them with a bound copy of my thesis. Before leaving Germany, I travelled to Hamburg with a commission from RTÉ to report on an opera performance by a company that had visited Dublin. Apart from enjoying the world openness of that great port city, and in particu-

lar the large saltwater lake, the Alster, at its centre, I went at night to the
Reeperbahn, the famous night-life and brothel quarter full of sex shops and
striptease joints. It was my first visit to such a place and I was deeply upset
by this 'festival of the woman's body' as I called it in the article I later
wrote, 'Aifreann, Opera agus Gnéas i Hamburg', for the Irish-language
magazine Comhar.

I travelled via Ostende, Dover and Holyhead back to Dublin, did an
exam in European diplomatic history (The Congress of Vienna) and was
awarded an MA. Opus Dei wanted me to go to Spain to teach English
in a secondary school they had opened in the port city of Bilbao, in the
Basque Country. I did that. The school was in Algorta, a wealthy sub-
urb on the sea. My colleagues were diverse and congenial Spaniards. For
the older boys I instituted visits to the concerts of the Bilbao Symphony
Orchestra. I accompanied the head, Isidoro, to the US for a study tour of
American schools. Because our school was starting from scratch most of
the pupil intake was very young. At the end of three years there—by then
speaking Spanish fluently—I was aware that I wanted to teach young
children about as much as I had wanted to play rugby! I wanted to write,
freelance journalism for a start—I had done some in Spanish—and I
obtained permission to return to the Rhineland.

ABOUT BEHAVING NORMALLY IN
ABNORMAL CIRCUMSTANCES ★

It was…Lessing who did a man's part in giving the
German nation confidence in itself and in its star.
Ireland's present condition is incomparably worse
than Germany's ever was; and not one but an entire
battalion of Lessings would be needed to establish a
normal state of mind among us. One can but predi-
cate not one Lessing nor a succession of them, but
rather a succession of nationalistic movements, rising
and falling, each dissolving into a period of reaction,
of provincialism, yet each for all that leaving the na-

★ From book of that title (Athol Books, Belfast, 2007) as retrospect on my writing life.

> tion a little more sturdy, a little more *normal,* a little
> less provincial than before. —Daniel Corkery, 1930
> [*italics added*].

IN LITERATE NATIONS it has long been normal that someone occasionally travels to places and peoples quite alien to the nation's way of life and frame of reference and writes about them for his or her compatriots. But in modern times up to 1959, when my book *Mainly in Wonder* appeared—dealing initially with my travels in Central Europe, Italy and Communist Yugoslavia, but devoted mainly to Japan and India—no Irish writer had done this. I say 'Irish' in the unhyphenated sense, and with reference therefore to those Irish, the great majority, whose ancestors were colonised and whose typical religion or cultural background has been and is Catholic. True, Kate O'Brien and Sean O'Faolain had written about journeys in Spain and Italy respectively; but those two countries were seen by the authors and their compatriots as 'Catholic countries like Ireland', and therefore as formally related to the essentially Gaelic, Catholic nation that the Irish of those days believed they constituted. On the non-Catholic world, Irish writing, as I have defined it, was silent. Most strikingly, the intense involvement, over forty-years, of thousands of Irish missionaries in pagan sub-Saharan Africa and in the Far East had not resulted in accounts of those countries or scholarly studies of their pagan, Muslim or Buddhist cultures.

The instinct to think, write or do things which had not been thought, written or done before by any compatriot (though not for that reason) had been part of my make-up since my student days. From *Mainly in Wonder* onwards, I was regularly thinking, writing and doing things which had not been done before in my social environment. That was true not only of those writing excursions into 'alien' territories which began with *Mainly in Wonder;* it was also true of another innovative feature of my writing which emerged in the late 1960s and which I will deal with in its place. The fact that these two features became recurrent resulted in a dual conflict of my writing with the norms of Irish writing generally. I understand better now, in retrospect, the nature of that conflict. I can now throw this greater explanatory light on my writing for those who have followed me all or part of the way.

My Asian journey was followed, a few years later, by visits to two countries which were proclaiming their post-Christian breakthroughs: Sweden, then regarded as the avant-garde country of the West on account of its innovative social welfare system and its 'pagan' sexual mores, and the officially atheistic Soviet Union. Having persuaded the London publisher of *Mainly in Wonder* to commission a book on Sweden, I spent a year there researching and writing it. From Moscow, under Khrushchev, I sent a series of fifteen articles to *The Irish Times*, the first account of Soviet life by an Irish writer to appear in an Irish newspaper.

What caused me, a Gaelic-speaking, Catholic Irishman to travel to that succession of 'alien' places and to write about them? My interest in the human condition in its various presentations—present, past and possible future—and the fact that I was a writer. More precisely, being a writer and with that general interest in the back of my mind, I became successively interested in those particular human realities to the point of entering into them, investigating them and reporting on them, with judgments and conclusions. In so doing, I did what many men and women of many nations had done when similarly impelled, though not always necessarily by travelling. I behaved normally. But in so doing I was stepping outside the norm of writing that held sway in Ireland.

That norm, tacitly accepted by writers, academics, publishers and the public at large, was to the effect that Irish writers and academics wrote only about Ireland or, very occasionally, about Ireland-related matters abroad. I am not talking about fictive writers who might well, on occasion, set a novel, a poem or a play in a non-Irish milieu; such writing is not an account of any reality. I am talking about realistic writing about the non-Irish world—that is, description, judgment and definition of it, historically or in the present—and my point is that, in the prevalent Irish way of seeing things, that was a role proper to members of that alien world; or more simply, to Anglo-Irish people, Englishmen, and other foreigners. So omnicompetent indeed was the role assumed by these non-Irish categories that they might also, if they so wished, join with Irish writers in writing about Ireland. In the prevalent Irish view, the world of mankind was *their* oyster. As a consequence, my normal behaviour was abnormality, had an alien flavour. Without intention or even awareness on my part, but simply by following where my interest led me, I was breaking a tacit rule of my tribe.*

What was it that caused the Irish, in the matter of writing about the world, to perceive that division of roles between themselves and all others? I want to answer that with some precision, and with the view of hindsight. Generally speaking, during the Revolution and the decades that followed it, the Irish saw themselves, collectively, through the prism of an inherited nationalism which in that period took its definitive republican shape. That nationalism depicted them as members of the essentially Gaelic and Catholic nation that since ancient times had owned and inhabited all of Ireland, and was therefore entitled to exercise dominion over it as an independent republic. 'Essentially Gaelic and Catholic' paralleled British nationalism's view of its multi-ethnic monarchical nation as essentially Anglo-Saxon and Protestant. (Both nationalisms allowed for membership of the nation by persons who, by descent or religion, lacked the essential attributes, provided they gave their allegiance to a nation and state characterised by those qualities.)

The Irish nation, thus immutably characterised and with 'anti-imperialist' added, was in its nationalist vision further distinguished by something like a superior racial quality from humanity generally, as represented by the Anglo-Irish, the English and other foreigners. Its nature, thus effectively *non*-human, was superior to human nature because, while in worldly—intellectual and practical —respects its endowments might be less than the norm, in what really mattered, the spiritual and moral spheres, they were greater.

It was a colonised nationalist vision, dwelling in unreality. Colonisation dispossesses a people of reality by taking from them the perception of themselves as human. More precisely, it induces them to regard themselves as constituting a version of humanity which differs radically from the norm; a version which is seriously deficient

---

* It is nevertheless true that, because of the physical and mental outreach of their work, I have felt a kinship, as among Irish writers, with the poet Desmond O'Grady and the novelists Brian Moore, Francis Stuart, Aidan Higgins and John Banville. And inasmuch as 'the world' also comprises abstract realities, I was later to feel a colleaguely, Irish kinship with Richard Kearney for the uninhibited adventurousness in the world of ideas which he would exhibit from the 1970s onwards.

in those intellectual and practical faculties, and related autonomies, by means of which human beings tackle and control the world. Colonised by the English, the 'native' Irish shaped a nationalist self-image which took as given this effective dispossession of humanity. But in order to motivate them towards regaining their lost political dominion, that nationalist image transformed their non-humanity into a positive value by affirming the higher nature of spiritual and moral endowments and Ireland's more-than-human possession of these. Thus, Irish non-humanity became a two-tiered thing: an affirmed superhumanity resting on an assumed subhuman base. By not perceiving normal humanity as present in themselves, and thus appropriating it, the nationalists appeared to confirm the absence of man in Ireland which the English had alleged.

The point to note is the unreality of this Irish self-image and the logical consequences of that. People who are guided by an unreal idea of their nature use judgment, thought and language abnormally. The Irish, guided by their colonised nationalism, judged that, because humanity and its various cultural worlds—the Catholic parts excepted—were radically alien to the Irish nature, they lay beyond the competence and jurisdiction of Irish mind and word. (It was much as in the matter of government, where the asserted rightful dominion of the Irish was confined to Ireland and its offshore islands; so, too, in the matter of thoughtful language, where the 'related Catholic parts of the world' corresponded to our offshore islands.) And even those related parts, though not entirely alien, were seen as connected only inasmuch as the Pope recognised them as Catholic; that is to say, in a formal manner, not intrinsically. That these were abnormal judgments for human beings to make is obvious, and that they led to abnormally restricted use of investigation, thought and writing, not surprising.

When I wrote *Mainly in Wonder* and made those other forays abroad, I was, for reasons unknown to me, unaffected by all that. I was absorbed in a personal quest and making progress in it. It is only in retrospect that I see my quest in its relation to Irish nationalism, and how that made my writing deviant. In *Mainly in Wonder*, particularly in the Foreword, it is obvious that in my approach first to Continental Europe, then to Asia, I was very conscious of belonging to the Irish Catholic people and their peasant history. Obvious, too, is my experience of those non-Irish worlds as, in a certain sense, alien; hence the 'wonder' of the book's title. Both those sentiments are partly explained by the fact that in the 1950s—I had gone to Germany in 1951 as a student, and subsequently worked there and in Spain and travelled widely—Ireland was still many years away from becoming a member of the European Community. Irish people rarely travelled to the Continent; fewer lived there. I was aware, moreover, that 'travelling' as an activity was uncharacteristic of the Irish: 'The Irish,' I wrote, 'become exiles but seldom travellers…your Irishman as a traveller is not a known quantity.' So I felt myself both a pioneer scouting for my tribe, and an unknown quantity, in alien territory.

However, the alienness I registered, first in Europe, later in Asia, was not that which the Irish, collectively, perceived in the non-Irish, non-Catholic world. Its nature was spelt out in that Foreword. It was not a radical alienness, as of another kind of being. Casually conscious of myself as a human being, and of the people I encountered as human beings like me and my countrymen, I took our common human nature as the basis of my observations. The alienness I registered, and found food for wonder in, was a merely circumstantial thing within that shared humanity. Modern Europe was a social reality the Irish had taken no part in building; it had 'made itself without our asking', bore no Irish mark. And again, its richness of inherited cultural forms and rituals struck me forcefully as in contrast with our poverty of these. As for Asia, well, obviously, it was culturally a quite other world. But in addition, there was my awareness that, in the partial shaping of it in recent centuries by European colonisers, my people collectively, individual instances apart, had played no part. So it was in no way, its humanity apart, my world.

A couple of years after returning to Ireland in 1961, I became interested in a debate then going on in England about how Britain was now to proceed, with the Empire gone and a sense of purpose absent. On the one hand, there were the 'angry young men', as they were called; on the other, intellectuals such as Richard Hoggart, Martin Green and Raymond Williams who were publishing books that both analysed and offered prescriptions. I decided to write a pamphlet about this, and with the help of Liam Miller as designer and printer, I published it under the imprint 'Sceptick Press'. It was entitled *The British Problem: a radical analysis of the present British troubles and of possible ways of ending them*. By then—this was 1963—I must have become aware of the transgressive nature of my previous writings, for I chose that title and published the pamphlet 'with intent', so to speak. I took pleasure in breaking the self-imposed Irish taboo on serious writing about English or British matters—as distinct from the British-Irish political relationship. I particularly enjoyed, in the title, 'the British Problem' and 'the British troubles' as, so to speak, literal reverse action.

Although it came about by accident, there was a certain logical progression in my four years, 1964–8, working for *Herder Correspondence*, first in Freiburg, then in Dublin. As some will remember, it was a German Catholic magazine which played a leading 'progressive' role in the matters of the Second Vatican Council. Truly international in its contents, it sold in all five continents. When its office moved from Germany to Dublin, with me as editor, I derived satisfaction from the fact that, for the first time, such a magazine was being edited and printed in Dublin. As well as having translations made of articles from our German edition on near and far-flung places and developments, I was commissioning and editing similar articles. Because we had a well-informed correspondent on Chinese affairs, we were particularly strong on Mao's 'Cultural Revolution'! While seeing to it that Ireland was well covered—I did most of that writing—I once again took piquant pleasure in writing an article on an English theme, 'England's Troubles and the Catholic Left', which went on to be included in an American book.

However, since my return to Ireland after my Sweden year, Irish matters—contemporary Irish painting and religion, a debate about Scandinavian industrial design and the approaching fiftieth anniversary of the Easter Rising—had become central to my attention. After my move to the Conamara Gaeltacht in 1968, this homing change of focus was completed: Ireland in all its dimensions became the main theme of my writing until the 1990s. This happened despite the fact that I had gone to Conamara with the intention of writing a book about the contemporary western world and ultimately wrote *Beyond Nationalism: The Struggle against Provinciality in the Modern World*, published by Ward River Press. It was the first Irish book to deal broadly with the modern West, and it contains the first study of nationalism by an Irish author. Given our history, that was an odd omission by Irish scholars, but it was also a telling one. Thinking and writing about nationalism *as such* would have meant seeing Irish nationalism in context, as a mere local instance of a common phenomenon, rather than as yet another feature of our *sui generis* and therefore incomparable reality.

To be continued in Part 3.

MY ENCOUNTER WITH 'DER MENSCH' ⋆

FOR SOME YEARS before 1960, probably since 1951–2 when I was a postgraduate student at Bonn University, I had been interested in man and was investigating him intermittently. Eventually my interest in his future would take me to Sweden, but his future had not been my initial concern

My first desire was 'to know man': to know the essentials of his nature, which I assumed had been constant throughout history and was the same worldwide, regardless of its many historical and contemporary cultural forms. If my assumption were true and my quest successful, I would end up knowing the essentials of man. Then, I imagined, I would return to Ireland and write novels—fiction being the accepted Irish way of discoursing about reality!

I am now articulating clearly that desire I had to know man, but for years it was a subconscious, barely formulated curiosity which I pursued haphazardly. Only gradually did I become conscious of it and pursue it deliberately, as I finished my MA in Modern History in Bonn and Dublin, taught English for three years in an Opus Dei secondary school in Spain, made on its behalf a study tour of US schools, worked as translator and newsreader on German Overseas Radio, wrote about Continental theatre for the London *Times*, contributed to Radio Éireann and *The Irish Times*, travelled in Asia,

---

⋆ From the Introduction to *The Turning Point: My Sweden Year and After*, Sanas Press, Dublin, 2001.

became the first Aer Lingus sales manager in Germany, visited much of Europe and, finally, Israel.

I said above that my active interest in man 'probably' began from the winter and summer semesters I spent in Bonn and the Rhineland in 1951-2. I have a hunch that it had to do with encountering the words *der Mensch*, meaning 'man' or 'the human being', as a commonplace of everyday language.

Two things came together there. First, there was the verbal handiness of *der Mensch*, ranking alongside *der Hund* (the dog), *der Tisch* (the table), *der Mann* (the adult male), as a normal noun. In English, by contrast, neither 'man' nor the only other way of saying it, 'the human being' is a normal noun. 'Man' is treated, grammatically, like an abstract noun, such as 'courage', 'wickedness' or 'heat'; like them, but unlike ordinary nouns, it does not take the definite article. 'The human being', for its part, is a cumbersome noun-plus-adjective, and is given an abstract flavour by the ambiguity of 'being'. Again, *der Mensch* has a normal plural, *die Menschen*, which can mean only what it says, whereas the plural of 'man' confuses it with 'adult males'. But as well as this handiness, clarity and concreteness of *der Mensch,* and doubtless connected with that, was the fact that the word occurred frequently, in talk and writing. In English there was no comparable common usage of 'man'; apart from religious language, it was rarely used. Irish has in *an duine* and its grammar and usage an exact equivalent of *der Mensch*. It has occurred to me that if Irish had been my everyday language, my interest in man might have burgeoned sooner. But English was my everyday language, and it was therefore in Germany, when I was 22, that I first heard people talking about this being called *der Mensch* in the same way as they talked of 'the world', 'the rhinoceros' or 'the weather'.

From my teenage years I had liked to believe that my view of things was utterly personal, unideological, unaffected by received opinion. I considered this the necessary cast of mind for the free person I aspired to be. But of course it could not be so and was not so. Later, in retrospect, I realised that my view of the world and my presuppositions about it were generally of that British Liberal kind which, with Irish Catholic and Irish nationalist modifications, had been second nature to most Irish people since Daniel O'Connell's time. For a youth growing up and attending university in Dublin in the late 1940s, that was inevitable. Moreover, even as I became conscious that my worldview was indeed (in that traditional or classical sense) 'Liberal' and therefore ideological, I still continued, generally speaking, to see the world that way, in the belief that it was the 'normal', true and right way. So in fact, as distinct from my fancy, it was only when I deliberately applied my mind to some specific human matter that I put my personal ideal into practice. Then, by an act of will making my mind a *tabula rasa,* I would discount—insofar as I could!—all received views and judgments on that matter.

The first notable case of this had to do with the 'Irish nation'. When, as an undergraduate, I began to think about that topic, I disregarded the certainties of Irish nationalism that surrounded me. On the basis of what I knew of European nations and their history, and my observations of Irish life, I concluded that the Irish were not a nation, but merely a 'people'—and argued that view in a student magazine.*

It was not that, in forming a judgment about something, I was prejudiced against received opinions. I recognised such prejudice as the prejudgment it was. And if it were directed against opinion inherited from the past, I identified it, as I grew older, as a specifically Liberal prejudgment. My approach was simply, when I wished to understand a particular matter, to suspend judgment on the received view—which might be right or might be wrong—because I wanted to find out about the matter for myself, and to know it in that direct way. Christian teaching did not rank for me as received opinion; it was authoritative revelation through the person and words of Christ transmitted to me by the Catholic Church and made my belief by faith.** By received opinion I mean doctrine, hearsay or belief of merely human origin. But while I was not willing to find Christian teaching ultimately wrong, I found that, in the investigation of a particular matter, I could substantially discount my knowledge of it,

---

* See 'Vocal at UCD' on p.8 above.

** That came easily. During my years in Opus Dei, part of its regime was a twice-daily half-hour meditation in the presence of Christ. That yielded a personal companionship with Jesus which remained with me permanently.

and let experience, observation, and imaginative sympathy—*Einfüh-lung*, 'feeling-into'—do their work autonomously.

The conclusions I came to by such means were 'truth for me', the best I could do, sufficient to work with. 'Truth as such' lay out there, beyond my personal reach. It would emerge out of my communicating my finding publicly, others commenting on it, my revising it and restating it publicly, and so on. I believed that truth was a social product. (Unknown to me, for it was only many years later that I would glance at modern philosophy, my mental tackling of the world was Lockean, with a touch of Descartes and Kant!).

Accordingly, when man, *der Mensch*, became the topic I was most interested in, my approach was that of a 'know-nothing' testing the hypothesis 'that man has been, and is, in all cultures essentially the same'. In practice this meant verifying that, *despite many current opinions and assumptions to the contrary*, the single nouns 'man, *der Mensch*' indicated what they implied: a single reality. With that in view, I wanted human beings to teach me about their shared nature by their presentations of themselves. This meant, in pre-modern cultures, presenting themselves through relevant writings and material remains. In the contemporary world, it meant presentations of a more or less direct kind.

Twenty years growing up in Ireland, much reading in Greek, Roman and European history, three years teaching English in a secondary school in Spain, a two-month roaming visit to the US, a total of two years in Germany, close attention to European painting, sculpture and architecture, and travels ranging from Skoplje and Bari to Warsaw, Birmingham and Gothenburg made me feel that I had a tentative grasp of European or western man. That was important for my purpose for two reasons. Europe was the broad manifestation of man that I could know best—because I was part of it. It was also one of the two areas of the world where man had developed his capacities most fully and continuously. The other was Asia. In a year-long journey to the Far East, I consciously tried to discover how it was with man there, and to draw general conclusions from the features shared with Europe. The book I wrote about that year paraded my empirical method emphatically, both by its title, *Mainly in Wonder*, and by the agnostic approach to Asia that it explicitly practised.

As I made progress I found myself conceiving of man in terms of his needs and their satisfaction, his capacities and their realisation. For example, man was a being who needed to eat and name, to see coherence and find sense in life, to trust and to be encouraged, to organise socially for survival and celebration, to have security for the raising of his young and a means of annulling death. There were basic necessities such as these, which enabled people to live and reproduce themselves indefinitely. Beyond these there were other things, not needed for survival, that enabled people to live fully, to be at ease and to flourish; to live well.

In sum, man was a being who flourished, observably, when he was supplied with certain necessities and facilitating amenities, which I could more or less identify. When he had these, and in the degree that he had them, that was a good human life.

Because he could have them in many different ways—ways called cultures—a good human life could and did take many different forms. But I believed that Western Europe, in all its variety, had been the best life so far; it had shown this by its supreme accomplishments in every field of human possibility and by its proven ability, partly to coerce but mainly to persuade, every other culture to respect it, learn from it or imitate it.

Based on a flat in Cologne, on the Rhine a short distance north of Bonn, I wrote articles for The Irish Times *and found work with Die Deutsche Welle (German worldwide radio), translating news into English and reading it to distant places. But my mind was set on getting to the Far East. Researching for cargo ships that took passengers, I found that a Yugoslav ship that did so was to sail in a few weeks time from Rijeka on the Adriatic to Hong Kong with stops en route. The full journey would cost £175—which I could pay. So after saying 'See you in a year' to my Deutsche Welle colleagues, I covered the Berlin and Vienna theatre festivals for the London* Times, *travelled from Austria through Yugoslavia to Italy, and after a goodbye-to-Europe Christmas in Cologne, left on the long train journey to Rijeka where at age 28 I boarded ship for Asia.*

THE ROAD TO MANDALAY *

WHEN WE CAST anchor in the Rangoon River, where the ship was
to remain for eight days, the usual officials came aboard. I noticed
when they left again in a group that the security officer, a man of
about forty-five wearing a Burmese *longyi*, approached our second
officer and asked for cigarettes for himself and his companions. They
had previously been sitting in the lounge where they were liber-
ally entertained to beer and cigarettes, as was the custom. The second officer had little alternative but to comply. He went away and
then came back with some packets of American cigarettes, which he
distributed among the grown men who represented the Union of
Burma and were engaged in the fulfilment of their duty.

I started looking for a lorry to take me to Mandalay and a Burmese Muslim businessman got to hear of it. He searched me out
and told me he was going there himself by jeep and would be glad
to take me, for he wanted company. Besides, it would be a pleasure
for him to show the visitor Burma and, in particular, Mandalay. He
would be accompanying one of his own lorries and I gathered that
that would hold us up a bit. But it would allow me to see the country better, so I agreed.

U Soy was of Indian-Burmese parentage, a rather small man,
dark-haired and thick-set, with coarse but not unpleasant features
and a bullish kind of strength. He spoke English fluently in a rather
weird brand of the Oxford accent. He had learned it in the Church
of England school in Rangoon. He was an army contractor supplying foodstuffs to the army in the field, especially in the remote hill
regions of the northeast frontier. The disturbed state of the country
made it necessary to maintain a large army on combat footing.

Some of those details I learned later, but what he told me on
the drive to his cousin's house in the suburbs on the night before
his departure was how lucky I was in having met him and in being enabled to make this trip with him, and with what knowledge
and enthusiasm he would point out to me the things of interest and
beauty. I was to spend the night in his cousin's place so we could
make an early start.

I awoke some time after five and U Soy was nearly ready. There

* *From Mainly in Wonder*, Hutchinson, London, 1959.

was coffee and I took it standing and went out to the jeep. An elderly woman and a young couple were sitting in the jeep among a pile of baggage. The elderly woman turned out to be U Soy's aunt, the frail but cheerful boy her son and the wispish young girl her daughter-in-law. When U Soy came out he said the young man had better travel in the lorry so there would be room for me in the jeep. U Soy and all the others were wearing *longyis*, ankle-length, cylindrical skirts which you twist at the waist. That is the normal Burmese dress.

We moved off while it was still dark and passed people washing their faces at street pumps, vendors lighting fires near their stalls. The lights in the great Shwedagon Pagoda were still burning but were paling as the red dawn broke. It was bright half an hour later when we joined the day's traffic on the northbound Pegu road. Heavy lorries mostly, many of them ex-British military lorries; some jeeps packed with people and a few cars. U Soy's lorry had met us and we kept it in sight in front. At the first customary halt, the lorry-drivers stopped to buy flowers and sprays, which they offered at a Buddhist shrine and then fixed on the front of their lorries to gain the favour of the *nats* or guardian spirits. U Soy pointed this out to me. He thought it very funny. We passed scores of people lining the road for a stretch, holding boxes and bags of foodstuffs. They were awaiting the arrival of the local abbot who came once a year to accept their alms-giving.

We drove fairly steadily until after eleven, waiting for the lorry now and then. There were armed guards and militiamen at most of the bridges. Usually they sat in huts of bamboo matting and had telephones. In some places there were stockades and at one bridge the local villagers under their headman were building a road obstacle. A lorry full of military passed us at high speed, one of the road patrols that kept mobile from dawn to dusk. There were villages of bamboo hutments with shops and eating-houses.

At Pegu we were diverted through the town because the bridge was being repaired. Six hundred insurgents had raided the place a month previously. They had spent a few hours in the town, harangued the citizens and blown up part of the big bridge as well as the railway station. Their declared policy in such raids was to harm only Government property and take no life unless they were resisted. On this occasion the insurgents had asked all the railway officials to leave the station. Two remained inside, afraid to come out, and were blown up with the station.

Beyond Pegu we reached the Mandalay Road proper. Since we had left Rangoon, old trees had given shade in many places, though some were being cut down to widen the roadway. It was so narrow that we often had to stop to let lorries pass us in the opposite direction. Paddy-fields, banana groves and rubber plantations continued on both sides. We reached Pyayagyi village, which had been raided several times, the last time four days previously. Four hundred insurgents had made off with the spoils of the Government liquor shop and pawn-shop. After midday we stopped in one of the villages and had a hearty Burmese lunch—called 'breakfast' in Burmese-English. U Soy paid for everyone.

We took the road again. Now and then we passed derelict British and Japanese tanks. Under the hot sun water-buffalos sat embalmed in cool grey slime and looked very contented. The petrol was ten pyas dearer in each village as we got farther from Rangoon. At Benwegon we saw the burned-out market and fire-tower. In the raid a couple of weeks previously the defenders had fled.

Paddy-fields had predominated for a while, then came a lot of scrub country. In the late afternoon we reached a tract of sugar-cane. Indians had been settled there by the British and it was they who had brought the sugar-cane. U Soy stopped the jeep and sent the wisp of a girl to one of the sugar-cane fields with a long knife. She cut a few stalks and we cut them into chunks and ate them as we went along.

Once we stopped to wait for the lorry near a cool well, just outside a Buddhist monastery. I could hear the monks chanting. The engine wanted cooling down. I found a damaged tin and it was a great pleasure after the heat of the day to draw up the water and carry it slowly and pour it and go for more, while U Soy looked at the road and the women chattered.

The police closed the entrances to all the towns at six in the evening and no traffic was admitted afterwards. We reached the entrance to Toungoo at 5.55. We passed the guard and crossed the long bridge and stopped on the far side hoping the lorry would catch up in time.

We got out and I sat on the grass and looked at the reddish sky in the west, where a wraith of a new moon was rising behind a tall palm. A boy came cycling out of a lane loosening his neck-tie. He had on long trousers. I wondered what visit he had been doing that he had needed to dress up like that. The sky above the red glow became a deeper blue-black and we kept looking towards the bridge. It must be after six we were thinking but didn't say. How many minutes extra would they give? The last minutes...the last minutes...of the day and of the flow of traffic, of that red glow and of the colours in the things around us. Would the end of the world be more final than this, more definitive in its ending? Would the people know it was the last passing or would they believe as we did that in twelve hours it would all begin again—the light and the colours and the movement and the fights for this and that? U Soy walked back across the bridge and I joined him. The shallow stretches of water were fiery red. When we reached the guard-house we found that the lorry had just come and found the way closed. U Soy said something about 'army supplies' and showed documents. It was all right. We recrossed the bridge and I saw the water beneath us as a dark sheen touched by moonlight. *We continued towards Mandalay.*

MY ENCOUNTER WITH ZEN *

IT WAS ALSO in Daitokuji Temple, Kyoto, that I spoke to the Zen master and priest, Kobori Solaku. A young, dynamic man, he lived in a lovely old garden house, the Ryoko-in. Like any good Japanese host he began by pointing out to me the fine screens, the austere little tea-room and other details of house and garden. There was a single flower in a vase. He had chosen it for the occasion. We drank green tea.

It was a memorable interview for me in many ways, but the things which made it memorable are such as one feels ought not to be spoken about. They are perceived and felt and appreciated. They make you feel that life is very much worth an effort, that its secrets

* From *Mainly in Wonder*. This full chapter, from which I present the core, was twice republished with permission by a Dublin martial arts group.

can be discovered and that wisdom can really be learned and lived. But such perceptions become ungainly when put into words and the attempt to do so is unseemly.

Kobori-san did not agree with Dr Suzuki's view that the approach to Zen is through art. Practicality must come first, he said. There must be years of meditation, in which the world gradually opened to you and the smallest things acquired meaning. Zen was first and foremost a method, a striving. Zen was not art nor joy of life, but it was based on a passion for life. It was great earnestness.

He believed that the turning back to Zen in Japan these last years was due to two factors—its success in the West and the desire of the Japanese to meet the challenge of the West by drawing strength out of their own native resources. The place Zen occupied in Japanese life, he said, was concrete on the one hand, vague and general on the other. A small number of persons consciously made Zen a part of their lives. But at the same time, most Japanese, even those who believed themselves to be opposing Zen, were influenced by it in a hundred ways through its partial expression in the tea ceremony, poetry, flower arrangement and the general tone of Japanese ethics and cultivated living.

I tried—others who have tried will appreciate the futility of it—to gain some rough outline of the doctrine or moral views of Zen. When I had asked Mrs Sasaki what, according to Zen, becomes of the soul after death, she had answered that Buddhism could not be read off a tree while passing in a train! Now I asked Kobori-san about right and wrong. But he rejected the whole idea of enunciating principles.

'Let us leave principles,' I said. 'If you go out on to the street now and knock a man off his bicycle—what then? Is that right or wrong?'

'But you posit an "if",' he said. 'I have not done that. We must keep to what is here and now. I take this little dog up and fondle it.' He did so. 'Is that good or bad? I drink tea.' He drank. 'The garden is darkening. It will rain now and that will make the moss look very bright and green. Perhaps later this evening I'll feel hungry and eat something.'

But as I questioned I sensed his reluctance and that he was being polite, while believing his talk futile. He acted as a person does who has a precious secret and resents the curious questioner who is not prepared to buy that secret by a personal commitment, but wants the gist of it for its sensation value and as a conversation piece. In fact Kobori-san said to me, gently, 'I don't like talking about these things. I like to work at them, make progress and then, when the occasion demands it, talk plenty—with accumulated force!'

I have often recalled every minute of this lesson.

Since my return to the Rhineland from Bilbao my link with Opus Dei had been loosening. I did not connect with their organisation in Germany, though I continued for a time to perform some of their daily devotional 'norms' as they were called. In India, more precisely in the Hindu holy city of Benares on the Ganges, I had my last conscious association with a member, the learned and holy Indian-Spanish Catholic priest, Raimundo Pannikar. I spent three weeks with him. He was living alone there, exploring by living it what he found to be shared by Hinduism and Christianity. I would remember with gratitude the day he pointed out to me in a Benares market, among the stalls, the devotional image of the god Ganesh as a small elephant-headed man, and told me he was the god of literature and wisdom and that such images, popping up in public places, had the function of inducing contemplation amid the hurly-burly of life.

After my return in 1958 from the Far East to Cologne, I was shocked and saddened to hear that the amiable 30-year-old woman colleague in the radio station whom I had asked to retain for me any incoming correspondence had committed suicide on Rosenmontag, the joyous, flower-bedecked opening day of Karneval. On a sunny May day I went to her grave, prayed for her and laid flowers on it.

I continued doing theatre criticism for the London Times *(e.g. Tennessee Williams in Dusseldorf and Brecht in East Berlin) and did radio talks for Francis McManus in Radio Éireann. Then, essentially because of my knowledge of German, I was employed by Aer Lingus as their first sales manager for Germany. I found a head-office in Dusseldorf and a girl secretary, and took a flat in that city. Our routine work consisted in seeing to overnight accommodation and general caring for hostesses on overnights after Aer Lingus flights from Dublin, as well as keeping account of Aer Lingus expenditure as it arose and dealing with enquiries to the office. My own main work had to do with the fact that a Volkswagen car came with the job. I was to use it to visit travel agents throughout West Germany, making them aware of Ireland and its attractions. I did this far and wide. I found to my surprise—the travel agents said so—that, quite unlike the Irish case, Germans living outside the big cities regarded flying as not a thing for them. This accorded with the standard airline publicity on billboards which generally showed a smart young businessman-cum-briefcase striding towards a plane. I may not have been a good salesman, but more importantly Aer Lingus head-office found that sales did not increase sufficiently. Besides, it had done me no good that the Irish manager for Europe reported to head-office that I had attended a meeting of the area managers in Switzerland in duffel-coat and sandals. After a year I was informed that my services would not be further needed and the manager of the Frankfurt office, a German, would take over in my stead. Because of my job I could fly for free on most airlines. Taking advantage of this, in my last days of employment I flew to Israel. My primary motive was to visit a kibbutz or two; in those more innocent days the Israeli kibbutzim were the main reason apart from Jerusalem why young people visited that country.*

I was not dismayed by my employment with Aer Lingus ending. Sweden was on my mind and I had saved some money. I had persuaded Hutchinsons of London, who had published Mainly in Wonder, *to commission a book on Sweden.*

At the time Sweden was notorious internationally as an affluent and 'pagan' country that had broken free from European norms, most notably in sexual matters and nude bathing. Over the years I had made two short visits there. A conversation with young Swedes on a beach in summer had remained tantalisingly in my mind. No one was nude, but the free range of the conversation about life and death—more the feeling I drew from it that these were young humans starting out again as if on the Moon—left me with an idea of Sweden as both the Future and an attractive prospect. Having observed humanity West and East as of now, it seemed to me that for a full picture I must take a long look at its nascent Future!

So I went to Sweden, took a flat in Stockholm; after three months I could speak the language and thereby get really close. During the year I spent there I visited Moscow for a fortnight and, back in Sweden, sent fifteen articles about life in Moscow to The Irish Times—*the first reportage from the Soviet Union to be published in an Irish newspaper.*

MARRIAGES IN MOSCOW *

MRS SOYA NIKOLAYEVNA, a kindly woman of about thirty-eight, with a round, smiling face, is marriage registrar for the Kiev ward of Moscow. When I enquired at the registry office, she invited me to attend on a Saturday afternoon and I took my schoolteacher acquaintance Kora with me to interpret. We stood chatting before the first couple arrived, and Mrs Nikolayevna told me that she sometimes marries forty couples in one day. I asked her if, with all her experience, she still considered marriage 'a Good Thing'. 'Yes,' she said, 'having a family is part of Communism,' 'Why not part of life?' I said. 'Communism is life,' said Mrs Nikolayevna.

You passed through a couple of ante-rooms with open doors before reaching the room where the marriage takes place. In those outer rooms music was relayed, and that was where the excited groups arrived and took the wrapping-paper off the bouquets. Mrs Nikolayevna took us to the inmost room. In front of us was a desk and, to either side, the flags of the Soviet Union and of the Russian Republic. The room was tastefully decorated and furnished. There were paintings of flowers and country scenes.

The first couple came in, dressed in ordinary clothes, and we stood to greet them. We also stood while Mrs Nikolayevna read out the following: 'Today, 21 January 1960, in the marriage registry office of the registry office of Kiev ward, Moscow, in accordance with the Soviet Marriage and Family Laws of the Russian Republic'—and mentioned the names of the couple). 'Dear bride and bridegroom, do you know the Soviet marriage laws?' (The couple

* From a 15-part series, 'Life in Moscow', in *The Irish Times*, 1961.

answered.) 'Do you agree to be his wife?' (The girl answered) 'Do you agree to be her husband?' (The man answered) 'Since you both agree we fulfil the act of marriage.'

At this point Mrs Nikolayevna asked the couple to sign a book. She then stepped down off the platform, congratulated them—asking me to do so also—and said, 'Now kiss each other!' They did so hastily.

After that, they came trooping, couple after couple, impersonating abstractions as in a medieval mystery play. Here love was anaemic and there robust; some looked as if they were condemned to death; the faces of others shone with youth and anticipation. This couple came alone, and another with a group of friends, girls in the background holding flowers and giggling, and making the bride giggle as she answered the questions.

There was a working-class couple, the man with shy humour in his eyes, the girl, full-lipped, wearing a blue woollen dress. When asked would she have this man to husband, she said, somewhat startled: 'Of course, why not?' and when Mrs Nikolayevna said, 'Kiss now!' they kissed each other joyfully and went out hand in hand. But mostly the couples were shy about kissing, and some girls feigned horror at the suggestion, so that several men were made wait for a less public moment.

Some couples came dressed for the occasion. There was a boy in a black suit with silver tie, and a girl in a white satin dress. After the ceremony they invited myself and Kora to a little celebration with their families in the ante-room. They told us they were both engineers and had studied together. The girl's father opened bottles of champagne and we drank to the couple's health. Someone asked me if marriages in my country were like this, and I said they were usually in a church and there was a bit more fuss and to-do. The girl looked at her husband and said, 'This is enough for us.' Then we had oranges and they left. There was a slender girl in a simple white dress with a shy bridegroom in a black suit. They, too, asked me to have champagne with them. A girl in the party spoke good English and asked me if registry offices were like this in Ireland. That stumped me; I had never been in an Irish registry office. The couple were both railway-workers. Chocolates were handed around.

I told Mrs Nikolayevna I was satisfied and would be going, but she said four couples were waiting and would be most offended if I didn't stay for their weddings. I glanced rather anxiously towards the couples and noticed that one couple was dressed in black and white—that meant another glass of champagne. I went back to my platform and looked solemn again. The couple in formal dress asked me to their celebration, but I don't think we talked about anything important. One of the couples had been very young, and when the day's marrying was finished I asked Mrs Nikolayevna what she thought of such a marriage. She said that if a young man were being posted to some remote part of the country, it was good for him to be married. 'But don't you have the same trouble here as in other countries, that such marriages often don't last? I think a man takes a risk in marrying a very young girl.' 'But he can teach her to grow up,' said Mrs Nikolayevna. 'And then,' said I, 'when she knows her mind she'll want another man.' 'Not a Soviet woman,' said Mrs Nikolayevna. 'She would be too grateful.' She told me that especially festive marriages were organised in the Palace of Culture and she officiated there too. 'We can do that, we're not capitalist, we're masters of our own property'—she meant of the Palace of Culture.

Smiling, she asked Kora if she worked for Intourist (the State tourist agency)—I understood her though she spoke in Russian. Kora's face showed embarrassment as she answered that she did not. Mrs Nikolayevna, with a worried look, asked her what she did, and Kora, now in great embarrassment, told her she was a teacher and explained how we had met. 'Show me your papers,' said Mrs Nikolayevna sternly. As Kora, in distress, found her identity card in her handbag and handed it to the woman, my mood had changed too. I felt strongly tempted to slap Mrs Nikolayevna's face. I had seen my companion shattered and reduced to trembling by the woman's officious bullying. She looked at the papers, delivered a lecture—about associating with foreigners, I assumed—and we left. It took a long time for me to recover some equanimity.

I heard that many young people in Russia—especially girls—would like more ceremony and colour at their weddings, and that even some unbelievers get married in church for this reason.

★ ★ ★

That evening, in my room in the hotel, I was alone with Kora, talking. She was sitting on the floor, her back to the bed where I was seated. In a pause in the conversation she said, 'I didn't know that, talking about politics, you could fall in love.' During the few days we had been meeting we had talked about more than politics, but I got her meaning, with sharp surprise and then abashment. I reached out my hand to caress her hair but she brushed it away; very properly, for I had not felt attracted that way, and she sensed it. She had simply wanted to make her statement. It was part of my learning that, in their dealings with men, Russian women, more often than their western sisters, take the initiative in showing amorous interest or declaring love.

DISAPPOINTED IN SWEDEN ⋆

IN THE 1830s a Swedish writer could tell his fellow-countrymen that Swedish poverty was a byword in Europe and that their strength lay in accepting the fact of their poverty once for all. Today the Swedes are the richest people in the world. They are the first entire nation of rich people in that they enjoy those comforts, pleasures, freedoms and securities that fifty years ago were still the special privilege of a very small number of human beings. All Swedes, to the extent of their capacity and circumstances, have shared in the new wealth— engineers and lorry-drivers, writers and miners, teachers and teenagers, old and young, mothers married and unmarried, priests, prostitutes and printers, the mentally sick and the physically disabled. The only inequality in the sharing of the new wealth is that the poorest have been given a greater share—proportionately—than the people who were already rich.

Sixty or seventy years ago the King and the Lutheran Faith represented the sum of human values for the majority of Swedes. But neither the King nor the Faith—nor the State Church which taught it—seemed to have much relevance to the new Sweden; so they have been abandoned as values, but retained as useful relics—the King as master of public ceremonies, the Church as a dispenser of

⋆ From 'Goodbye to Summer', *The Spectator*, London, 9 Feb. 1962. This article, while eliciting a furious response from the Swedish media and to a lesser degree in *The Spectator*, was reprinted in the *Washington Post* and referred to admonishingly by President Eisenhower.

socially useful private ceremonies and as a bureaucratic device for keeping the register of population.

Though a small country, Sweden has acquired the material appanages of the great nations—a worldwide market for her industry, a worldwide airline, de luxe railways, a television network, an important film industry, big operatic and ballet ensembles, well-equipped armed forces, an underground railway more modern than Moscow's in the capital. Industrial productivity quadrupled since 1900. Since 1913 real wages have trebled. There is a car for every six people—only America can beat that. The consumption of coffee has increased 30% in the last five years. Though the Swedish television licence is unusually dear, the first million licences were acquired in Sweden quicker than in any other country and no less than ten years sooner than had been estimated. Swedes even have double-leaf lavatory paper for luxury lavatories. The outer leaf is coarse, enabling the fingers to get a grip; the inner leaf is of fine tissue for contact with the softer skin. Swedes consider themselves (with justice) to have outclassed Europe; their statistics and economic writings normally compare Swedish conditions with those of America. But America has not eliminated unemployment; Sweden has.

At the same time all has been done which money and laws can do to implement some old European and Christian ideals. There are now luxurious homes for old people, homes for alcoholics, unmarried mothers and the mentally ill; fine hospitals and resplendent day nurseries. Sweden has given economic and legal expression to the dignity of her womenfolk. The wages of women in industry have more than trebled since 1900 and women are now, for the most part, economically independent of men or able to become so at short notice. This is a far cry from a hundred years ago, when women' living in cities were so dependent and unprotected that—for example—of the babies born in Stockholm around 1850, 45% were illegitimate, against a present-day rate of 12%. Here, then, is a society which has eliminated poverty, the great defeater of human dreams. Two short visits had made me curious, so I went back for ten months, learned the language and spent all my time watching Swedish life and getting to know Swedish people.

The Burden of Riches

'The floor-tiles of the Big House are slippery,' says an Irish proverb. And Horace preferred his little farm in the Sabine hills to 'most burdensome riches'. What is life like, I wanted to know, when everyone is rich? Sweden is the most complete example we possess. I was quite clear in my mind that Swedish life would not be the way that people must live when all are rich, but it would show me the way that people *could* live.

Did people love each other more when poverty had ceased to cause contention and bitterness in society and in the family? When everyone was assured of life's necessities from the cradle to the grave, were families more united? Did society pursue other, less grubby, goals than before? And if not, why not? Was important new truth being discovered—new meaning for life? Was beauty of a kind never seen before being created? Did economic and legal buttresses to woman's dignity help women to become happier, fuller persons? When money considerations had almost ceased to influence the choice of a marriage partner, did love between man and woman become a finer, stronger more tender thing, something closer to the ideal—not the botched job it had so often been in the past? In short, were the great dreams and hopes which animated European society and drove it forward during 1,500 years of poverty brought any nearer to their fulfilment now that riches had come?

The first impression, if you arrive from Denmark or Northern Germany, is of a tightening of the strings which control life, a large-scale disappearance of permissiveness, imagination and common hilarity. You are forbidden to smoke in trains or buses or when you go to a telephone call-office or when you enter a large shop. In restaurants waiters give you directions about what you may drink or not drink, what you must eat if you drink this or that. Restaurants have a strange silence as of a church full of people awaiting the priest's appearance. There are many small tables and at most of them sits a single Swede. To buy liquor you must go to special state shops, massive and unadorned; people queue at the counter: a notice warns them that they may be required to produce proof of identity; you are made to feel that these shops are houses of shame. The big windows display typewriters or tyres, disguising the truth within;

the assistance looks at you horrified if you make to leave the shop with an unwrapped bottle.

Just as in Spain or Ireland people worry about their soul's salvation, so that you have many small shops selling statues, holy pictures and prayer-books, so in Sweden people worry about their sex life. Many small shops sell nothing but contraceptives and handbooks on sex problems and practice. White-coated women stand ready to offer you advice. Slot-machines on the streets provide contraceptives; it's easier to find a contraceptive than a postage stamp (you will notice, probably on your first day, that newsagents and tobacconists charge extra—make a small profit—when they sell you a stamp.)

Although Sweden prides itself on being a rationalist society, Swedish life is full of irrationalities. Government is controlled by the 'workers' party', but the fact that a man works does not legitimise him as a person. He is much better legitimised by being clean-shaven, by not drinking or by wearing a tie; only two per cent of workers' children get higher education. 'Irrational taboos' are officially frowned upon, but there are more of them now than ever before: you may not drink a toast to your hostess, or whistle a tune in the street.

Religion and shame are things you must feel ashamed of. Swedes repeat frequently that they possess freedom of speech, but they talk less than ever before and there is no satire of the sanctimonious Establishment of liberal rationalists, puritanical libertines and respectable money-makers. They assert continuously that there is freedom of thought, but no new thoughts have emerged in years and both philosophy and radical debate have died. The only people who disagree radically with the reigning orthodoxy—Communists and Catholics for their different reasons—are regarded officially as bad Swedes. Babies are scarce and the industries have to send as far as Greece to get workers, yet public policy promotes the limitation of families. Women are said to be emancipated. But a woman is regarded as a full person only when she has lain with a man and when she practises (or has learnt to practise) a trade or profession that commands a money wage.

Fifty years ago—and even more loudly thirty years ago—the liberal rationalists set out to free Sweden from the shadow of death, which was Christianity, and to open a new positive era of human development. But the annual converts to Catholicism are mostly intellectuals and artists, and the poets are writing poetry which is increasingly elegiac. They hint that the society they live in is going nowhere.

Summer Worship

Dr Mårtens, a Stockholm psychiatrist, told me that the Swedish myth of summer causes much frustration and depression. 'Many people live only for summer, they plan all the year what they will do then,' he said. Summer is to bring them perfect happiness—which often includes blissful love; when summer comes and goes and happiness has eluded them, they feel bitter and cheated—they regard themselves as failures, since they believe that they alone have missed what everyone else has found.

This myth has been created by modern Swedish city-dwellers. At least three Swedish films in the last fifteen years have drawn on it and strengthened it. The three have an identical theme—young love in summer landscape ending in autumn tragedy. In two of the films the tragedy is violent death; in the third, the squalid death of love in a hellish marriage. In *Summer Interlude* and *Summer with Monika* the summer landscape is in the Stockholm Archipelago, where tens of thousands of Stockholmers, especially the young and dreaming, seek every summer the Isles of the Blest. In the films *Summer with Monika* and *One Summer of Happiness* the moment of complete surrender to love and to nature is identical and is given a quasi-ritual force by the complete nakedness of the boy and the girl and the bathe which precedes their love-union.

For the purposes of the myth the year is simplified into two seasons—an immensely long winter and an agonisingly short summer. It is a Swedish myth, not a myth of a cold climate, for neither the Finns nor the Russians have it. It is a myth made by modern Swedish city-people who find social life hateful and hostile, but who still have to live together in large numbers. The juxtaposition of Winter and Summer is the juxtaposition of Society and Aloneness—or rather, Aloneness with Dialogue, which is the pleasurable Aloneness, where a person is fully himself.

Summer and Nature are not desired for what they are, but because they allow the person to do two things which many Swedes today find difficult or impossible in the society of people—to get outside themselves into something bigger and to communicate themselves. When alone with Nature (as they often are in the holiday season on remote islands or near quiet lakes) they can give themselves to something bigger and they can speak out their souls without fear or inhibition, without people to catch them in a phrase or to reprove their sentiments for being irrational. This freedom is also present between lovers so that, in the summer myth, supreme happiness includes both forms of communion.

The summer cult is the nearest thing to a religion that post-Christian Sweden has produced. It constitutes a sort of mystic Trinity, with the sun and the sexual union as aspects of Nature, Nature being present in both of them and both of them in Nature, yet Nature is greater than both. It is significant that the sun and love (meaning loving sexual union) are the focal points of the summer cult. The oldest gods who were adored in Sweden were Ull, a sun-god, and Njord, a goddess of fertility, and the cult of these gods included a ritual act of sexual union. In the present-day summer cult the erotic principle (Njord) is sublimated through association with a purifying spiritual principle (Ull) and becomes a parody of *agape* or spiritual love fulfilled carnally. It is a religion for puritans who produce their wealth mechanically and regard female fertility as a curse.

A special consequence of the thesis or the assumption 'There is no world but this' is the importance which death acquires. If there is no life after this, then, obviously, the most important event in life is death. That is one reason why the Swedes are fascinated by it. But another and complementary reason is that life in their present circumstances, and in the interpretation of it they have been induced to accept, seems hateful to them. It is the democratic life, it is the enlightened life, it is the rational life, it is the fully employed, wealthy and civilised life; but it is still hateful. So the fascination of death as the biggest event is met by a longing for death as a release from the pain of living.

The most beautiful modern work of art that I saw in Sweden was the Forest Cemetery at Stockholm. When I had discovered the

fascination with death, I looked at Swedish faces with new understanding. I knew the source of the sad and delicate lyricism of the
glass art, the poetry and the ceramics. I remembered the faces in
the Pompeian paintings which I had seen in the National Museum
in Naples and I understood their affinity with the faces of modern
Swedes. Both show the same dim, hopeless premonition; both seem
to encase human organisms without being human persons. I recalled the drinking cups with skull-and crossbones and 'Remember
Death' inscribed on them, which were found in the volcanic ashes
after having been passed around at banquets, and those paintings of
men and women on low beds, posturing tensely, with rapt faces, in
the acrobatics of carnal zeal. Everything had its place and its consist-
ency. Frenzy which leads to a simulation of dying is a necessity in
modern Sweden.

When death instead of life holds and fascinates the living, then
will, the active fashioner of life, gives way to cupidity, the involun-
tary response to external stimuli. Both result in much activity, in the
appearance of being busy, but for the death-haunted it is the fact of
being busy that is the important thing. You notice this in Sweden—
work is the other anaesthetic.

MIDSUMMER ★

IT WAS MIDSUMMERNIGHT in Södermanland, the province south of
Stockholm, all rolling farm country and lakes. Stealing away from
the music and dancing. I walked the short distance to the manor
house and past it towards the lake. The house stood in bright moonlight, the door open and lights burning in the empty rooms. Hearing the music still, faintly, from beyond the trees, I recalled the scene
in the film Miss Julie where she and the butler, fleeing from the
dancing, arrive at the house and find it like this. A terraced garden
led down to the lake, and on one side of it was the small house for
the sauna. It was handy having it there, where you could rush out
of the hot air into the cold lake water. At the lake edge was a small
wooden bathing-house with a platform for diving and sun-bathing.
Normally a boat-slip would have been there too, but this stretch of

★ This and the following piece are from my fullest account of my time in Sweden in The
Turning Point: My Sweden Year and After, 2001.

water was only an arm of great Lake Målaren, and the channel leading to the open water was blocked by rushes.

I went into the house and looked at the silhouettes of the Paus
family on the wall of the sitting-room. They showed Herr Paus'
parents and brothers and sisters in open-air settings. He had brought
them with him from Norway when he came to Sweden and married Tanya Tolstoy, granddaughter of the great Tolstoy. Tanya does
some painting, and a portrait she had made of one of her sons was
hanging in the study. It showed a small boy, and I was not sure which
of them it was. The two eldest are now big lads who run the farm in
the summer. The eldest, who is twenty, has a cottage of his own in a
wild part of the estate, with pines and rocks all around it. It used to
be quite literally a pig-sty, but it has been done up in sturdy, rustic
style, and from the outside looks like something from a fairy-tale.
Standing in the door, he was able to shoot two deer.

I went upstairs to the formal dining-room, which they use when
they have more than eight guests, and looked out through a window
at the terraced garden and the lake very silvery in the moonlight.
Beyond this room Tanya has her studio. Her latest pictures recall a
visit to Moscow and to Zagorsk monastery. I went downstairs and
left the house by a back-door, on the side away from the lake.

A maypole was standing in the middle of the yard, and beyond it
an avenue of tall pines extended. To the left was the children's clubhouse. It had become a problem having them and their friends and
records in the house every night, and the clubhouse was the solution. They had their books and records there, and pictures of their
favourite film-stars and of other temporary idols covered the walls.
I walked up the avenue, coming nearer to the music. Some people
were standing together, drinking out of bottles. The great shadow of
the barn with its drive-up ramp towered above the old stone store-
house where the dancing was going on. Just inside its door you
mounted a wooden stair.

All the neighbourhood and friends from other estates and nearby
towns were welcome here every Midsummer night. Tanya, lean and
handsome, full of verve, was moving among the guests collecting
for the bank. Christine was dancing with Gordon. I had never seen
her so hearty and gentle as earlier that evening, in shorts, in the

field below her house at Mariefred, leading children by the hand in dances around the maypole. Her house is a stone's throw from the Gripsholm Castle; her father is steward of the royal lands in the neighbourhood. My Stockholm friends, Ann and Gordon, were spending the night in Ann's parents' house, which is next-door to Christine's. Ann and Gordon had given us a meal at long tables in the garden, and then there was a hectic taxi-ride through the darkening countryside, looking for Herresta, the Pauses' place. The ride left memories of dusty roads, mist moving slowly over fields and waters, swallows darting against a sky still blue but tinged salmon-pink on the horizon.

THE WRONG MAP

IN OCTOBER 1960 I decided it was time to start writing the book on Sweden. A sculptor, Erik Höglund, lent me a house he had in the south, in Småland. It was said that once, when he was drunk, he had taken a hatchet to his wife. If it were true, it did not surprise me. His work was unusual, it showed emotion. In the new Sweden, if unconventional artists did not kill themselves, they got drunk and did things like that. It was a wooden house in a forest near a village that had a glassworks, a few kilometres from the town of Nybro. It gave me peace and quiet, and a useful sense of apartness after all I had seen and absorbed. I had been working for about six weeks when I took a walk one evening after dark.

Suddenly on that narrow road among the trees, all that I had experienced in Sweden came to mind and made me stop. The spiritual suffering—the sharpest I had encountered in any country in my travels—presented itself as the core, and was accompanied by its explanation: a false life-image. This people was living, or trying to live, in accordance with a false life-image, and suffering the consequences. Sweden appeared to me crucified by its false image of life. Then, less dramatically, I saw it like this. A man, leaving a friend's house at night, in a boggy countryside with which he is unfamiliar, has been given a map to guide him across the bogs. By mistake his friend has given him the wrong map, and he, trusting it, falls into bogholes, encounters unexpected barbed-wire fences, gets scratched by many thorn bushes; in general has a painful time.

I was very happy after I had this flash of vision on the country road. Everything I had experienced in Sweden began to fall into place. (Only later would I realise that, having seen what it could lead to, my own inherited Liberal life-image had been smashed).*

Given my previous belief that Sweden represented the emerging future of the West, or indeed of mankind, I spent the next years without any clear understanding of where in history the West was or where it was heading. At the start of 1961 I returned to Ireland and stayed in Dublin with my Aunt Lena, a sister of my father. He had kept us out of touch with his Sligo family except that once when his father—my other grandfather— died, he took me to Sligo to the funeral. Lena was one of his many sisters and brothers from his father's two successive marriages. Some time before my showing up in her life she had come to live in Dublin with her two daughters, Deirdre and Gráinne. She and I became good friends.

During my travels my Belfast grandfather had kept in touch with me occasionally by letter. On a visit to Dublin prior to my final return I had sought out a Northern Ireland painter, Terence Flanagan, and commissioned him to make a portrait of the old man. Grandad died a month later but Terence had done the job. He offered me a choice between a pastel portrait and one done in oils. I chose the pastel because it was more true to life. I rejoiced that I had paid that due homage in time.

The Government had established an Arts Council with a Jesuit, Fr Dónal O'Sullivan, as Chairman and the writer Mervyn Wall, long a civil servant, as Secretary. A post of Exhibitions Officer was advertised. On my travels I had seen in museums most of the great painting of Europe.

---

* It was smashed and I had no image of the present age, no understanding of it, to replace it with. The Swedish government was nominally socialist but people sometimes spoke of Sweden's guiding ideology as 'liberal'. I was dismayed that Liberalism could evolve into this. It was only years later, when it ruled the West, that I came to hear of 'left-liberalism' or the neo-liberalism called by its American propagators plain 'liberalism'. My reaction to the Swedish use of 'liberalism' to describe their system had been irrational. The fact that centuries ago some idealistic European Christians derived Puritanism from Christianity and called it Christianity was not the fault of Christianity.

I had written somewhere that I had learned more about life from looking at paintings than from reading books. I applied for the job and got it. The Arts Council premises then consisted of two rooms on Merrion Square. Mervyn occupied the inner room, a girl secretary and I had desks in the room with windows onto the street.

I got busy visiting Dublin commercial galleries to see their shows while occasionally suggesting one. Many Dublin artists became my friends. But after three months Fr O'Sullivan informed me that my services would not be further needed. I gathered informally that I had done, or said something, which displeased a very influential member of the Arts Council, the wealthy businessman and collector Sir Basil Goulding. Mervyn Wall, drawing on his civil-service wisdom, said to me, 'Desmond, you should have sat at your desk reading a novel until someone asked you to do something.'

But I was very annoyed. I had tackled my job with enthusiasm. In a spirit of revenge I published a pamphlet, Art for the Irish *(printed by Mount Salus Press), dealing with Modern Art in a historical context and with Scandinavian Design for which there was a sudden Government-sponsored enthusiasm. And I became art critic for the daily* Evening Press *and a writer on art for the fortnightly* Hibernia. *For regular income I took the job of sales office manager for Gaeltarra Éireann, an Irish-speaking semi-state company, which sold tweeds, dolls and other products manufactured in the Gaeltacht.*

DUBLIN PAINTING IN THE 1960s *

IN THE SUMMER of 1962 in Dublin I began to write art criticism regularly. Then, as for a decade before that, contemporary Irish painting was held to be virtually synonymous with the work of those painters who were associated with the Irish Exhibition of Living Art. Increasingly, this was coming to mean 'abstract' painting in the so-called 'international' manner, which was really only the manner of post-war Paris, New York and London. Writing in August 1962,

* *Arena*, Gorey, Spring 1965, a leading arts journal co-edited by James Liddy, Michael Hartnett and Liam O'Connor.

the *Irish Press* critic, Miss Marian Burleigh, could refer, without fear of public contradiction, to 'the increasing acceptance by the intelligent public of abstraction in art and the confidence that can be safely placed in the selection committee of the Irish Exhibition of Living Art...'

For several years previously, since Father Dónal O'Sullivan S.J. had become its Director, the Arts Council had given most of its attention to the plastic arts and had been supporting the Living Art painters and their kind of painting. Although the council numbered no artist among its members and showed little respect for the only artists' institution, the Royal Hibernian Academy, it had established such close working relationships with the internationalist painters and sculptors that it had in fact largely replaced the Academy as the 'official' body for the plastic arts. What had begun as a painters' rebellion had thus become a sort of orthodoxy.

Most paintings which were exhibited in Dublin were not 'abstract'—they bore some obvious relationship to visible reality—but the greatest names were being made fastest by the abstract painters, and there was a corresponding pressure on all painters to 'go abstract'. Richard Kingston, for instance, 'regretted' in print that a certain painting of his of a bird in a bush was representational, and John Kelly, at the start of his career, discovered that, when he left the representational style (which suited his talent) and made a few awkward abstracts, the collector and member of the Arts Council, Sir Basil Goulding, became interested and bought them.

The Academy painters had long felt defeated, rejected by the larger section of fashionable patronage, as they were by the critics writing in newspapers and magazines. The *picture* as such, the painting which *depicted* something in a more or less straightforward manner, was out.

When paintings were non-figurative, critics would wax eloquent about 'structure, 'texture' and the like. They usually ignored these aspects of representational work. Willy-nilly, this gave the public to understand that these qualities of craftsmanship—of what Berenson would call the mere 'cooking'—were peculiar to abstract paintings and not present to any comparable extent in representational ones. Representational paintings tended more and more to be dismissed as run-of-the-mill stuff, which anyone could turn out, and not worth analysis either on the 'metaphysical' level or from the point of view of painterly technique.

To illustrate this, here is a review of an exhibition of Richard Kingston's paintings by an *Irish Times* critic, 'W', published in September 1963:

> The paintings, which are oils and cover the last three years of his work, are, whilst in manner abstract, essentially representational, the majority taking their inspiration from natural landscape. In the most recent, however, the abstract manner predominates, and as it predominates their success as paintings increases. The striving for simplification which the process of abstraction generates has led in certain of the works, particularly 'Shore Shapes' and 'Near the Top', to an astonishing increase in their structural sureness and power which makes a brilliant painting such as 'Erosion' seem loose and uncertain by contrast.
>
> The contrast between these paintings is further underlined by their difference in technique, the latter ('Erosion') being constructed with essentially rectangular elements, the former with curvilinear. If the curvilinear technique which is the basis of the majority of the paintings gives the artist more personal satisfaction, this apparent sympathy of his with these forms, which are so much harder to handle and which can so easily degenerate into an almost oozy oiliness devoid of precision, has led in 'Near the Top' to a great success and achievement.
>
> This painting, whose interest is increased by some similarity of compositional theme to Patrick Scott's 'Sun on Horizon' series, consists of two ovals, a dark one (in the sky), a light one (a lake), simultaneously displaced by and jointed by a falling sweep of paint (the brow of the hill) which forms a near horizontal division of the canvas. In the junction of the two ovals at the horizontal band, the great structural strength of the painting becomes most evident, and the solution of this jointing problem by means of hard rectangular elements of paint, modelled to establish a relationship of planes between the three main elements of the composition, adds to the contrasts of forms and compels the viewer to grasp the idea of movement and height conveyed by the relationship of the elements.

'Sea Memory', almost purely abstract, is one of a few paintings which indicate, perhaps, a change in the artist's approach to colour by being composed with clean primary colours on a white ground. This use of primary colours is certainly part of his increased concern with abstract form, the most notable feature of the exhibition, which must firmly establish itself, containing as it does many works in his previous more representational manner, of profoundly great interest.

In her review of the Living Art exhibition of 1962, Miss Burleigh dealt with Cecil King's work in these words: 'Cecil King explores, with confidence and sensitivity, the varying effects of thickly encrusted and always sombre paint'.

Critics, and the public who listened to them, took for granted that an abstract painting was *ipso facto* deep in psychological content and meaning. This assumption gave critics free scope to say anything they liked and to establish themselves as initiates in esoteric knowledge, not only of painting, but, much more so, of the Soul and of quasi-mystical Reality. Often the intrinsic spiritual importance of abstract canvases was simply assumed without being analysed and criticism consisted in relating them to the work of other painters or to other kinds of experience, while avoiding all direct assessment and analysis of their place within art or outside it, of their nature, content and social meaning as works of the painting art. What was written about paintings might often just as well have been written about sunsets or about textiles or motor cars.

Mr James White, commenting on the French paintings in the 1961 Living Art exhibition, had this to say: 'They are all abstract conceptions in which the development of surface with agile and delicate brushwork is apparent. Most of them have the tender reflection of light and the almost pointillistic range of colour which was the rage in the days of Seurat and Signac. Bathed in warm sunlight, the objects are not seen. They shimmer and suggest, and remind one of the music of Debussy. Is it coincidence that two of the artists are named Ravel and Cortot?...'

Sentiment was often confused with sentimentality, and both were out. Patrick McElroy, the sculptor, was praised by Mr White for his 'uncompromising contempt for the least indication of sentiment in religious figures'. Oddly, however, the same critic often praised abstract painting as 'lyrical' and constantly used the word 'tender' as a term of praise. It was assumed that abstract painting was *per se* 'bold' and that it could not therefore be sentimental—though it might well be 'lyrical' or 'tender'! On the whole, then, a great deal of assuming was done.

Criticism was sympathetic towards all 'innovation', but there was in fact no innovation, only a great deal of copying of new styles or variations on old styles, all of which, whether old or new, had reached Ireland from abroad. The value set on style virtually replaced all regard for content—this was the 'academic' mistake in new guise! The imitation of what were contemporary stylistic fashions elsewhere was confused with originality or innovation and was praised as such. It was often called 'reflecting a contemporary trend' and this was assumed to be a positive quality. In other words, Irish painters were encouraged to paint like painters elsewhere, not to show their difference or to offer anything really new.

There were, of course, among painters, extreme opponents of the fashionable extremes, though they were seldom vocal in public. In the summer of 1963 Mr Harry Kernoff, R.H.A., published privately a broadsheet in verse, from which I quote with his permission. It was entitled 'After an Exhibition of Abstract and Subjective Art' and it began as follows:

> Bilious, amorphous, gangrenous muck.
> Negative, crapulous on canvas stuck.
> Any results a mere matter of luck.
> Inchoate, nebulous, mystical stuff.
> Quality infantile, crude and rough.
> This absolute and incoherent bunk.
> A pile of incompressible junk.
> Coprolitic, scatalogical punk—
> In which some people have their money sunk.

In defence of 'academic' painting, and in somewhat more moderate vein, Lady Beatrice Glenavy, R.H.A., had this to say (November 1961) about a critique of paintings by Patrick Hennessy, R.H.A., which had appeared in *The Irish Times*:

Your art critic seems to have a very mistaken idea of what concerns a painter when confronted with something which he wishes to paint, some object which absorbs his attention and compels him to search it out in all its details and subtleties and find, in doing so, an increasing beauty and mystery. Your critic writes that Mr Hennessy uses 'tricks of technique' to 'deceive the eye' and he is 'not convinced that such tricks are necessarily art'. These statements suggest that Mr Hennessy is a sort of musical-hall entertainer or a television magician playing for public amusement.

Surely a painter is unconcerned with the eye that may be 'deceived' or the mind which thinks it can decide 'what is art'. Your critic alas says: 'We must ask ourselves, does he in fact convey a heightened appreciation of landscape by showing the very hairs which cover the spines of plants or the tiniest cracks in the woodwork of walls?' Surely a painter sees his own truth in these things and is under no obligation to convey 'a heightened appreciation of landscape' to the viewer.

I cannot see why a picture of a rose 'whose species is recognisable' should show 'a disdain for the warmth of humanity'. This sounds rather like nonsense. Perhaps Mr Hennessy had no disdain for the warmth of the supernatural—but now I may be writing nonsense, it is infectious. Perhaps your critic is in sympathy with painting which is concerned with the modern cult of personality, as opposed to the humility of the painter who still finds in visual things all the wonder of those evenings of the days of creation when God looked at what he had done and found it was good.

The intentions of the critics and of the art-tasters on the Arts Council were often the very best. Mr James White, especially, had started with the desire 'to give a chance to the moderns', something which many would have wanted to do in the 1940s in view of the weariness of much academic art, the restrictive attitudes of the Academy and the burgeoning talent of the younger painters. He wanted Irish painting to find a place on the world map of painting and was often lenient in his criticism in order to promote the emergence of an Irish modern school.

If, however, the maintenance of artistic standards and the promotion of *good* painting are the proper concerns of art criticism, the mistake which Mr White and other critics made was to regard 'modern' styles as an end in themselves or as necessarily connected with good painting. To do so and to accept without question values concerning painting which had been worked out elsewhere in different human circumstances was to be uncritical and to encourage superficial mannerism. Besides, to promote the emergence of an Irish school of 'modern' painting merely so that Ireland might take part in a prestigious international art movement was to put nationalistic considerations before standards in art. It could only lead, as it has in fact led, to artistic frustration for those who went with it wholeheartedly and to our *failing* to gain a place on the world map of painting. In the world's eye (whatever about Irish eyes) no such thing as Irish painting exists—there is merely an Irish branch-office of 'internationalism', as undistinguished and as undistinguishable as branch-offices usually are.

No Irish painter was included in the exhibition of the '100 Leading Painters of the World' which opened in the Tate Gallery in London last December. Of the 'Twelve Irish Painters' shown last October in New York in an exhibition organised by the Arts Council and Córas Tráchtála, the painter most praised by the American critics was Barrie Cooke, who was born in England, grew up in Bermuda and began his painting career in America. This would seem to show that 'international' *people* are more likely to succeed in internationalist art than we are; which is not surprising. The fact that five of the twelve painters chosen were women and that this reflects the extraordinary prominence which women painters have achieved of late in Irish painting would also seem to indicate something which is not surprising: that when keeping up with world fashions is a criterion of 'good' painting, women are apt to be extraordinarily successful. Indeed, our recent period in art can be described as a 'feminine' one. Even among male painters, the more 'feminine' talents, in the sense of those most apt at fashionable decoration or at 'creating a scene' in paint, have had a heyday.

If instead of encouraging Irish painters to be modern (as if that were a value) so that Ireland (meaning some people in Dublin) would get connected up quickly with the big world and appear to play a part in it, our critics and connoisseurs had forgotten the 'modern' and 'Ireland' parts of their ambition and had simply and relentlessly demanded good art, we might now have, not only good and important painting, but—through it and because of it—a *new kind* of modernism. This alternative, a renewal of painting arising out of our own needs, beliefs and life, was available but was ignored. Such a modernism had been exemplified by the Irish literary renaissance, our only substantial artistic achievement in this century apart from the painting of Jack Yeats and Evie Hone's and Harry Clarke's stained glass. The literary renaissance represented (and represents) the only known process by which first-class art has emerged or can emerge anywhere. Perhaps, however, such an ambition—more a desire than an ambition—would not have suited the urgent *non-artistic* needs of our modernist art promoters and would therefore have been impossible for them to entertain.

By regarding in a critical spirit both academic values (in the vulgar sense of the word) and the modern values in vogue elsewhere; by applying the perennial artistic values in the light of our aesthetic needs and human circumstances and by encouraging our painters to give us in their art their undiluted selves, their uniquely personal vision, our critics and connoisseurs would have remained true to real artistic criteria and have trained the Irish in them. This would have been for the good not only of art, both in Ireland and in the world, but for the good of our souls, for the good of the humanity in us which art is made to serve. By the providential irony of all true and integral human striving, it would have achieved, without trying to, the ambition of our Modern-Irelanders-in-a-hurry. We would have found our place on the world map of painting not by extending its indeterminate grey, but by changing it—by painting onto it a new colour.

This can still be done. The critical pressure to do as others do has lessened; this 'feminine' period of our art history may be ending. The evidence on canvas in the Independent Artists' exhibition last December shows that we have a number of young painters who are in touch with the art of painting, who are not 'taken in'. Their conservatism is, in the circumstances, the most-needed form of rebellion. The continuation of painting must have its roots in the old masters from Giotto to Matisse and Kandinsky. There are also some senior painters who have known all along what the art of painting is, who have made concessions under pressure, but who have never sold the ultimate pass inside them. They will now feel freer to be themselves unashamedly.

Critics and patrons can advance the cause by realising once for all that academic or unacademic, modern or unmodern, figurative or non-figurative, contemporary trends or old-fashionedness, this style as against that style, are not real values in art. The only real values are those of good art—of good painting—and this is not the place to set them down. But only those critics and patrons who know them, either consciously or by instinct, can be of use to painting and they will be of use by judging according to them, by giving praise only when they believe that they see them applied and by demanding them when they are not evident. Knowing what art is, asking for it and praising it when it is present are all potent factors in bringing it into being. If mistakes are made in good faith, they do not matter. Or rather, they matter very much because they become part of a necessary and fruitful dialectic that is rooted in concern for truth. The fear of being shown wrong, of being found against good new art, has been the basic cause of wrong judgment and of the abandonment of judgment in contemporary art criticism.

Dublin has never yet had a full generation of painters devoted to the mainstream of European painting and at the same time to the direct experiencing and rendering of *life as such*. Not life filtered through genteel drawing-rooms or *cliché* Irishness or synthetic Celtic mist, not a selectively ideal life such as that of the idealised Gaelic West, but life quite simply and seriously as men find it in themselves, in woman, in their God, and in the world of people and things around them; life both real and ideal as understood by European Christian humanism.

Two provincialisms have to be overcome: that of imitative eye-over-the-shoulder up-to-dateness and that of mediocre craftsmanship.

Sometime in the early 1960s I applied for the then vacant job of art critic for The Irish Times. *I was interviewed by two friends, Editor Douglas Gageby and Assistant Editor Donal O'Donovan. Towards the end of the*

interview, Donal said to me, 'We're afraid you'd bring your philosophy into it.' (It was the second time, but not the last, that I heard 'philosophy' mentioned in relation to my writing. The first time had been by my Uncle Bonnie in Belfast. A lover of travel books, he commented after he had read Mainly in Wonder *that there was 'too much philosophy in it'.) Neither of them meant any particular philosophy for I had none; they meant 'your philosophical way of writing'. I supposed it had to do with my frequently evident consciousness of man in whatever I was writing and my evident fascination with him.* The Irish Times *gave me a try-out as their art critic and it so happened that my first job was the annual exhibition of the Living Art group about which I wrote two articles. I think it was not because of any 'philosophical' prose that* The Irish Times *did not make me their permanent critic, but rather because in one of the articles I dealt bluntly and disrespectfully with two fashionable abstract painters, something which the* Irish Times *readership would not have liked.*

Around this time Thomas McGreevy, the modernist poet who was Director of the National Gallery and with whom I was friendly, was thinking of retiring. Considering me as a possible successor, he chose to decide the matter by inviting me to his office and presenting me on an easel with an oil painting of a girl frolicking, which I recognised as eighteenth-century French. I was required to identify the painter. Recognising that it was either Fragonard or Boucher, I guessed wrongly, and that perhaps decided that my subsequent life did not take a very different course than it did in fact take.

In Dublin as throughout the West it was, of course, the famous Sixties. With rising prosperity (and an end to the decline of the Irish population), a new social dynamism filled the air. We got to know espresso coffee; a couple of cafés in the city centre (mine was the New Amsterdam) became places to meet. A previously non-wine-consuming people had the Portuguese Mateus Rosé wine on every restaurant dinner-table; the hold of Catholic sexual morality loosened. There were many house parties.

At one such party in 1962 I met a girl I liked talking to and fell in love with. She was Mary Troy, a 21-year-old student of Semitic Studies

(Hebrew and Arabic) and German at Trinity College, daughter of a widowed Limerick doctor. In February of the following year we married. We had a brief honeymoon in Conamara and Ballinasloe with the intention (fulfilled) of a 'real' month-long one in Greece the following summer. We made our home in a cottage I had rented from Brian Inglis in Dundrum, on the southwest edge of Dublin. (Brian was then editor of the London Spectator.) *Our social life was mostly with Dublin artists.*

That autumn Mary was in St James's Hospital awaiting the birth of our first child. As the birth drew near I hovered with journalist Patrick Gallagher or writer John Jordan in the streets near the hospital. Our firstborn was a boy, Oisín. Because Mary was still attending Trinity College, I left my Gaeltarra Éireann job and looked after him in his first year while she was doing that. Mary knew Dermot Ryan, who was then Professor of Oriental Languages at UCD and would later, in 1972, become Archbishop of Dublin. He told her that a certain Herbert Auhofer, editor of the new English edition of the German Herder Correspondence, *a monthly Catholic journal of ecclesiastical affairs and general world affairs, was coming to Dublin every month to oversee its printing; and that said Herbert Auhofer was looking for an Irish assistant who knew German. So I became assistant editor of* Herder Correspondence *and in 1964 moved to Freiburg, Germany, where the publisher Herder Verlag was situated. Mary and Oisín joined me there after Herder Verlag had found a flat for us on Friedrichsstrasse. From then on, all articles on Irish matters were written by me and were unsigned, as was the practice with all articles in* Herder Correspondence. *Our friends were members of the Herder staff. Mary and I enjoyed the early Bond films. I gave her a present of a ten-day bus tour to Russia, which as it turned out had an unfortunate consequence for one of our children. I will come to that.*

IRISH CATHOLICISM GOING STRONG *

WHENEVER ROME CALLS for radical renewal of the Church, the most vigorous immediate support comes from those parts of Christen-

---

* From 'Time of Decision for Irish Catholicism', *Herder Correspondence*, November 1964.

dom where the Church is in acute crisis and where theology is alive. It is therefore hardly surprising that when Pope John called for a Council that would lead to a radical *aggiornamento* or 'updating' most of the leading personalities of the Irish Church showed little interest.

Measured in terms of the number of religious vocations, of popular and voluntary participation in the Church's liturgy, reception of the sacraments, voluntary financial support of the Church, missionary enterprise, effective lay apostolate, relationship of the Church to civil society in five-sixths of Ireland, and imaginative, practical expansion of the nineteenth-century formula of Catholicism, the Irish Church was flourishing. Measured by the standards of that late Tridentine Catholicism—of which modern Irish Catholicism was the most thorough-going, full-blooded and successful embodiment—this was more or less what the Church should be. What the modern Irish Church had received from its formative period in the nineteenth century has been conserved at home, while being made to bear fruit in fifty-three countries. The point had been reached where three out of every four priests ordained in Ireland were leaving to work in Britain or overseas—300 priests were being 'exported' annually. The lay Legion of Mary, which had been founded in Dublin in 1921 and which had provided the backbone of the Church in China in face of Communist persecution, was publishing its bulletin in twenty-one languages and extending its apostolate in 1,300 dioceses at the rate of fifty new 'praesidia' a week.

For over a century six major seminaries have been training priests almost exclusively for English-speaking countries abroad. One of them, St Patrick's College, Carlow, sent out priests as follows between 1920 and 1956: U.S.A. 334, Britain 274, Australia 131, New Zealand 16, South Africa 10, France 2. Between the revolutionary years (1916-21) and the 1950s, the missions to Africa and Asia were developed. 'Between 1933 and 1953 the number of missionaries sextupled,' exclaimed the French magazine *Missi* in a broad survey of Irish Catholicism (April 1962). New Irish congregations of nuns, streamlined for modern missionary work (e.g. the Missionary Sisters of St Columban, the Missionary Sisters of the Holy Rosary, the Medical Missionaries of Mary) covered the English-speaking world with their foundations and established hospitals, missions, and schools throughout Africa and Asia, breaking down the canonical and other taboos which hindered women's mission work, producing women of extraordinary character: to name but two, 'Mama Kevina' of Uganda and Mother Mary Martin, foundress of the Medical Missionaries of Mary. When the Council opened, hundreds of lay professional people were in Africa as mission-helpers.

To put it another way: when the call for *aggiornamento* reached the Irish Church, those members of its élite and of its rank and file who had remained in Ireland were very busy. There were heavy tasks of organising the missionary work and of training the great numbers of novices and seminarians: 75 seminarians per 100,000 Catholics—as compared with the next highest figures, 36 per 100,000 for Canada and 33-26 per 100,000 for Australia, Spain, Britain, and USA. (*Herder-Korrespondenz*, May 1955). Moreover, most of the secondary education of Irish Catholics is provided in schools run by priests, nuns, or brothers. Although the number of Catholic priests in the Republic and Northern Ireland had increased by 87% since 1871—despite a 23% fall in the Catholic population through emigration—the absolute ratio of priests to people was not extraordinarily high: 558 Catholics per priest in 1960. This figure includes non-diocesan priests, whose numbers had increased between 1871 and 1961 by 396%. In Holland the ratio of Catholics per priest was 494, in Britain 507, in France (which is said to be very short of priests) 751, and in Italy 766, although 28 Italian dioceses had a ratio of less than 400 to 1. In the Anglican Church of Ireland the ratio of church-members to ministers was 180 to 1.

Besides, in order to interpret the Irish Catholic priest-people ratio correctly, one must take into account that almost the entire Catholic population are regular practicants. The demands made on the 58% of priests who are directly engaged in pastoral work are therefore unusually high. 'Our position is quite extraordinary,' writes Daphne D. C. Pochin Mould. 'We are a people who take the existence of God for granted and, I suppose, alone in the modern world, a nation that attends Sunday worship regularly as a taken-for-granted universal custom.'

In an article in *Études* in May 1964 Fr John C. Kelly, S.J., tries to take a sober view of Irish religious practice. Remarking that some people would say that social pressures play a part in the large attendance at Sunday Mass and that there may be some truth in this, he goes on to say:

> On the other hand, in Dublin, and certainly in the country, people undergo real hardship, without complaining, to attend Sunday Mass. They are present Sunday after Sunday in circumstances which, in the opinion of even the strictest moral theologian, would excuse them from attendance. There are some more facts that give one pause. The most important of these is the number of people in Dublin who attend morning Mass on weekdays before going to work. This is one of the phenomena of Dublin (population 650-700,000). From 6.30 in the morning until about 8.30 there are large congregations at Mass and many receive Holy Communion. This is certainly sincere…On feasts of the Church and particularly at the Easter liturgy, in more than one Dublin church as many as ten thousand hosts must be consecrated so that the huge numbers of people present may receive Holy Communion. It is impossible to think that most of these people are not genuine and sincere. They are under no obligation. They act freely.

Attendance at weekday Mass increased rather than diminished during the 1950s. Most urban churches have at least six Masses on Sunday morning. The scene outside a Dublin suburban church between two Sunday Masses, with police on special traffic duty, special Mass-buses arriving and departing, and perhaps 200 cars parked or moving slowly through the crowded streets, is one which explains many things about Irish Catholicism—about its strength and its problems—to the sensitive observer. (There is a common misconception that Irish Catholicism, almost entirely urban in its foreign transplantations, is still closely connected with agriculture at home. In this regard, it should be taken into account that only 35% of the working population of the Republic are engaged in agriculture.)

However, amid all this activism and partly because of it, theology and philosophy slumbered. Theology was accepted as something finished and given, not as something in need of constant re-making through the personal confrontation of knowing Christians with the truth of Christ and his Church. It was not, as the cliché would have it, that Irish priests were 'unintellectual' or 'anti-intellectual'. They included all types, and some of them could be thus described. Many, on the other hand, have been outstanding scholars in various spheres of secular learning. For many decades past, all of them have received a thorough theological training. It was the attitude to theology of the 'intellectual' priests which was the real fault. Their concept of intellectual endeavour in the theological sphere was too narrowly rationalistic and too exclusively bound up with scholastic textbooks and commentaries. The intellectualism which they practised was typically Late Tridentine—legalistic, positivistic, academic. Their arid, doctrinally correct sermons were often too abstract, too untouched by life—by the lives of the individual preachers to begin with. Due to this stagnation of theology, there were few voices in Ireland to say with authority that Late Tridentine Catholicism, however 'successful' in its Irish embodiment, was not enough for Christian men and women, that it omitted too much of life. While this was being said by a growing number of theologians in the French- and German-speaking parts of the Continent—while the present radical restatement of Christianity was being prepared by men deeply involved in the acute crisis of their own local churches—the leaders of the Irish Church seemed intent merely on holding the bastion of Irish faith and practice; most of the innovating personalities and tendencies were channelled (some might say forced) into missionary activism abroad.

During the period between 1920 and the Second World War the single far-reaching innovation in the strictly internal life of Irish Catholicism was, oddly enough, the work of laymen. The establishment of the Irish State and the framing and implementation of the Constitution of 1937 not only effected a radical change in the temporal circumstances of Irish Catholicism and opened new possibilities for its redemptive action. As the work of Catholics, assented to by a Catholic people, it ushered in a form of Church-State relations and of Catholic relationship to modern civil society which had no precedents. There have been other changes in the life of the Irish Catholic people since 1920 which, in their cumulative effect, were pointing towards the necessity for a radical restatement of the Christian message: increasing access to secondary and higher education; widening experience in all fields; the weakening of Irish nationalism as a buttress to Catholic belief and practice; the consequent ideological vacuum and the impact of liberal material-ism both on the people at home and, even more so, on the mil-lion Irish-born Catholics now living in Britain; increasing affluence; large-scale movement from the country to (Irish and English) cities. Due, however, to the stagnation of theology, the Irish Church failed to make an adequate creative response to these changes (cf. Nivard Kinsella, in *Rural Ireland*).

True, in the years between the Second World War and the Coun-cil a movement towards the intensification of Catholic life in Ireland got under way. It was not a 'movement' really until the Council came and gathered all its forces together. It was a series of decisions and initiatives which were not inspired by any new theological vi-sion of Irish origin, but which implied a new concern for the qual-ity of Irish Catholic life. Perhaps it was partly due to the imposed isolation of the war years, when Ireland remained neutral. During these years certain imaginative personalities of the Irish Church may have been forced to be interior, to turn in on themselves.

In the fifteen years before the Council two journals were found-ed which were to act as literary focal points for the new currents: *The Furrow*, edited from Maynooth by Dr J. G. McGarry, and *Doc-trine and Life*, edited by Austin Flannery, O.P., in Dublin. New insti-tutes and congresses were founded: an annual Irish Liturgical Con-gress in the Benedictine Abbey of Glenstal; the Dublin Institute of Catholic Sociology, sponsored by the Archbishop of Dublin, Dr John Charles McQuaid; the Christus Rex movement of priest so-ciologists (with its journal of the same name edited by Dr Jeremiah Newman of Maynooth); the Social Study Congress in Dublin. The Jesuits opened a college for trade unionists. Irish publishers, with the Mercier Press of Cork in the lead, translated many German and French theological works. Old-established Catholic journals passed into the hands of new editors and showed marked improvement. Biblical studies made some progress despite episcopal restraints. Pre-marital courses for engaged couples and young married people were established at several centres. *Doctrine and Life* began the publication of a special journal for nuns. Summer courses and study meetings of all kinds multiplied. An excellent vernacular Ritual in Irish and English was adopted. Some architects, priests, sculptors, and painters began to collaborate fruitfully for the renewal of church architecture and sacred art.

Far from producing complacency, this new 'movement' was accompanied by growing dissatisfaction with the status quo and by increasing concern about the future. From about 1957 onwards sharp public self-criticism began: by priests of themselves and their fellow-clergy, by laymen of the clergy and of the Irish Church structure as a whole. This criticism was encouraged by the Council and by the progressive propaganda which accompanied it. At present it is both widespread and intense. The well-known negative criticisms of Irish Catholicism by Irishmen and by foreigners have been faced up to and analysed by priests (cf., for example, Denis Meehan, *The Furrow*, April 1957 and August 1960; Kevin Smyth, S.J., *ibid.*, March 1958; Seosamh Ó Nualláin, *ibid.*, April 1958).

The contribution by Fr Smyth, a theologian and biblical scholar, was especially significant, since it was originally read as a paper to the Maynooth Union Summer School in 1957. Some of his introductory remarks offered a basis for the further critical discussion and could have helped to make it constructive—if they had been heeded:

> The healthy state of the [Irish] Church is so obvious that anything like an orgy of self-criticism would be unbalanced and pointless. Whatever may be called for in Latin America, in Italy, or France, there is no need here for a dirge to a decaying priesthood, an estranged and dechristianized people. However, we priests are perfectionists…we echo Mao Tse-Tung in China recently: 'Let a hundred flowers of criticism bloom, let schools of thought contend.' There may be some defects in what Continental Catholic intellectuals call '*le catholicisme du type irlandais*'. There may be certain manifestations of anticlericalism in our country which are depressing if not terrifying. There may be instances of a lack of soundness in the moral fibre and religious sense of the Catholics whom we produce. While listening for the discords, we must not be deaf to the great fundamental harmonies which have produced what is perhaps the most

solid achievement of Catholic culture in the world, an achievement hard to parallel elsewhere, except in Catholic bodies which are precisely modelled on the *type irlandais*, namely the Church in England, America, and Australia.

Other writers have gone beyond the well-worn lines of criticism to formulate personal critiques (cf. John C. Kelly, S.J., *Doctrine and Life*, October–November 1959; Desmond Fennell, *ibid.*, May 1962; John A. Dowling, *The Furrow*, March 1964). The debate eventually spread to the seminaries, the universities, the newspapers, and television. The *Evening Press*, *The Irish Times*, and *Hibernia* made useful contributions.

Television discussions of Irish Catholicism by young lay people brought shocks, amazement, gratification, and displeasure into many homes. If the participants had been chosen because of their knowledge of Irish Catholicism and of Catholic life generally, these discussions would have been even more useful than they were—certainly more constructive. As it was—and as so frequently happens when Irish Catholics are discussing their country or their religion—intensity of feeling was often mistaken for knowledge and thought both by the participants and by many who heard them. A great deal of this widened public debate was bedevilled by ignorance and provincial-mindedness. Very little effort has been made by Irish lay Catholics to study their Catholicism systematically, to amass or to publish rationally ordered knowledge of it. Hence, the provincial assumption that it was the best thing in the world shifted easily—under the impact of fashion and unhampered by knowledge—to the even more provincial-minded conviction that it was the worst thing and that the proper norms of human and of Christian living were all to be found elsewhere.

The reaction away from the inherited Catholicism has been accompanied by a reaction away from nationalist ideology. This coincidence and the resulting ideological vacuum have confused the issue very much indeed. Unfortunately, Irish churchmen had failed to supply the practising, believing Catholics who govern and administer the country and who live in it as citizens with positive Christian inspiration for their temporal concerns and activities. The Prime

Minister, Mr Seán Lemass, had to wait for Pope John's encyclicals to get effective Christian guidance for his Government's social policies.

Thus the reaction away from nationalism has been accompanied in many cases by an atavistic return to reliance on England for ideological inspiration—and this means a turning towards liberal materialism. Irish liberal materialists and anti-Catholics have had a heyday as soured Catholics gathered round them. Trinity College, the more or less Protestant university which has not quite outlived its colonialist tradition, has acted as a focal point for negativism. *The Irish Times*, a Protestant-owned newspaper and a sort of Irish version of the English *Guardian*, has played a provocative 'outsider's' role, publishing variations on the theme that 'you Irish [Catholics] are not as good as you think you are'. Part of the vogue is to look 're- alistically' at Irish (read 'Irish Catholic') life. This is tacitly identified with looking at its seamy side and, in the light of secular criteria, not of Christian supernaturalism. Some have discovered that 'lib- eral and enlightened opinion' is the norm which Christians should conform to. Amid such confusion students, journalists, and others can be heard lecturing clergy and people in these terms: 'Listen to Pope John and Karl Rahner, do what the Labour Government did in Britain (in the late 1940s) and approve of those things which *The Guardian* and the London *Observer* approve of.' In short, provincial- mindedness is having a fresh innings under new forms.

Amid the welter of self-assertion and of ideological manoeuvring many Catholics whose first concern is that their Church increase in Christian fruitfulness look expectantly and apprehensively towards their bishops. Clergy and laymen, they form a sort of a seething un- derground. They want to graft the best of the new Church life on to Irish Catholicism. Most of them now believe that this is not merely a desirable thing but the only way to save the Irish Church from a sudden, acute crisis.

This more urgent note was heard in the writings and public statements of Irish Catholics some time after the movement of self- criticism had got under way. The transition to this view of the future can be noticed in a lecture which Fr P. Corcoran, S.M., gave in 1958. Fr Corcoran said:

The danger, I think, is that we have made vast progress with our secular education; we have not made anything like the same progress with our religious education in relation to new needs…I am aware that we possess a vast capital of strong faith inherited from the ages of persecution…(but) we cannot afford to live just on this capital, otherwise it will be eaten away imperceptibly.'

When, in *Doctrine and Life* of May 1962, Desmond Fennell published an essay entitled 'Will the Irish Stay Christian?', his question was still so unspeakable and impolite that the title was changed on the cover of the magazine to the innocuous 'Ireland and Christianity'. Yet such was the positive response to this article that a few months later, when a comment by James Scott on the same theme was announced on the cover, that dread question was printed fearlessly. Mr Fennell's thesis was that Ireland could follow the rest of Europe away from Christianity through the failure of its Christian leaders to 'know the times', through a failure of intellect and charity combined. In March of this year (1964) John A. Dowling, speaking on behalf of what he called 'interested, fair-minded, and educated Catholics', wrote: 'We fear, from personal experience, observation, and report .. that Irish Catholicism has a predictably limited future as the faith of the mass of our people.'

His essay was a meditative reflection on the present feelings of the committed Catholic intelligentsia about their bishops. The Irish bishops had gone to the Council and had said very little. It seemed they had been taken by surprise. They returned and said very little.

★ ★ ★

If the renewal proposed by the Council and by the reforming element in the Church is to become effective in Ireland, this should mean a new theology resulting in a new kind of priest and a new kerygma. Elements of the new kerygma would be liturgical and catechetical renewal, ecumenical initiatives, and a new evaluation of the layman's role. What are the chances?

To the extent that the renewal consists of external activities, forms, new words and phrases, assent to certain attitudes, the signs are that it will pass into Irish Catholicism without much ado. To a considerable extent, it has already done so. The new theological language has become normal in the better journals. *The Furrow* and *Doctrine and Life* have been so active in things ecumenical that the names of non-Catholic clergymen in their tables of contents no longer cause any surprise. There have been a few theological study meetings of Catholic and non-Catholic clergymen. Disinterest and reserve are still widespread, but the only real opposition comes from a section of Belfast Presbyterianism.

The bishops met in June 1964 and took decisions about the use of the vernaculars in the liturgy. During the thirteen years of its existence the Irish Liturgical Congress has spread liturgical education among a considerable number of priests. It is difficult to gauge the attitude of the people and of the priests in general towards liturgical change. To judge by the laity's responses to minor innovations during the past decade, they are willing to adapt themselves to anything. There is a deep trust of the Church and, among the more educated, an experimental, expectant frame of mind. In secular affairs an experimental, innovating atmosphere is abroad. The Republic is experiencing an industrial boom, and the population is at last increasing. The people feel that their country and their society have still to be made—so that open-mindedness in regard to religious forms does not require much effort. The shyness—even secretiveness—of Irish Catholics about their religious life may put obstacles in the way of some liturgical innovations.

In the course of his ninth world tour in 1964 Fr Johannes Hofinger, the expert on modern catechetics, gave courses in Ireland, Britain, and Africa. He attracted his biggest audiences to date when he gave two complete courses in Belfast and Waterford, plus a special three-day session for priests in Dublin. Both Belfast and Waterford were compelled to refuse hundreds of applications due to lack of space, while the former had to have recourse to closed-circuit television to accommodate its 1,300 participants. In all, Fr Hofinger delivered eighty hour-long lectures in twenty days. It was by far the biggest catechetical event ever held in Ireland. The simple explanation is that Irish catechists were better prepared than many realised. Much quiet work had been going on behind the scenes. For example, many of the orders of nuns and brothers had been sending their members to study at such centres as Lumen Vitae, Jesus Magister and Regina Mundi. A few bishops had also sent priests abroad to study catechetics. These and other contacts with the movement had prepared the way.

One consideration which argues against the fear that the Church in Ireland is heading for disaster is the enthusiasm—the absence of 'weariness'—among the pastoral clergy. High ambition, however naive sometimes, is met with everywhere. The Primate of All Ireland, Archbishop Conway, stated some months ago (in an interview given to *The Word*) that Irish Catholics, because of their later, more gradual approach 'to the newer forms of modern civilisation' had an 'opportunity to christianise this oncoming civilisation to the core'. Such ambition does not seem inordinate to many Irish Catholics.

In the course of an interview, Fr Hans Küng has said:

> I saw in America and England how important is the position of the Irish in the Catholic world. I saw the great heart of the American and British hierarchy was Irish…A great deal depends on Ireland as to how the renewal of all Christians is put into practice in a large part of the world. On the Continent people often think that the Catholic Church in Ireland is very 'conservative', but I know that the Catholic Church in Ireland has a very, very great tradition and I know…that it is a living thing in the faith and practice of the people. At one time it was so on the Continent…I think we have done very many good things too late.

For the birth of Oisín, Mary had needed a Caesarian section and was likely to need that for subsequent births. So because there was a doctor in Limerick whom she specially trusted, in early 1966 when she was expecting again, she travelled to Limerick, leaving me with Oisín in Freiburg. I missed her greatly. She returned five months later with our second son, Cilian. Half-way through that same year Herbert Auhofer had a fatal car accident. I was appointed Editor of Herder Correspondence *and was permitted to move the editorial office to Dublin. I gave notice to the Breandán Ó hEithir family to whom we had rented our cottage in Dundrum; but they delayed leaving it so that when I returned to Dublin—with Mary*

and our two sons following after—we had to stay for a while with Augus-
tine Martin and his wife, Clair.

That year, 1966. was the fiftieth anniversary of the 1916 Rising
and with that in mind I had been reading the writings and speeches of
the leading revolutionaries and noting that their common leading theme
was the restoration of man in Ireland. The following essay, (from About
Behaving Normally in Abnormal Circumstances, *Belfast, 2003)*
marking a later anniversary, is the most comprehensive piece I have written
on that subject.

THE HUMANISM OF 1916

I BELIEVE THE best way to honour the men of 1916 is to recall pe-
riodically what they were about and to consider its continuing relevance to us. Those of them who were articulate—who wrote and
spoke for all of them—were by their own words humanists who
directed their efforts to restoring the broken Irish people to proper
humanity. They wanted the Irish to live humanly again, and took
measures to bring that about. By living humanly they meant living as men and women who, freed from the psychological, material
and political obstacles to being their normal human selves, use their
freedom to be that.

Two French travellers in Ireland, writing seventy-five years apart,
give us an idea of what the rebels found themselves up against. Gus-
tave de Beaumont, in 1835, had observed the Catholic Irishman as
he moved out of the period of the Penal Laws. He noted in him
'that *laisser aller*, that carelessness of his person, that total absence of
self-respect and personality, which are the direct results of his former
condition'. But again later, in 1908, when the Revolution was gathering force, Paul Dubois saw little change: 'A fine talker, but devoid
of the critical sense, vaunting and verbose...Full of physical courage,
he is often deficient in moral courage: he lacks confidence in himself, initiative, and energy, and has lost the habit of looking things in
the face. He quails before responsibilities, and has forgotten how to
will, for his soul is still a serf.'

More profoundly than against the British state in Ireland, the

1916 Rebellion was against that inhuman condition of the Irish. In his poem 'The Rebel' Padraic Pearse has a political rebel who is 'of the blood of serfs' express his motivation with the line: 'I that have a soul greater than the souls of my people's masters.' Thomas McDonagh wrote a poem, 'The Man Upright', about a man who was distinguished by that characteristic from the others in his village. Pearse interpreted Irish nationalism as fundamentally a humanism. He wrote:

> One loves the freedom of men because one loves men. There is therefore a deep humanism in every true Nationalist. There was a deep humanism in Tone; and there was a deep humanism in Davis.

James Connolly wanted victory for the workers, not in the first place because it would mean higher pay or better housing, but rather, as he wrote because 'every victory for labour helps to straighten the cramped soul of the Irish labourer'. Proudly he said of the Irish Transport and General Workers' Union:

> It found the workers of Ireland on their knees, and has striven to raise them to the erect position of manhood; it found them with all the vices of slavery in their souls and strove to eradicate those vices and replace them with some of the virtues of free men; it found them with no other weapons of defence than the arts of the liar, the lick-spittle and the toady…and it taught them to abhor these arts.

It was for the sake of this rehumanisation of the Irish that the rebels rose against the British state in Ireland in pursuit of a free and sovereign Irish state. Like everyone in Europe at the time, the insurgents regarded such a state as the necessary environment for human beings to realise themselves.

They were in accord with Terence MacSwiney who wrote: 'A man facing life is gifted with certain powers of soul and body… In a free State he is in the natural environment for full self-development.' For Pearse, the political and human goals were one: 'Independence,' he wrote, 'one must understand to include spiritual and intellectual independence as well as political independence.'

The rebels, along with the rest of nationalist Ireland, assumed that in a free Irish state there would naturally emerge the material basis for 'full self-development': a prosperous Irish economy. All the free states of Europe had flourishing economies.

While most of the leading men of 1916 believed that the creation of a sovereign, prosperous republic would suffice to realise their rehumanising aim, a few of them saw the need for a prior act on the way to that. In subsequent years, what these men envisaged has been called, inaccurately and meaninglessly, 'blood sacrifice'— a term applied by the English to their soldiers killed in the Great War. For accuracy, at the very least, 'redemptive' should precede that term. Redemption, rather than sacrifice was at the core of the rebels' thinking. They envisaged a redemptive bloodletting in imitation of Christ's death on the Cross.

Pearse, like some others in Europe at the times, was eloquent about the redemptive efficacy, in a spiritually desiccated age, of the shedding of blood in battle. In his play *The Singer*, he has his self-image, the freedom-fighter MacDara, say, 'One man can free a people as one Man redeemed the world.' In some of the mystical religious poetry of Joseph Mary Plunkett there lurks the hope, variously expressed, that the poet's own blood would make 'the dark rose (An Róisín Dubh)...redden into bloom'. Connolly made the most explicit statement. In March 1916 he wrote:

> Deep in the heart of Ireland has sunk the sense of degradation wrought upon its people...so deep and humiliating that no agency less potent than the red tide of war on Irish soil will ever be able to enable the Irish race to recover its self-respect...Without the slightest trace of irreverence, but in all due humility and awe, we recognise that of us, as of mankind before Calvary, it may be truly said: 'Without the shedding of blood there is no redemption.'

That the republic they wanted to bring into being would not be an end in itself, but an instrument for the people's sake, and that the economy they wanted to build would not be an end in itself but a means to that people's human fulfilment, all the leading rebels were in accord.

Pearse wrote, 'Man is not primarily a member of a State but a human individuality.' Liam Mellows, speaking in the Treaty Debate for the entire revolutionary struggle, said:

We would rather have this country poor and indigent, we would rather have the people of Ireland eking out a poor existence on the soil, as long as they possessed their souls, their minds and their honour. This fight has been for something more than the fleshpots of empire.

Michael Collins spelt that out:

What we hope for in the new Ireland is to have such material welfare as will give the Irish spirit the freedom to reach out to the higher things in which it finds its satisfaction. The uses of wealth are to provide good health, comfort, moderate luxury, and to give the freedom which comes from the possession of these things. Our object in building up the country economically must not be lost sight of. That object is not to be able to boast of enormous wealth or of a great body of trade, for their own sake. It is not to see our country covered with smoking chimneys and factories. It is not to show a great national balance-sheet, not to point to a people producing wealth with the self-obliteration of a hive of bees. The real riches of the Irish nation will be the men and women of the Irish nation, the extent to which they are rich in body and mind and character.

Looking back in his famous radio address of 1943, Eamon de Valera, Commander of the Boland's Mill garrison, concurred:

That Ireland we dreamed of would be the home of a people who valued material wealth only as the basis of right living, of a people who were satisfied with frugal comfort and devoted their leisure to the things of the spirit.

All of that, broadly speaking, is what the men of 1916 were about. Their aim and their striving towards it are, insofar as we assent to them, their legacy to us in the different circumstances of today.

In the Christmas 1965 edition of the Dublin monthly Comhar *I had published an essay in Irish, 'Cuireadh chun na Tríú Réabhlóide' ('Invitation to the Third Revolution. A Humanist Essay'). The title was taken from an essay by the contemporary Yugoslav writer Mihailo Mihailov in which, after an extended visit to the Soviet Union, he wrote—and was*

jailed for publishing—that after the completion of the economic and social revolutions Communism's third, humanistic revolution was now required.

In 1968, because I was tired of the job, I resigned from Herder Correspondence. *Mary and I decided to move to South Conamara on the Atlantic coast, an Irish-speaking district, part of that group of districts known as the Gaeltacht. I will come to that move. But because it was to result in our getting involved in Irish-language matters, and specifically in the effort to restore Irish as the language of the Irish nation, I quote from my article published in 1970 in* Twentieth Century Studies, No. 5, *University of Kent, which gives some historical background.*

THE IRISH LANGUAGE MOVEMENT:
ACHIEVEMENT AND FAILURE

WRITING IN *The Irish Times* in January 1969, I said of English-speaking Ireland as a whole that after many years of Irish-language 'revival' 'not a single street, not a single pub or shop or café in Galway—not to mention Dublin or any other city—has become *even predominantly* Irish-speaking during the past fifty years.' When I wrote that, I had already been living several months in Irish-speaking Conamara, almost 50 miles north-west of Galway city. It was a statement which, I regret to say, no one could contradict.

The Irish language movement depended for its efficacy both on *the suitability of its structure* for its purpose and on *the will to an Irish-speaking life* in the movement itself and in Ireland generally. The structure contained, as well as some useful features, several in-built impediments to success. As for the will to an Irish-speaking life, this was widely strong in the early period of the Gaelic League (founded 1893), but grew progressively weaker after the new state was established.

In the early period, for the space of a few years, the League was able to point to an image of the Bright and True Life and make Irish speech seem the kingpin of that life and the way to experience it. It was this image, and the movement of Irish men and women towards it, which irrupted like a whirlwind into Irish history, changing its course in a way which the League had not consciously intended. But when this image, and the faith it evoked, disintegrated and died, the language movement was left going through the same motions as before, without getting the same or even similar results.

The period in which the Gaelic League was founded was a high period of Celtic and, specifically, Gaelic scholarship. German, French, English and Irish scholars were engaged in exploring and sifting the ancient Gaelic language, literature and history with the enthusiasm of discoverers. Growing out of this, a poetic movement had arisen, in which Protestant Irishmen, such as Samuel Ferguson and Standish James O'Grady, were the leading figures. In verse and prose in English these writers cultivated in Gaelic terms the con-temporary European myth of ancient heroism and nobility.

The Gaelic League inserted itself into this context. Under its influence, another contemporary myth—that of the genuineness and nobility of peasant life—became a central theme of the Irish literary renaissance. The Gaelic districts of the West were seen as the place where ancient nobility and peasant nobility fused into a single Bright and True Life. Yeats, Synge and Lady Gregory were captured by the spell. Socialists, such as James Connolly, discovered that ancient Gaelic society offered a model for the socialist society. Theosophists, such as George Russell and Yeats, hoping for a return of holiness or divinity to the earth, found inspiration in the gods and other supernatural beings of the ancient Gaels.

The Gaelic League moved at the heart of all this, vending its language-primers, teaching its night-classes, founding new branch-es, organising historical excursions and festivals of Gaelic song and dance—drawing the intellectual cream of the rising generation from the cities and towns to the soul-shattering, liberating romance of summers in the Gaeltacht. To the dream-image which illuminated the Gaelic way of life, the League added the rational and cogent humanism of Hyde and others, showing by reasonable argument the desirable life which the restoration of Irish would restore to the Irish.

During those years the active mind of Ireland looked west with hope and longing. It disassociated itself from the mainstream men-tality of modern Irish history—that of a broken and depressed peo-ple valuing material power and status above all else. Guided by the League, several thousand Irish men and women saw integrity and honour as the prizes most to be sought for. When in 1916 a few of them, uniting this conviction with the older Fenian aspiration, planted Cuchulainn's standard in the Dublin GPO, they did not know that they were releasing a train of events which would dissipate the Gaelic vision and restore the mainstream mentality to ascendancy.

The logical course for the language movement after the establishment of the new State would have been to build its restoration of Irish on the foundation offered by the Gaelic districts. Its 'obvious' political course would have been to press the new state to make that foundation secure and to rebuild the nation around this old Gaelic nucleus. This obvious course was not taken because the language movement, now left visionless, was afflicted by a paralysed and divided will.

If the language movement, the people of the Gaeltacht, and of the new Irish state as a whole, had *effectively desired* to give Irish, at the very least, the status of Flemish in Belgium, they would have taken the obvious course of building on the available Gaeltacht foundations. In fact, however, there was no such effective desire, either in the Gaeltacht or among the people of the new state as a whole.

There was merely a vague wish, almost entirely confined to urban English-speakers; and this wish was rendered impotent by that older more effective desire which had characterised Irish life (more specifically, Irish Catholic life) for nearly a century previously. This was a desperate, overriding desire, both of individuals and of the collectivity, for *material power*, whether financial or political, and for the *status* which goes with such power. Since these could be had more quickly and more easily by speaking English, than by speaking Irish, and in cities rather than in the country, we could not seriously want to restore Irish, least of all in the rural Gaeltacht. We could only wish sentimentally for an Irish revival, make guilt-ridden and uncoordinated gestures in that direction, and employ Irish as a shibboleth in our revolutionary state-building—much as Marxist-Leninist language was employed in Soviet Russia.

But our dilemma was even greater still. For the mentality I describe (which still predominates), any serious idea of living in an Irish-speaking milieu day-in day-out—and hence of *creating* such a milieu throughout Ireland—was traumatically abhorrent. Most of us feel that an Irish-speaking milieu would not only be inferior to, but the very opposite of that 'modern', 'urban', 'sophisticated', 'enlightened' and 'not-native-Irish' life that we predominately desire. Deep down, Irish is bound up in our feelings with that world of things 'native', 'narrow', 'old', 'peasant', and 'poor' which we have been struggling desperately to get out of. We feel that a 'native Irish' mentality and way of life betoken insecurity, insularity, intellectual impotence and lack of status in contemporary circumstances.

Since the Gaeltacht, with its small farmers and fishermen, was (is) that alarming world incarnate to an extreme degree, there could be no question of our wanting seriously to build on the Gaeltacht, or of our seeing any useful future for it.

This applied to language enthusiasts almost as much as to anyone else. Except for learning Irish, for summer holidays, and (a few of them) for occasional missions as do-gooders, they have avoided the Gaeltacht. Love of the language was a fine thing, but it must not mean sacrificing city life, a well-pensioned job, a substantial income or the corridors of power and status. Let the Government save the Gaeltacht but no one except the natives live there!

Finally, as it so happened, the Gaeltacht was on the opposite side of the country from England. For a mentality which saw England as power and status incarnate—as the living image of what we most keenly hungered for—that finally sealed the Gaeltacht's fate. Today more than ever, we still regard distance from England—in a geographic-economic sense or intellectually—as a black mark and as something to be avoided at all costs.

This unbalanced craving for power and status above all else was a normal enough reaction in a people so ground down and broken as we had been. Consider the case of the Germans after both World Wars, or of the Jews in Europe during the past century and a half. But however normal in the circumstances, our single-minded devotion, individually and collectively, to getting on top made the restoration of Irish a lost cause. Useless for our primary purpose, it had no hope against our bitter hatred of our inherited condition.

Such was the analysis of the situation which I offered in the aforementioned article in *The Irish Times*. I concluded by pointing out the 'instructive parallels' to be found in the recent history of the Jews:

> As growing numbers of Jews, leaving their ghettoes, struck out for social and economic power, Yiddish gradually became a badge of inferiority and of the bad old life. The successful among them discarded it in favour of the major European languages. It was not until Hebrew, by its association with the saga of the state of Israel, acquired new status, that successful Jews were willing to speak 'Jewish language' again.
>
> In explaining the revival of Hebrew, too much has been made of the need of the diverse bodies of Jewish immigrants for a *lingua franca*. If that had been the overriding consideration, any one of several major languages would have served just as well and would have seemed more advantageous and less troublesome. Obviously, it was a strong spiritual force that made archaic Hebrew the chosen language. Obviously, too, the spirit which made the desert bloom in Israel, and swept Hebrew to new status, was a breakaway from the main Jewish stream upwards and westwards to the fleshpots of New York. Some few thousand who believed deeply sank their all, and revived their language, in their Promised Land.

After that kind of talk the next logical step (which I took) was to propose a 'New Israel' in the Gaeltacht. My friend Professor Augustine Martin of UCD, writing in a new South Conamara paper, Iris Iarchonnacht★ *(May 1970), called it 'The Last Ditch':*

> The people of Irish-speaking Ireland must change from objects into subjects—turn themselves inside out. The first sign of this happening was in the anger of the young men who objected to the Teach Furbo affair [a protest against the recording by RTÉ television of a programme in English in a Gaeltacht hotel that led to the foundation of the Gaeltacht Civil Rights movement]. They were no longer willing to be acted upon by an outside and alien world…and, how-

★ By then I was in Irish-speaking South Conamara and taking part in its 'revolution' and had persuaded the activists to revive the old name of that district, namely Iarchonnacht. *Iris* means 'Journal'.

ever harmlessly, misrepresented. This is new and it is good…It is a last-ditch stand…If it is to succeed the impetus must come from within the Gaeltacht, inside Iarchonnacht.* That impetus can only be generated by a revolution and there's an exciting possibility that one is on the way.

THE GAELTACHT REVOLUTION *

IN THE AUTUMN of 1968 I moved with wife and three young children (our first daughter, Natasha, so named after the character in Tolstoy's *War and Peace*, had been born the previous January) from Dublin to Maoinis, a small island connected by a bridge to the mainland near Cárna village in South Conamara. The immediate reason for moving was Dublin city's intention to widen the road (Churchtown Road) in front of our cottage. Somehow we got it into our heads that we would move to the West, and we chose Maoinis principally because it was a beautiful place and a house to rent was available there. Mary, an enthusiastic swimmer, liked living beside the sea, and both of us were attracted to the idea of living in the Gaeltacht—it was like going abroad again. We could afford the move because I had saved some money and Mary was offered in nearby Cárna a temporary teaching job in the nuns' secondary school which became permanent. I wanted to get on with my book on the present age and Maoinis seemed a good place to write it. Within a year we had bought a half-acre in the Meall Rua quarter and got a local builder, Jackie Dowd, to build a house on it on rising ground with a view out to sea.**

Years later we discovered that in 1968, in West European countries and the USA, a trickle of families and individuals began to move voluntarily from the power-centres to the peripheries. In France, 1968 is looked back to as the year when a resurgence of the depressed cultures on the French periphery—Breton, Occitan, Alsatian and so on—began. In Paris there was a revival of interest in

---

* From 'The View from Maoinis' in *Beyond Nationalism: The Struggle Against Provinciality in the Modern World*, Ward River Press, Swords, 1985.

** Later, also from Dublin, Tomás de Bhaldraithe built a house near us and Maurice Manning bought land to build a house.

these cultures, and a drift of young intellectuals and artists from the capital to the regions in question. All of this, it seems, was connected with the 'May Revolution' of that year which rattled the French state to its foundations. In France, as elsewhere in the western world, there was a sharp loss of faith in 'the centre' and a corresponding movement from the centre to the periphery. It was around this time, too, that Welsh, Scottish, Cornish and Breton nationalism began a period of resurgence. Unknown to ourselves, therefore, when we moved west, we were being moved by the 'spirit of 1968'.

The Gaeltacht itself was being moved by the same spirit: it began to assert itself, politically, for the first time in the spring of 1969, here in South Conamara, and I participated in that assertion. But of course the chief peripheral stirring in Ireland in those years occurred among the Six-County Irish who, feeling abandoned by Dublin and cast on their own resources, launched the Northern Ireland Civil Rights Movement.

It transpired that our baby daughter Natasha had very poor eyesight and needed glasses. Medical advice was that she was infected by toxoplasmosis and that she had received it during pregnancy from an infection which Mary had probably got during her previous pregnancy with Cilian when she made the above-mentioned bus tour of Russia; and that the infection came most likely from a cat. Years later in her early teens, Natasha would lose sight altogether and treatment would restore it to thirty per cent. She would subsequently live with that, not wearing glasses but seeing adequately for daily life and using a magnifying glass for reading or other similar activities, while becoming a successful businesswoman and author.

Mary and I had made a resolution that, for a year at least, we would 'not become involved in anything', meaning any local 'cause'. There was as yet, when we arrived, no local indigenous Gaeltacht cause, but we knew, in a general, Dublin sort of way, that 'the West' was a cause because of its depressed economic circumstances, and that this Western cause included many local causes. Hence our deliberate resolution.

Our two boys attended the island primary school. One night, about three months after taking up residence, Mary and I in the house's sitting-room heard through the open door of the boys' bedroom that they were talking—very normal—but that they *were talking Irish*. Spontaneously, they had made the language shift. Given that Mary and I knew Irish well, from then on we became, except between Mary and me, an Irish-speaking family.

I worked daily towards the new image of the age that I was seeking. I saw it as an age that was 'not bad really, only depressed'. I drew on contemporary American, English, Irish and continental examples to illustrate this. At the same time, I found this general view of the age confirmed by what I saw around me in the microcosm of Maoinis, with its 175 inhabitants, and in the larger microcosm of Cárna parish to which Maoinis belongs.

Here, in this 'traditional rural community' of good neighbours and friendly people (friendly, that is, to us despite our being *stráinséirí*, strangers) community life had disintegrated, households lived their own lives; individualism was the dominant mode; individuals lived their own lives; there was little communication within families; celebration had almost vanished. For most of those who stayed at home, the standard of living had become good and continually rising. Money, the local party (Fianna Fáil), and distant bureaucrats were the powers that ruled life, or rather, the powers which were felt to do so. The greatest power was the people's image of their life and that was a depressive image which falsely portrayed many desirable things—including 'real' life—as possible elsewhere and for others, but impossible 'for us here' (and even impossible 'for us, as individuals, elsewhere, except by becoming other than we are').* As a consequence, people lived below their capacity as persons, insulated from the life they shared, diminished by unnecessary dependence, and suffering unnecessary fear.

Working on my picture of the present age viewed from Maoinis, Cárna, and South Conamara, within the general setting of Ireland,

---

* Running through *Beyond Nationalism,* which I am quoting from, was a theory of representation, set out at the beginning, which posited roughly that people live in accordance with how their collective circumstance is represented or imaged to them. Probably this view of things was influenced by that vision I had had in Småland of the Swedes suffering because they were being guided by a 'wrong map'.

I was stretched on a sort of rack. In order to depict the present age intelligibly I had to sketch the last few hundred years of European history; set this present age off against other ages; and relate it to a general picture of man in world and history. At the same time, in order to give the picture a foreground and relate it to where I stood, I had to sketch the contours of Irish life in the recent past and in the present, and centre it on the life immediately around me. This gave me a sharp eye for the life immediately around me, and to look at it was to encounter, necessarily, the oppressive images which weighed on it. As the days passed, and I experienced these images—or their effects rather—with increasing keenness, I felt impelled to do something about them straight away.

Two months after settling in Maoinis, and a few weeks before Christmas, I was asked to join the choir preparing songs for Christmas in Cárna parish church. I am no singer, but the choir was small and I didn't like the thought of Cárna at Christmas, with many sons and daughters home from England and Dublin, feeling perhaps that its choir, like so much else about it, was a poor, inadequate thing. That would do its image of itself no good. So I joined and went to practices.

Shortly before Christmas, so that the congregation could take part in the singing, I went to Galway and got a few hundred stencilled copies made of the words. On Christmas Eve and on the following day I went around the church before Mass distributing them to the people. As I did so, I became aware that, in their eyes, this was a remarkable initiative for a layman to take in church, and that my doing it gave them a realer image of the Church, of the status of the laity within it, and therefore of what was possible for lay people including, vaguely, themselves. At the same time I knew my action didn't represent those realities very effectively to them because I was a *stráinséar* and not one of themselves. But I mention the incident because it was the first time I realised that, besides language, other symbolic systems, and representative institutions, *significant personal behaviour or action* was part of the repertoire available for representing the nature of things and circumstances, and the possibilities immanent in people.

The Church was misrepresented in Cárna by a pious but eccentric parish priest who was as famed for the effectiveness of his curses as he was for his faith-healing. His Mass, nominally in Irish, was an unintelligible gibberish of mispronunciation lasting from one and a half to two hours. In order to counter this misrepresentation somewhat, I got the reading of the Lessons by laymen introduced into the Mass. So as to remedy it more comprehensively, and to establish *some* representative body for the parish, I took steps to get an elected parish council set up. More precisely, since the parish actually functioned as two half-parishes, Cárna proper and Cill Chiaráin, each with its own church, I tried as a first step, to get an elected council for the Cárna half-parish. My idea was that the council should have both ecclesiastical and general functions, albeit without any legal power. In the ensuing public debate organised by the parish curate throughout the parish, this became known as a 'broad' council. The local Fianna Fáil party organisation opposed it, and advocated a 'narrow' council , confined to the ecclesiastical sphere. The majority of people opted for the broad council. Along with fourteen others, I was elected to it. A similar council was elected for the Cill Chiaráin half-parish.

★ ★ ★

The holiest place in Cárna parish is Macdara's Island. St Macdara is venerated along the Conamara coast and is the patron saint of the local fishermen. On the island there is a twelfth-century church built in his honour and called Macdara's Church. Every year, on 16 July, a pilgrimage is made to the island, and this is followed by festivities on the mainland.

The church, at the time I am talking about, was in a semi-ruinous state, largely because the roof had fallen in a long time previously. This was accepted by the parish as an irreversible circumstance. I wrote to the National Monuments Commission asking them to restore the church. The director, Percy Le Clerc, came to Cárna and I took him to see the church and introduced him to the chairman and secretary of the parish council. He agreed to restore the church as nearly as possible to its original condition.

The work began a couple of years later. Then, with the approach of European Architectural Heritage Year in 1976, the authorities decided to include the restoration of Macdara's Church among the eight Irish contributions to the Year. The completion of the work was made the occasion for a three-day festival centring on the saint's day in July 1976. The chief feature of the festival was a race for the class of old Conamara sailing-boats known as 'hookers', of which about fourteen still survived in the entire country—most of them in a dilapidated condition. That race of three or four hookers marked the beginning of the great revival of interest in all classes of old Conamara sailing-boats. The dilapidated hookers were refurbished, and there is now a season of regattas for hookers, *gleoiteogs* and *púcáns* in various Conamara venues every summer. Subsequently, in 1982, when a new set of standard Irish postal stamps was issued, celebrating Irish architecture, the restored church was featured on the 29p and 30p stamps.

To return to when the two parish councils were being established. I was asked to write an article on the Gaeltacht for a special supplement of *The Irish Times*. This directed my attention to the South Conamara Gaeltacht as a whole and to the Gaelic language movement based on Dublin. The South Conamara Gaeltacht, including the Aran Islands, is a district comprising seven parishes, and it had a population at that time of about 13,500

The article which I wrote hurled some brutal realities about South Conamara and the language movement in the direction of the latter. [I have summarised part of it above]. It concluded by saying that in order to make South Conamara into a stable, representative Irish community of Gaelic speech, two immediate measures were needed. Firstly, the Government must establish a Development Authority for the district which would promote its economic development and aim to provide it with modern facilities equivalent to those of 'three average Irish towns of 7–8,000 population'. With this yardstick in mind, the authority would draw up a list of the kinds of skilled and professional people—butchers, bakers, lawyers, engineers—likely to be needed over a period of, say, five years. Secondly, the Government would make the implementation of the plan dependent on the requisite number of fluent language enthusiasts, with appropriate skills, pledging themselves to move to South Conamara when required. In other words, the Gaeilgeoirí of Dublin and the other English-speaking cities and towns must be willing to fol-

Macdara's Chapel off the Conamara coast; right, before reconstruction.

low the example of the Jews in their revival of Hebrew. If all went well—if the volunteers were found and the plan went ahead—then, after five years, the Development Authority would transfer its non-technological functions to an elected district council based on a network of elected parish councils. By then, however, South Conamara would be passing from a mere catching up with Irish modernity to

The stamp featuring the restored chapel, issued in 1982.

a pioneering role as it became 'Ireland's laboratory'. In local government structures, scientific research, liturgical innovation and so on, it would be breaking into the postmodern—thereby putting its traditional sense of apartness and abnormality to positive use.

Shortly after this article was published I wrote a letter to *The Irish Times* urging that, rather than wait for the Government to take the initiative, Gaeilgeoirí with capital or skills should imitate the Jewish pioneers directly by establishing colonies in Conamara and founding a 'New Israel' there. I said I would be available on a particular day at Professor Gus Martin's telephone number in Dublin.

In response to my call, a committee emerged in Dublin, headed by Seán Ó Muireagáin and Séamas Ó Síocháin. Linked to it, subsequently, in Conamara was another committee of which I was a member. The purpose of this loosely structured association was to promote the idea of Gaeilgeoirí moving from Dublin and elsewhere to the 'Gaelic frontier' in the West to found a 'new Israel', possibly in kibbutz form.

The area which I have referred to as the South Conamara Gaeltacht comprised most of southern Conamara and also the Aran Islands. The mainland part was referred to by its inhabitants simply as 'from Cárna to Bearna' (these being the villages at the two extremes). In short, this Gaelic-speaking district on the mainland and the islands, had no district name of its own. Obviously, if it was to be a representative unit of Irish life, and if its inhabitants were to have a clear image of it as a communal unit, it required such a name. So I resurrected an old district name, 'Iarchonnacht' (literally, West Connacht), which had lately fallen into disuse, and used it to designate the Gaelic-speaking district in question. This had the added advantage, in the context of the new movement and its propaganda, of breaking with all the mental associations of poverty, backwardness and defeat which were attached to the name 'Conamara'.

The slogan 'A New Israel in Iarchonnacht' became known throughout Ireland. By the summer of 1969 the group promoting the 'migration' scheme had decided on 1985 as the target year for the full emergence of the new Iarchonnacht, and it called itself, accordingly, 'Iarchonnachta 1985'.*

Meanwhile, in late March 1969, Gluaiseacht Chearta Sibhialta na Gaeltachta (The Gaeltacht Civil Rights Movement) had been founded in Iarchonnacht by a group consisting largely of young teachers, but including in Cárna parish a young factory manager, Seosamh Ó Tuairisc, and a young journalist, Seosamh Ó Cuaig. This was the first indigenous political movement to spring up in the Gaeltacht. I was consulted about the aims it should announce in its first manifesto and suggested two—a Gaeltacht radio station and democratic self-government for the Conamara Gaeltacht—which later became the movement's principal objectives. (As our range of interest and our ambition expanded, 'self-government for the Conamara Gaeltacht' became regional self-government for the entire Gaeltacht, that is, all the Gaeltacht districts and 'pockets' from Donegal to Kerry.)

Two months after the foundation of the civil rights movement, Iarchonnachta 1985 redefined itself as a joint venture of Gaeilgeoirí and native Iarchonnacht people. Both within the *Gluaiseacht* (as the Civil Rights Movement was commonly known) and in Iarchonnachta 1985, I established a close working relationship with Seosamh Ó Cuaig. A very intelligent and imaginative young man from Aill na Brún near Cill Chiaráin, he worked for the Dublin-based weekly *Inniu*. He was a great admirer of Lenin and was reading deeply in Castro and Che Guevara. We were both strongly attracted by the Cuban and Chinese revolutions because of their rural and peasant base; but where he leaned to Castro, I was more of a Maoist. I modernised the spelling of the island where I lived from Muighinis to 'Maoinis', which retained the word's sound and meaning ('Flat Island'), but which could be read, playfully, as Mao-inis (Mao Island).

Out of these beginnings there emerged the many-sided 'Gaeltacht revolution' of 1969 and the early 1970s. This is not the place

---

* The final 'a' added here to Iarchonnacht was an unnecessary archaism which I believed at the time to be 'more correct'.

to record its history, but some account of its main features, of my own part in it, and of what I learned from it, is relevant to my theme. While participating in the movement—as in other activities in these years which I shall come to presently—my view of what I and others were doing, and of its purpose, was usually influenced by my 'representationism', and was correspondingly different from my comrades' view. Very roughly, while they were doing things, and trying to achieve things, *for the people*, I was doing things so that the people, by re-seeing their shared life and its possibilities, would be *induced to do things which would make them a people, a community of communities, and thereby realised persons*; and I was trying to nudge our overall activities in this direction.

The Gluaiseacht, with Peadar Mac an Iomaire as its candidate, contested the general election of 1969 in Conamara. This helped to unsettle the slavish allegiance to the two main parties, and particularly to Fianna Fáil, which the rising prosperity was already loosening. Elected half-parish councils, on the Cárna model, spread throughout Iarchonnacht. They combined in a federation which, by-passing the official two-party structure, spoke for the district as a whole. For a time, there were two local journals, *Tuairisc* and *Iris Iarchonnacht*, representing the Gluaiseacht and Iarchonnachta 1985 respectively. *Tuairisc* lasted for several years. There was some bickering between the two journals, and some polemics between the two bodies that sponsored them, but this, far from detracting from the effectiveness of the movement as a whole, added spice and interest to it.

The Gluaiseacht demanded that the 'bilingual' signposts, which showed the Gaelic place names together with their anglicised corruptions, be replaced by signposts showing only the Gaelic forms. Activists painted out the offending signs. The Government agreed to change the signposts in the entire Gaeltacht. We called publicly on Ireland's Gaelic-language organisations to remove their headquarters from Dublin to Iarchonnacht. To their emphasis on *teanga* (language) we opposed our emphasis on *pobal* (people or community), maintaining that the language would look after itself if the communities which actually spoke it were stabilised through self-government. The principal annual festival of Gaelic literature and music, Oireachtas na Gaeilge, had been held for many years in Dublin. We demanded that it move to Iarchonnacht and, to back up our demand, organised a counter-festival, Oireachtas na nGael, in a field in Rosmuc. The Gaeltacht people and many Gaeilgeoirí flocked to it. Its proceedings were broadcast by a pirate radio, Saor-Raidió Chonamara, which also called on the government to establish a Gaeltacht radio. The Dublin organisers of Oireachtas na Gaeilge agreed to hold it every second year in the Gaeltacht. After more campaigning for the radio station—including more broadcasts by Saor-Raidió Chonamara—the government authorised RTÉ to establish Raidió na Gaeltachta with a studio in Iarchonnacht and two sub-stations in Kerry and Donegal.

In Cois Fharraige, the strip along Galway Bay which had the greatest number of activists, a multi-purpose co-operative was founded, and this was followed, through the 1970s, by the establishment of several more. There was a trickle of Gaeilgeoirí (language enthusiasts) settling in the Gaeltacht, either as freelancers or in the employment of Gaeltarra Éireann or the co-ops. (In 1968, Gaeltarra Éireann, the semi-state development company for the Gaeltacht which I had worked for in Dublin in the early 1960s, had moved its headquarters from Dublin to the eastern fringe of Iarchonnacht, and was steadily industrialising the Gaeltacht by importing factories.)

Among the freelancers who came to Iarchonnacht was Bob Quinn, the film-maker, who had resigned from RTÉ. No Gaeilgeoir to begin with, he soon became fluent. He set up a film company, Cinegael, which made a fortnightly video-tape of local events that was shown in pubs and halls. By making films of his own in Gaelic, he and his wife Helen (who became an expert in casting and locations) drew other independent film-makers to the district. Thus, within a space of five or six years, magazine-publishing, radio work, and video and film-acting had become part of the life of Gaelic-speaking Conamara, and to these the Cois Fharraige co-op added printing and book-publishing.

❖

To the extent that her teaching duties and her housekeeping allowed, Mary was at the heart of all this and attended its main 'events', as did Oisín and Cilian. She was my anchor and often, indeed, my car-driver. Occasion-

ally at night we took 'time off' in Meaic Mylotte's pub in Cárna on the mainland three miles away. The children, or rather the older ones, through attending Maoinis school and roaming the island with friends, had become fluent speakers of Irish. Two more daughters, Sorcha and Kate, who had joined them in 1970 and 1972 respectively, were on the way to that.

The children, especially the girls, liked sad stories. I told them sad stories. There was the Conamara man, a shopkeeper, who sold tobacco (I smoked a pipe, so they were familiar with tobacco) and who got a ship from Holland to bring him two tons of cheap tobacco to a cove in Conamara, and after he had stored it in a room in his house misfortunes to the point of destitution befell him. There was the Bó Liath, the Grey Cow, who was so depressed about her odd colour that eventually she stood on the road at night in the path of an oncoming car, and then, as her crushed body lay on the road, smiled and was, finally, happy. Or the more than sad story of the UVF man from the war in Northern Ireland who attacked me with a club in my vegetable garden and whom I felled with my spade and 'buried over there in that clay mound'. Horror-struck gazes at 'that clay mound' followed.

There were punishments and rewards. A misdemeanour entailed a run around the outside of the house; a serious misdemeanour three or four of those. The uprooting and presentation of designated weeds produced on Saturdays payments of pennies at a fixed rate, followed by a streaming of children down the road to Máirín's sweet shop.

After Natasha's blindness had been replaced with dim sight, I was worried lest this defect might damage her self-confidence. So at ten years of age, with me sitting beside her, I had her drive our car very slowly 100 yards along the road and turn successfully into a cul-de-sac. When the time came for the schoolchildren of her age to take a pledge not to drink alcohol until they were 18, I challenged her to a game of draughts on the kitchen table with an opened bottle of beer and a glass beside each of us and a beer toast as part of the game.

Then when Mao-Tse-Tung started shouting menacingly in China, I warned them that a Chinese army might well invade Ireland and its tanks cross the long bridge from Cárna into Maoinis. It was well to be prepared. So with them pretending to believe me, we used to drive towards the bridge and at a shout from me my passengers would smartly open the car doors and throw themselves prone on the grassy verges.

Not to forget—above all not to forget—an steamroller briste, the broken steamroller that lay abandoned and rusting on the side of the road north of Cárna. I lamented its state. When occasionally we drove past it, we stopped, the girls got out, and going to the old steamroller stroked it sooth- ingly and spoke kind words to it—while the boys looked superior.

During these same years, agitation for the chief aim of the whole movement—Gaeltacht self-government—continued errati- cally. Plans were produced and canvassed for an overall Gaeltacht regional council and administration based on district subdivisions in Donegal, the West and South. The Gaelic press in Dublin accepted and supported the contention of the Gaeltacht activists that this was a prerequisite for the survival of the Gaeltacht. Politicians began to pay lip-service to it, and ultimately, Gaeltarra Éireann was re-named Údarás na Gaeltachta (The Gaeltacht Authority) with economic development functions and a majority of its board members to be elected by popular vote. But self-government was not achieved— not even minimally.

We were aware that our campaign was the first occasion on which a concerted local demand had been made for a real change in the government structure which the Republic had inherited from the British. Our opponents, for their part—principally the Dublin bureaucracy and the English-language liberal media—were aware that to concede our demand would set a precedent which could be applied to other parts of the country besides the Gaeltacht. Since the foundation of the state, the Dublin establishment had been reso- lutely centralist and centralising, and the new consumerist liberalism now gave this resolution extra force. A pluralist Ireland, that is to say, an Ireland in which various communities shaped their lives as they saw fit, was anathema to the new liberals. What we called Gaeltacht self-government, they smeared as *apartheid*.

All in all, in the various phases of the movement in Iarchonnacht, there were about fifteen fairly constant activists and about the same number again who rallied on special occasions. We were helped *vis-à-vis* the authorities by the emotive force of the Gaelic language issue and the related, symbolic significance of the Gaeltacht. But the movement also derived strength from the fact that it was based on a group of parishes and half-parishes—each of them a distinct social personality—rather than, say, on a single town or parish. This enabled the movement to draw both on a variety of local circumstances, issues and perspectives which helped to make it multiform, and—to a lesser extent—on an internal dynamism of mutual example and rivalry which helped to maintain its impetus.

My own contribution to the movement was chiefly as a definer of concepts and realities, as a supplier of ideas for action, and as a projector of interesting and attractive images by all the means available to me. On the whole, I confined myself to these roles, partly because they were the things I could do best, partly for other reasons. On principle, I resisted the notion, which is common in Ireland, that because one proposes something, one should also actively lead its implementation. Apart from that, I lacked the patience and the native, Conamara cast of character which were needed for much of the 'committee work', and Seosamh was very good at that. After a few months on the Cárna parish council, I resigned because it had spent several meetings trying to decide to cut down some trees near the church and then, when we finally decided that we would do so, I was the only one who turned up, saw in hand. But the council went on to do several useful things without me. Then again, because my writings, TV appearances and so on, made me publicly prominent, I didn't want, by also having an executive role, to risk dominating, or to seem to dominate, what was happening. I believed that the long-term success of the movement depended on the emergence of a native Iarchonnacht leadership which would function without me—and let me get on with my main work. However, as time passed, I had reason to doubt the realism of the assumption underlying that belief: the assumption, namely, that an enduring native leadership *could* emerge out of such depressed circumstances. The fact seems to be that, in a depressed social situation, such as had existed for a long time in Conamara, enduring remedial leadership is most likely to be provided by a committed outsider.

My primary concern throughout was to represent the reality of things and to destroy illusions, particularly those fostered by the language movement, by the state's half-hearted commitment to it, and by the people's depression. This concern proved infectious to a considerable degree, so that the movement, generally, prided itself on its forthright statement of how things really were, whether the tidings were, in the short term, encouraging or deflating. In the interests of realism, I initiated trivial changes in language habits which were by no means trivial in their significance. When writing about the Gaeltacht in English, I used the Gaelic, rather than the English, forms of the place-names, because the Gaelic forms were those normally used by the inhabitants. On the other hand, when writing in Gaelic, I didn't gaelicise—as had been the Gaeilgeoir custom—the names of people who normally used the anglicised form of their names, but wrote them as they used them.

Maps were another instrument of realism. Since Iarchonnacht, like the other Gaelic-speaking districts, was located within the much wider boundaries of the illusory, largely English-speaking 'Gaeltacht' which the Government had defined in 1956, there was no map showing its own real boundaries. In Iarchonnacht, I investigated these, made a map showing them, publicised it widely, and displayed it at lectures and meetings in Iarchonnacht. Later, in 1975-6, I investigated the entire Gaeltacht and published a map showing its real boundaries and giving the real population figures (they totalled 29,000). We publicised its real size and emphasised its smallness. We believed that only by building on facts could we hope to achieve anything.

Similarly with the name for the Irish language. It was around this time that I began to call it Gaelic, habitually, rather than Irish. Partly this was a matter of verbal neatness and coherence: Gaelic, as the language name, coheres logically and intelligibly with Gaeltacht, Gaelic League, Gaeilgeoir, gaelicise, Gaelic civilisation, Gaelic-Irish, etc. But it was principally for the purpose of indicating, verbally, that in modern times 'Gaelic' and 'Irish' are in fact two distinct realities, with things Gaelic constituting only a part of what 'Irish' means, much as 'Hebrew' is not coextensive with 'Jewish'. (An immediate reason for my wanting to clarify this was that I was writing simultaneously about the Northern problem.)

Conamara was regarded as 'remote' because it was at a considerable distance from Dublin and on the 'far' side of the country from England. But in reality, I pointed out, it was situated centrally between Russia and America, near the major world traffic routes across the Atlantic, and on the side of Ireland facing America and Africa. Iarchonnacht saw itself, because of its Gaelic language, the attempts to 'save' it and so on, as an oddity in the world. From early 1974 onwards I countered this by representing Iarchonnacht as one of the struggling linguistic minorities of the West European periphery, and thus as part of the pattern of modern Europe.

My eyes were first opened properly to this European dimension of the place by a special number of *Les Temps Modernes* on the 'national minorities of France' which Pat Sheeran sent me from Paris. Shortly afterwards, my education was continued when Ruairí Ó Brádaigh, president of Sinn Féin, brought me back a stack of literature from a conference in Trieste on cultural and ethnic minorities. The *Temps Modernes* volume, edited by Yves Person (whom I was later to get to know well), introduced me to the advanced discussion on 'centre and periphery', linguistic imperialism, the nation-state, and regionalism, which was going on in France. It contained a map showing the areas where the various 'languages of the peoples of France' were spoken, more or less; and this, backed up by the accompanying articles, disintegrated France for ever more in my eyes and gave me a new view of 'French' history.

Moreover, extrapolating from France, I now saw Ireland as historically 'peripheral' *vis-à-vis* imperial London, and Iarchonnacht as peripheral *vis-à-vis* Dublin's sub-imperial power-centre. The documentation from Trieste reinforced these new views of France, the British Isles and Ireland, gave me parallel insights into Italy, Spain and elsewhere, and introduced me to West European ethnic and cultural groups which I had never heard of. I wrote an article in *Tuairisc* showing a map of Western Europe taken from the Occitanian paper *La Lutte Occitane*. Ireland figured in it—due principally to the struggle in the North—as part of a European periphery in rebellion against the centre. The caption read: 'The encirclement of rich Europe. The same exploitation, the same struggle.'

Within the Irish context, too, Iarchonnacht was represented as an oddity and felt by its inhabitants to be one. Its people were thought of as undifferentiated 'Gaeltacht people' characterised by Gaelic speech, rocky fields and old customs; people quite unlike 'normal Irish people'—and therefore not even potentially a 'representative segment of modern Ireland'. Shortly after the slogan 'A New Israel in Iarchonnacht' was launched, Liam Ó Murchú of RTÉ asked me to do a series of television interviews called *Muintir Iarchonnacht* (The People of Iarchonnacht). I used these interviews to present six Iarchonnacht persons—Seosamh Ó Cuaig, a landscape painter, a young man who had trained as a seafood chef in France, a publican who had served in the British regiment of the Irish Guards, and so on—as Irish persons who happened to live in Iarchonnacht and to be Gaelic-speakers. I was trying to convey to Ireland generally and to Iarchonnacht itself that, at least in respect of its people, Iarchonnacht was a part of normal Irish life.

I had a similar aim several years later when, with some publicity on the radio and in the local press, I organised courses of 'adult education' in Iarchonnacht. I was also having fun, providing instruction, and making some money. The bodies which normally provided adult education—University College Galway and the County Vocational Education Committee—regarded South Conamara as 'Gaeltacht', 'rural' and 'backward', and hence as a place where the only suitable courses were on such themes as 'community development', home economics and fishing. Now, instead, at three centres, I gave lectures, illustrated with slides, on the history of European painting, and organised beginners' classes in Continental languages. Bob Quinn, for his part, gave a well-attended course in film-making in his house in An Cheathrú Rua. One of his students, Cóilín Bairéad, a fisherman from Cárna, wrote a script during the course which, with some help from Bob, became the script of the film *Poitín*. During this same period, I edited a series of twenty-five short parish histories for broadcasting on Raidió na Gaeltachta. This meant finding suitable local authors from Donegal to Rinn, Co. Waterford, sending them a basic questionnaire as a guideline, and editing the manuscripts. As

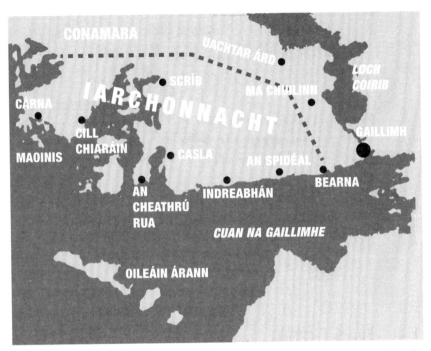

they were broadcast, I had them published in the weekly Gaeltacht paper *Amárach*. It was the first attempt ever to record and present the local history of the Gaeltacht.

Besides wanting to represent the Gaeltacht reality in the present and past, I wanted to represent and indicate *the possibilities present in it*. For example, in the very early days, I came across a picture of a flourishing Japanese fishing village in a magazine, and its natural setting looked very like that of the nearby village of Cill Chiaráin. I cut it out and used it in talks as an illustration of what the future Cill Chiaráin would look like. Conamara's legendary 'rocks'—its stony, rock-strewn surface—had become a symbol of its condemnation to poverty and dependence. I made a point of always referring to the rocks as one of Conamara's great advantages—excellent foundations for industrial estates, very useful for building deep-sea harbours. When I discovered that the Faroe Islands were both more barren than Conamara and more prosperous than *Ireland*, I wrote a pamphlet about them called *Take the Faroes for Example*. Mostly, however, the representation of possibility was mingled with the representation of present reality, and was, indeed, an intrinsic part of it.

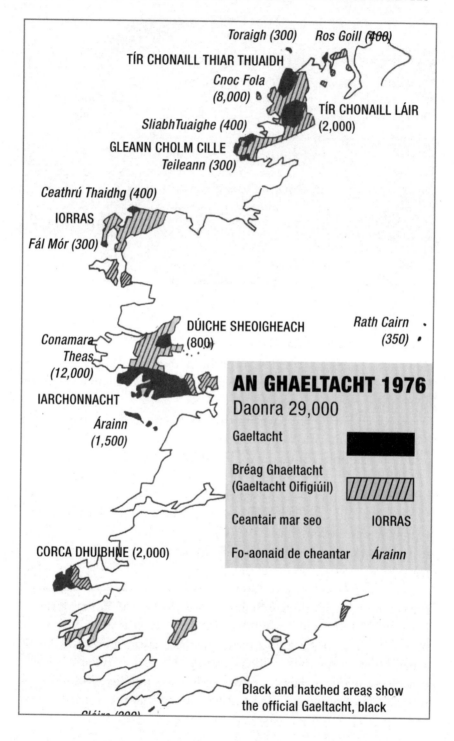

Toraigh (300)   Ros Goill (400)
TÍR CHONAILL THIAR THUAIDH
Cnoc Fola
(8,000)
TÍR CHONAILL LÁIR
SliabhTuaighe (400)   (2,000)
GLEANN CHOLM CILLE
Teileann (300)

Ceathrú Thaidhg (400)
IORRAS
Fál Mór (300)

DÚICHE SHEOIGHEACH   Rath Cairn
Conamara   (800)   (350)
Theas
(12,000)
IARCHONNACHT
Árainn
(1,500)

AN GHAELTACHT 1976
Daonra 29,000

Gaeltacht

Bréag Ghaeltacht
(Gaeltacht Oifigiúil)

Ceantair mar seo   IORRAS

CORCA DHUIBHNE (2,000)
Fo-aonaid de cheantar   Árainn

Black and hatched areas show
the official Gaeltacht, black

Since the possibility was present *there now* it was an element of the present reality.

A depressed people elevates impossibility, quite irrationally, into the ruling daemon of their environment. So one necessary way of representing present possibility to them is to make them sharply aware of this morbid self-abasement. I said and wrote on a few occasions—and it provoked anger—that the people of Iarchonnacht were sick: sick from inherited depressive illusions about themselves and their environment, which made them take a poor view of both, see 'impossibilities' everywhere, and regard difficulties as 'impossibilities'. They had made NÍ FÉIDIR ('It's Impossible') into a greater tyrant over their lives than landlords in the old days had ever been.

However, my most constant theme and aim was Gaeltacht self-government. I used all the obvious, practical arguments for it which others were also using; but I was interested in it principally because I saw it as a prime means of achieving good representation of reality. On the one hand, and very fundamentally, Gaeltacht self-government was a means of getting the real Gaeltacht boundaries officially and publicly defined. On the other hand, its institution and operation would enable the Gaeltacht people to see themselves, both *more clearly*, and *as the shapers and developers of their own lives*. In their present condition, they saw themselves, to a considerable degree, merely as objects on which others acted. Moreover, we had called on the bishops to establish a Gaeltacht diocese with a Gaeltacht bishop, and it seemed to me that the transformation of the Gaeltacht into a unit of secular self-government would make it difficult for the bishops to refuse an ecclesiastical counterpart.

With fourteen others, I walked the sixty-nine kilometres from Cárna to Bearna in a three-day demonstration of demand for Gaeltacht autonomy. (Our progress was reported on the national radio news bulletins). Fearing that my fellow activists were not bringing home the issue directly enough to the Gaeltacht people themselves, I wrote a one-page 'Discussion Document on Gaeltacht Self-Government', setting out concrete proposals for its structure, units and powers, got a thousand copies printed, and delivered it by hand to people in public places throughout the Gaeltacht, from Kerry to Donegal.

The Gaeltacht movement flourished vigorously until about 1972. After that, like so much else in the Republic, it was overshadowed and discouraged by the events in the North. The EEC (European Economic Community) referendum campaign about Ireland's entry into that body had something of the same effect. Moreover, as the years passed, the movement's achievement of many of its secondary goals, together with the rising prosperity in the Gaeltacht, lessened the numbers and enthusiasm of the activists.

★ ★ ★

Almost from the start, my Iarchonnacht activities branched out in two other directions—first, towards the entire province of Connacht, its economic 'underdevelopment', and the demographic and other social ills arising therefrom. In May 1969, on the invitation of the Castlebar Chamber of Commerce, I gave a public lecture in that town on 'Connacht's View of Itself'. Connacht, I told my audience, was held down, and prevented from realising itself, by its habit of seeing itself, its resources, its place in the world and so on, through Dublin's eyes. Look at Iceland, with its disadvantageous location, its resources less than Connacht's, its population half of Connacht's, and what it had made of itself! Look at Switzerland—or half of it, which would be about the size of Connacht! Those countries had succeeded economically because they looked at themselves through their own eyes, and therefore had a real view of their economic possibilities. Let Connacht follow their example!

The lecture was reprinted in full in the *Connaught Telegraph* under the headline 'Think for yourselves, Westerners!' 'Think for yourselves', it sounded familiar. Connacht's mental condition with regard to Dublin was Ireland's with respect to London. I persuaded the Castlebar and Tuam Chambers of Commerce to start preparing a Conference of Connacht which would invite 200 enterprising Connachtmen to gather in Tuam. First they would hear papers from specialists on the different aspects of Connacht's material circumstances—communications, transport, production, land and sea resources, the educational system. Then they would divide into specialised committees which would draw up five-year development plans and report back to a second session in Castlebar six months later. From this session would emerge Connacht's overall plan for Connacht—something no Dublin government could ever provide nor had ever asked Connacht to provide. For several months the two Chambers corresponded on the project; then it lapsed.*

However, the main area into which my Iarchonnacht activities branched out was the decentralisation of Irish government generally. I wrote regularly on the subject in my column in the *Sunday Press* and published a collection of these articles as a pamphlet, *Build the Third Republic.* Sinn Féin helped by publishing, as a solution to the Northern problem, its scheme for making Ireland into a four-province federation and by setting up four provincial comhairlí (councils) to prepare the way. Mary contributed nobly by becoming chairperson of Comhairle Chonnacht and by regularly driving a round trip of 140 miles to its meetings in the intended provincial capital, Tuam. For an understanding of the Irish administrative system, and for the general theory of decentralisation, I drew largely on the writings—signed and unsigned, always inspiring—of Tom Barrington, Director of the Institute of Public Administration. I was also greatly helped by Éamonn Ó Ruairc, who worked first with the Council of Europe, later with the EEC. Attracted, like so many others, by the stirrings in Iarchonnacht, he provided very practical assistance to this and other enterprises by putting me on the Council of Europe mailing list for local government and regional matters. Through the many publications which came to me from this source, and particularly those relating to the European Conference of Local Authorities, I was educated in the governmental structures of Western Europe, and kept informed about decentralist and regionalist thought and practice on the Continent.

Decentralising Irish government meant more than decentralising it. It meant making it coherent and democratic at the local and regional levels, and thereby making it more rational, efficient and humane. It meant ending the chaos and caprice of the existing governmental system in which scores of agencies of central government operated independently, dividing the country up pell-mell

---

* It reappeared a few years later in the bastardised form of a 'Western Conference' in Galway, sponsored by SFADCO and the Ballina newspaper, *The Western People.* Papers were read and published, but no decisions were taken or commitments made.

into criss-crossing, private systems of 'districts', 'regions' and 'areas' to suit their *respective* conveniences, and without regard for the convenience of the citizens or the well-being of communities.

Co. Leitrim was merely an extreme example. Down the years, politicians and others had talked of it as a demographic and economic disaster area. Yet in all that time not only had the people of Leitrim not been empowered to tackle their problem through their own representative institutions, but the local officials of the central agencies involved in Leitrim's affairs had not even got together, say, in Carrick-on-Shannon, to coordinate their activities or to draw up a plan of remedial action. The system forbade that, for various reasons, but essentially because, in the eyes of the administrators, no unit called 'Leitrim' existed.

In the bureaucracy's view, the nation (in the Republic) was a mass of 'individuals', each of whom had various administrative aspects which were to be dealt with separately by the relevant central agencies. The nation was *not* a community of communities, which the administrative apparatus existed to serve: each community particularly and coherently, and all of them for common purposes. In my view, the nation *was precisely that*. It was by nature a community of communities leading unrecognised and thwarted existences, but still existing by reason of the shared life of their members and their vague self-consciousness. For these embryonic, frustrated communities to begin to develop towards real communal being—as self-governing collectivities fashioning their own lives and world-views—they needed territorial definition and representative institutions with executive and decision-making powers; they needed this *representation of their reality to themselves*.

However, if the Gaeltacht question aroused my interest in the structure of Irish government, it was the Northern problem which led me to develop my ideas on this matter to the point of comprehensive and detailed proposals. Before the North exploded in Derry and Belfast in August 1969 I hadn't directed my mind seriously to it. In 1958, on the suggestion of Douglas Gageby of *The Irish Times*, I had gone there and written a series of six articles on 'The Northern Catholic', which were later published as a pamphlet. But that fell far short of an overall investigation of the North, and particularly of its political aspects. Now in August 1969, along with everyone else, I was compelled to think about the North daily. I found I had a lot to say on the subject, and Douglas obliged by taking three or four articles about it from me that month for *The Irish Times*. The first of them was called (inevitably!) 'The North: A Plea for Realism', and laid the basis for the vast amount I was to write on the subject in the following years.

❖

In the spring of 1970 a possibility had emerged and vanished which, if it had been realised, would probably have changed the course of my life. Fr Cóilín Garvey, a Franciscan lecturing on philosophy in University College Galway, approached me with the proposal that I join the department as a lecturer. I would deal 'with the kind of subjects you write about in your Sunday Press *column—Wolfe Tone, decentralisation, the Dublin "liberal agenda", the depression of the West and the like'. This would provide a bridge of ordered, interesting thinking between the academic philosophy course and concrete life, thereby adding a dimension of 'relevance' to the course as a whole. The shaping of my programme of lectures would be left to myself. When I responded with active interest, Fr Garvey brought me to meet the head of the department, Prof Edwin Rabbitt, who confirmed the offer. So it was agreed that I would take up the post the following autumn. However, in the course of the summer Prof Rabbitt wrote to me, with much regret, that they had not been able to secure the necessary funds from the College. Whether this was because, as some said, the philosophy department was inept at getting its share of College funding, or was because, as others later informed me, the President, Colm Ó hEocha, was opposed to the College giving me a permanent post of any kind, I never knew with certainty.*

Just as by contacting Aunt Lena I had become acquainted with my father's family, so in the summer of 1970 I went to the Sperrin Mountains in Co. Tyrone to find where my maternal grandfather, Francis Carolan, had come from. This resulted in my discovering a precious tribe of cousins reaching from Glenelly to Bournemouth.

FROM THE GLENELLY POINT OF VIEW*

I'M VISITING GLENELLY because my maternal grandfather came from here and because I have a countryside of cousins in and around the glen. Though I never lived here, it's the place which more than any other gives me my point of view on life. Let me explain.

Glenelly is a valley of middling to bad land in the Sperrin Mountains of north Tyrone, pretty high up and about eleven miles long. It is known for its sheep which graze in huge flocks for miles around. My grandfather, Frank Carolan, who died in Belfast ten years ago, was born here in the 1870s and grew up here speaking Irish. The family tradition is that the original Glenelly Carolan came from that fertile stretch of land called the Lagan on the Donegal side of the Foyle, in 1797. It is said he was evicted along with others when the land passed into the hands of Scottish settlers.

Shortly before he died, my grandfather told me his earliest memory. He was lying in a basket or something of the kind in one of these fields. He looked up and saw the moon and, in the field near him, through stalks of corn, people reaping and binding. I have looked around near the old house trying to guess which field that was.

When he was growing up his people were scattering over the English-speaking world and he himself went to Belfast. In due course I first saw the light of day in his house. My mother remembers that, when she was growing up, and the Glenelly relations came to Belfast, my grandfather used to talk Gaelic with them into the night.

I have reflected on his life's course and found in it the history of my entire people over the past century and a half. Frank Carolan, growing up in Irish-speaking Glenelly, still belonged, however tenuously, to the old Gaelic nation, driven back from the fat lands to the Glenelly's of Ireland. Then the great flight from that land began, and he took part in it, changing from Gaelic to English speech, moving from the familiar country to a strange, hostile city.

In the course of that move he became a man without status and of dubious identity. Or rather, he became a man sharing in the lowest identity that the English-speaking world gave to whites. From

* *Sunday Press* column, 2 August 1970; republished with some other articles from the column in *Build the Third Republic,* Foilseacháin Mhaoinse, Maoinis, 1972.

being a Gael, and thus a member of a great European nation, he joined the people of Paddy the Irishman, grimacing ape-like from the pages of *Punch*. All his hard-working life until his death in Belfast (where he achieved a degree of material comfort) he remained a second-class citizen in his own country.

Ninteen-sixteen came and went. My own father, whose father had spent some time in the RIC, took a small part in it. I grew up in the new Irish State, belonging to the first generation of my family, and one of the first waves of my people who got all the education they wanted to take. I saw a good part of the world, learned several of its languages, got to know something of its philosophies and great religions.

How did this leave me vis-à-vis Frank Carolan and Glenelly? I felt obligated. He was one of the wisest men I have known. But admiration and affection apart, he had been engaged in a struggle which was the struggle of my people out of ignominy and impotence towards a reaffirmation of themselves in new terms—towards a place again in the sun. And I saw that that struggle was far from over, far from succeeding yet.

I saw, looking around me, that we were as far as ever from stamping the world again with a distinctive form of life and thought drawn from our own Irish substance. We, the historic Irish of the Gaelic, Catholic tradition, are still victims of the world, still reacting to it merely, not fashioning it creatively, *even in our own island*. And most of us, even some of us who once cared, have stopped caring—gripped again by that despair of our own *dúchas* from which the Gaelic League temporarily roused us.

Well, as it happens, I do care and my caring gives my life its meaning. While I live, the struggle of Frank Carolan's people towards self-affirmation in new terms still goes on.

For a century and a half, the predominant view has been that the thing to do with the Glenelly's (whether Irish- or English-speaking) and with all that they stand for is to get away from them and from 'all that' as far as possible. Education has been seen as an escape-ladder, a way to get oneself out and away, upwards and upwards, to a point of secure indifference and sometimes of contempt—a point where you look back and down at 'them' and their old life, satisfied that you have made it. I understand only too well the fear and insecurity behind this flight, this rejection and this apparent selfishness. I don't blame anyone. But I dissent.

I believe that our people's struggle to assert themselves again in their own authentic terms is an enterprise which obligates each of us. Further, I believe that this struggle to achieve a form of life drawn from our own substance can succeed only if we go right back to the bottom of the escape ladder—to the Glenelly's and the Iarchonnachts—and find out how it all began, find what went wrong. But, of course, while finding this out, we may well be some use there, at the bottom of the pyramid of status and power.

TOWARDS PEACE IN THE NORTH *

AFTER THE PARTITION of Ireland in 1921-2, Irish political nationalism adapted to the new circumstances by maintaining:

- that Northern Ireland was part of the Irish national territory;
- that the entire population of Northern Ireland was part of the Irish nation;
- that the injustice perpetrated by Britain was the partition of Ireland—because this prevented a united, self-governing Ireland;
- that the division in the North was between two religious-political communities or traditions: Catholics or nationalists who wanted a united Ireland and Protestants or unionists who wanted union with Britain and who mistakenly believed they were British—an illusion that would disappear if Britain withdrew;
- that it was Britain's duty to withdraw from the North so that Orange and Green could come together as a united, self-governing Ireland.

A united, self-governing Ireland remained, as before, the primary aim.

When, as we say, the North erupted, in August 1969, I was liv-

* From *Heresy: The Battle of Ideas in Modern Ireland*, Blackstaff, Belfast, 1993.

ing in the South Conamara Gaeltacht, and my social and political
activity there had taught me certain principles of procedure in such
matters which I then began to apply to the Northern question. I
believed that, if you are faced with a disordered social situation, in
which the humanity of people is being oppressed, then the first
prerequisite—if your intention is to order the situation in a humane
way—is to reject and criticise the misrepresentations and confusions
that are obscuring its communal realities, and to represent those realities faithfully in words. In situations of the kind referred to, such
misrepresentations and confusions will always be found to exist.

When I looked at the way in which our traditional nationalism,
and the neo-liberal views that became fashionable in the 1960s,
represented the Northern situation, I found them seriously lacking
in realism, to the extent of including lies.

Not surprisingly, then, my first article for *The Irish Times* that August—an article that contained *in nucleo* all that was to come—was
entitled 'A Plea for Realism' (19 August). It began by saying that it
was up to us in the Republic, and to the Northern Catholics, to
make a realistic proposal for a lasting settlement; but that we could
not do this on the basis of the existing descriptions of the situation
and must first of all recognise the basic realities. The first of these,
which I spelt out—the first of four—constituted a rejection of the
notion that the two communities in the North formed part of the
same nation or 'historic people'. I wrote:

> The first basic fact that needs to be recognised is that Northern
> Ireland contains two historic peoples, or rather one such people
> (the Ulster Protestants) and part of another. Only the accident that
> both of them speak English obscures the fact that they are peoples
> as real and distinct as, say, the Austrians and the Czechs. But for an
> accident of history, they would differ in language, as do the Flem-
> ings and Walloons in Belgium.
>
> They did so differ less than six generations ago, that is to say, for
> a considerable time after the plantation of Ulster.* But language
> apart, they have different origins, histories and historical mytholo-
> gies. They are, moreover, very conscious of their respective histories;

---

* I later learned that this is an exaggeration: some Protestant communities, perhaps because they were of Scottish origin, spoke Gaelic.

they honour different and opposed heroes. Their social and cultural lives differ considerably. They have different understandings of Irish and British history. They also differ in religion. If the language difference had persisted, they would be known today, quite simply, as 'the Irish' and 'the Ulster Scots' (or 'na Gaeil' and 'na hAlbanaigh').

When the language difference went, religious adherence became the most obvious principle of distinction between them. As we have seen, however, the actual distinctiveness is far wider in scope. Captain O'Neill, as Prime Minister of Northern Ireland, was well aware of the nature of this distinctiveness and often referred to it in speeches and lectures. His way of putting it was that people of the Irish Catholic tradition and of the British Protestant tradition had been thrown together by history in Northern Ireland. This was fair enough, though greater accuracy would require us to speak of 'people of the Gaelic and Irish Catholic tradition' and 'a people of the Scotto-British and Protestant tradition'.

In other words, to say that the inhabitants of Northern Ireland are 'all Irishmen' gets us nowhere. It sounds good to most Irishmen; it expresses a generous intention; it is even true in a sense; but it stops short of throwing light on the real situation. The inhabitants of Europe are 'all Europeans', but there are many peoples in Europe, differing greatly in their history, culture and self-consciousness. The inhabitants of the neighbouring island are 'all British', but the Scots, the English and the Welsh are distinct historic peoples. Even accepting that all the inhabitants of Northern Ireland are 'Irish' in a general sense, we are still faced with the fact that there are two different peoples there: the Irish (or Northern) Catholics and the Ulster Protestants.

Those were the pretty conventional names that at the time I gave the 'two historic peoples', but it can readily be deduced from my description of them that I would soon become unhappy with those imprecise and misleading names. I had not as yet visited the North in conflict and listened to how the two communities really saw themselves.

I then went on to say: 'The second basic fact about Northern Ireland is that the struggle there is between the Catholics and the Protestants, but that it is not *about religion*, but about the relative status and power of these two historic peoples.' Arising out of this, I criticised the terms 'sectarianism' and 'religious war' as used in the Northern context, and pointed out that the flag flying over Derry's Bogside was not the Vatican flag but the Irish Tricolour.

Following from those two basic realities and two others that I spelt out, I proposed a political reconstruction of the North based on a western and an eastern region, which would contain, respectively, a Catholic and a Protestant majority, and the restructuring of local government to correspond to local Catholic and Protestant majorities—in other words, something like the successful cantonal solution that the Swiss found for their religious antagonisms. (The Swiss were agreed on their nationality.) In Belfast, Major Ronald Bunting, who was both an enthusiast for local government reform and Rev. Ian Paisley's right-hand man, found this article very interesting and praised much of it in a press conference. I went to Belfast, met him, and we agreed on five 'principles of settlement' which I published in *The Irish Times* on 26 August. At the time they were completely ignored, but in the light of all that followed and where we have arrived at now they are interesting. They were:

1. The issue is not about religion. It is a political issue, to be solved politically.

2. The two peoples are basically willing to coexist alongside each other, provided that they can each exist in their own way and on their own terms—as far as possible.

3. Threats to the security, status and cultural autonomy of either people should be removed.

4. The security, status and cultural autonomy of each people should be guaranteed by an adequate share in political power.

5. Neither people should be expected or forced to abandon any of its traditional loyalties, provided that it recognises the constitution of Northern Ireland.

The 'constitution of Northern Ireland' would be based on the sort of regional and local restructuring I have referred to.

Starting from the elementary new analysis in those principles, in my column in the *Sunday Press* I spent the next two years refining and modifying their pattern and vocabulary, arguing for them and criticising the traditional approach, and—since the two governments and all parties had ignored the cantonal proposal—casting around for some other structure that might reflect the communal realities.

In April and July 1970 I was criticising our refusal to take the unionists at their word when they described themselves as 'British' and pointing out the 'imperialism' of this. Such imperialism would make sense if, as in the internal imperialism of many other nation-states, we were prepared to impose our nationality on the dissident ethnic group by force and re-education; but since we, the Republic, that is, rejected the use of force, it made no sense and was counter-productive. While offering the provocation of imperialist rhetoric, it lacked imperialism's teeth.

Usually, while recognising their Britishness, I continued to refer to the unionists as 'the Ulster Protestants'; but as I took account of the fact that there were some Catholic unionists, as well as North-ern Protestants who were Irish nationalists, I became increasingly dissatisfied with the religious naming of the communities. At the same time, I wanted names that would describe them not merely as political groups, but as communities or peoples—names therefore that were independent of political allegiances or circumstances. For the unionists, I occasionally tried 'West British', but was unhappy with its derogatory connotation in the Republic and the fact that its established usage there made it not specific to them alone.

As the state in the North was rent asunder by the nationalist re-bellion, I had ceased to believe in the possibility of a solution within the UK. Consequently, from July 1971 onwards I was proposing an *Irish-British condominium of Northern Ireland* as the immediate way of satisfying the basic nationalist demand, while doing justice also to the unionists. In September 1972, the North's Social Democratic and Labour Party (SDLP), in consultation with me, adopted con-dominium, renaming it joint sovereignty, and recommended it in a policy document, *Towards a New Ireland*. From correspondence I received, I found that the principal support in the Republic for condominium came from Protestants. (As it happened, the SDLP man who had initially contacted me was their only leading Prot-estant member, Ivan Cooper; he had invited me to join them at a meeting in Gaoth Dobhair, Co. Donegal). The idea launched by the

Unnameable One was not popular in the Dublin establishment, in particular not in RTÉ.*

While campaigning for condominium, I had begun to write of the 'ethnic identities' of the two Northern communities; of the need to 'respect' and recognise both identities (see 'Open Letter to [the Northern Protestant lawyer] Desmond Boal', *Irish Press*, 21 September 1971); and of the assertion of Irish identity being the principal force motivating the nationalist rebellion. During a visit to the North I had seen (*Sunday Press*, 19 March 1972) young nationalist men and women 'daily risking their lives and freedom to assert—not an abstract claim to an all-Ireland state—but the identity, and the right to honourable recognition, of their own nationality and people'. The IRA, I wrote, were 'misrepresenting the struggle'—more precisely by their dogmatic united-Irelandism allowing it to be misrepresented—'as a mindless attempt 'to bomb a million Protestants into a united Ireland'. (That expression was Cardinal Conway's.)

I think it was not until 1975 that I hit on 'Ulster British', or perhaps adopted it from an Englishman, T. J. Pickvance of Birmingham University, who in a pamphlet published the previous year, *The Northern Ireland Problem: Peace with Equity*, used that term. Since there were 'Ulster Irish' on both sides of the Border, I called the Northern nationalists 'the Six-County Irish'.

My predominant concern was to make attractive, and to further, *any* constitutional arrangement which, by recognising the national identities of the two Northern communities, would bring peace to the North and thereby allow normal life and politics to take their course, both there and in the Republic. Consequently, from autumn 1971, I had been helping to put flesh on the Sinn Féin proposal for a four-province federation, insisting that such a federation must provide for explicit—as well as implicit or political—recognition of the Ulster British identity, writing occasional articles about it and speaking for it at public meetings in Connacht. The four-province

---

* When the SDLP policy document was published, RTÉ, alarmed, was at pains to convey to the public that 'joint sovereignty' was quite different from 'condominium'. Actually at the bar in Óstán Gaoth Dobhair, I had agreed with John Hume that, in the SDLP's intended policy document, 'condominium' could be more intelligibly rendered as 'joint sovereignty'.

federal scheme, as it evolved, seemed to me the best proposal, not only for the North but for Ireland as a whole, to emerge in these years. However, I regarded condominium as having a better chance of winning acceptance in the short term.

Later, in 1975, when the Ulster Defence Association and a few others in the North began to favour an independent Northern Ireland, I wrote two articles in *The Irish Times* (29-30 July) outlining—with some help from the Belgian way of dealing with Flemings and Walloons—how an independent North might be organised so as to give recognition to the bi-national nature of the population. Although I regarded this project as far from ideal from an Irish national viewpoint, I believed that it could be implemented in a manner that would advance the national interest and bring peace. Once again, the only significant public support came from a Protestant, Senator Trevor West (*The Irish Times*, 2 September).

From the start, the Dublin ideological and political establishment, and most ordinary citizens, had been hostile to any verbal breaching of the dogma that saw the Ulster unionists as an intrinsic part of the Irish nation; this hostility extended, logically, to any political arrangement that would recognise ethnic plurality in Ireland as a whole or in the North specifically.

It was a conservatism springing partly from genuine adherence to the traditional nationalist view, partly from support for that view by the consumerist liberals who had risen to power in the 1960s, particularly in the media. These, for their own ends as auxiliaries of commerce, wanted to promote homogeneity as idea and reality, not only in the North but throughout Ireland. Both for that purpose, and for their related aim of secularising the Republic, they found the 'one-nation theory' useful. Of course, no one denied that the Northern nationalists were Irish; so what it boiled down to in practice was a general unwillingness to recognise the Britishness of the unionists.

In *The Irish Times* commentators and letter-writers called my line of argument 'sectarian' and 'divisive'. I also heard myself described as 'West British' and 'unrepublican'. Official Sinn Féin and its leader Tomás MacGiolla coupled me with Conor Cruise O'Brien as a disreputable 'two-nation theorist' (a believer that there were two nations, Irish and British, in Ireland). Indeed the party organ, the *United Irishman*, of March 1971, writing about O'Brien at the Labour Party Conference, mistakenly credited me with 'spawning' that heresy. If, the paper said, O'Brien's line on the North represented Labour Party policy, 'then the Irish Labour Party finds itself allied with the Irish Communist Organisation and their new convert Conor Cruise O'Brien in accepting the two-nation theory spawned by Desmond Fennell and Major Ronald Bunting'.

Apart from myself, the small Irish Communist Organisation (ICO) was then the only voice in the Republic publicly rejecting the one-nation theory. It openly espoused the view that there were two complete nations in Ireland. An article by Jack Lane in its journal *Irish Communist*, April 1971, depicted me as in this respect a fellow-traveller, but one whose lack of Marxist vision had led to a distorted understanding of the matter. Although I had never written of 'two nations' in Ireland, I was content for a time to accept that this did not misrepresent my position—that there was an 'Ulster Protestant 'nation' forming part of the British nation'. But I sharply rejected the deduction from this made by the ICO—that we should cease pressing for a reunited Ireland—and the similar line taken by O'Brien. I regarded it as entirely legitimate that the Irish nation, existing throughout Ireland, though not comprising all the inhabitants, should aim at political unification. 'If the all-British state [in Britain] contains three nations, why shouldn't there be an all-Ireland state containing two?' (letter to the *Irish Press*, 6 November 1971). Later, however, I would reject the two-nation theory outright, maintaining that Ireland did not contain two nations but only one nation, 'the people of the Tricolour' and part of another (namely the British nation.*

---

* More precisely, this was my view 'for practical purposes'. In a subtler, more philosophical vein, I put forward—in the pamphlet *A New Nationalism for the New Ireland* (1972), in 'To Have a Nation Once Again', *Atlantis* (April 1973) and in 'The No-Nation Theory', *The Irish Times* (16 May 1973)—a no-nation theory which depicted Irish nationalism as an unfinished project to reconstitute a new Irish nation in place of the Irish nation which had disintegrated in early modern times. This line of thinking brought me close to the thinking of John Robb (see 'Breaking the Old Moulds', *The Irish Times,* 18 November 1972), particularly in his pamphlet *Sell-Out or Opportunity?* (Belfast: New Ireland Movement, 1972), but also subsequently.

The secularists (and these included those traditional nationalists who were also secularists) were attached to the one-nation theory because it made the Northern Protestants part of the nation, and usable therefore in that capacity as a very cogent argument, given the national aim of reunification, for de-Catholicising public life in the Republic. If the Northern Protestants were to be seen as a British community, not part of the nation but merely sharing Ulster with it, they would represent a much weaker argument for this purpose. It followed that any scheme of reunification which envisaged regional self-government for the Northern Protestants, or any reorganisation of Northern Ireland—whether by cantonisation, condominium or whatever—which suggested or recognised the ethnic distinctiveness of the Protestants would be opposed by the secularisers. For one reason or another, then, Dublin's view of Ireland and its project for were passionately unitarian and anti-pluralist.

I had more than the Northern question to teach me this, because I was at this time in South Conamara battling along with others for Gaeltacht self-government, that is to say for the practical political recognition by Dublin of the distinct identity, needs and interest of the Irish-speaking minority. Much of the rhetoric that was used against a pluralist view of the North was used also against our Gaeltacht demand for self-government. *La République une et indivisible!* In Iarchonnacht we came to feel sympathy and a sort of kinship with the *dílseoirí*, as we called the Northern loyalists, in their attitude to Dublin.

In 1972 my weekly column in the Sunday Press, *which had been my main public platform, ceased due to a quarrel with the Editor, Vincent Jennings, who said I was saying he was a liar. The Northern Ireland peace solution finally arrived at in the 1990s was a sort of tacit condominium with Britain still in direct control, the Republic's role ancillary.*

SKETCHES OF THE NEW IRELAND ⋆

Introduction: The New Thinking on Government

1. OVER THE past few years a growing number of individuals and groups have been expressing radical dissatisfaction with the present structures of government in the Republic and proposing far-reaching changes.⋆⋆ Some have been concerned only with the structure of government in a particular locality, say, Ballyfermot or the Conamara Gaeltacht. Others have directed their criticism at the state as a whole, proposing changes in its entire fabric.

Both movements have been interrelated, not so much actually—in terms of persons or organisations (though that has occurred)—as logically and by cross-fertilisation. The local movements for change have raised the general issue by implication. When the argument for district self-government in *Irish-speaking South Conamara* is based (as it is) not merely on linguistic, but also on socio-economic grounds, then some case is being made, willy-nilly, for a similar structure

---

⋆ From *Sketches of the New Ireland*, (text with maps written and drawn by me) published by the Association for the Advancement of Self-Government, Galway, 1973. It was the 'text' for an all-Ireland conference organised by the Association in the summer of that year in Athlone.

⋆⋆ See Addendum to the Devlin Report; various writings by Mr Barrington and Desmond Roche in *Administration*; submissions by various bodies arising out of the White Paper on Local Government—most notably, the Report by the Institute of Public Administration's Study Group entitled 'More Local Government: A Programme for Development,' but also the recommendations published by the Local Government and Public Services Union, the ICTU, Muintir na Tire, the Community Consultative Council, ACRA and the short-lived Council for Local Government Reform (Dublin); unpublished lectures by Prof Ivor Browne, Dept. of Psychiatry, St. James's Hospital, Dublin, on 'Man, His Environment and Mental Health' and 'Draft Outline for a Living Centre and Human Development in a Municipal Housing Estate' and my own pamphlets, *Build the Third Republic, Take the Faroes for Example* and *A New Nationalism for the New Ireland*. A plan for Gaeltacht self-government has been published by Gluaiseacht Chearta Sibhialta na Gaeltachta, and a scheme for new structures of government in Connacht by Comhairle Chonnacht. Representative bodies in Ballyfermot, Finglas and the Dublin Liberties have been calling for self-government for their districts. Finally, in the more strictly political field, regional governments have been advocated by the Christian Democratic Party and supported in principle by the Labour Party, while the Provisional Republican Movement has made the complete re-structuring and decentralisation of government the basic plank of its political programme.

of government in English-speaking North Conamara or South Leitrim. When it is maintained that Ballyfermot should be a self-governing township within the city of Dublin, then something to the same effect is being said about Crumlin and Clontarf. In this respect therefore, the generalised proposals for a re-structuring of government have represented the working out of the particular, local demands to their logical overall conclusions.

2. This new thinking on government does not merely seek structural 'changes' or 'reforms'. If that were all, it could not properly be described as new. Since the first half of the nineteenth century, many changes (usually described as 'reforms') have taken place in the structure of government in the 26 Counties. The most decisive of these occurred before independence, but further modifications have been made since 1922. The new thinking on government wants changes *of a different kind and degree* than those which have been occurring: changes which would substantially transform *the structure and ethos of government as these have developed in Ireland over the past hundred years*—first, under the British regime, then under an Irish regime which substantially retained the British system, and its direction of change, in all essentials.

3. A more precise way of putting it is that the new thinking on government wishes to change the *direction* in which change in our government structures has been moving. Thus, instead of the unco-ordinated proliferation of separate governmental agencies (Departments, Departmental offshoots, semi-state boards, county developmental teams, county and urban councils, county committees of agriculture and vocational education, regional health boards, etc.), *the gradual coordination of all governmental and semi-state services in a hierarchy of agreed local centres*; instead of the progressive concentration of powers at the centre of government, the co-ordinated *decentralisation of powers* throughout the land; instead of government trying to cater, in a fragmentary fashion, for an increasing number of fragmentary needs of individual citizens, government increasingly exercised *on behalf of communities for the overall needs of each community and of its constituent families and persons;* instead of government becoming more incomprehensible and irrational, government becoming more *intelligible and rational;* in short, instead of government

rendering itself structurally more inhuman, government being rendered *structurally more humane*—more like a work of rational, feeling, caring, social man.

4. The basic reason why the new thinking on government wants this change of direction is that it has a philosophy of man and government which differs radically from that which has *de facto*—even if often unconsciously—shaped the present system. Consequently, it has a different set of values from that which has shaped the present system. Etc.

❖

The 'new thinking on government', however widespread, came to nothing. Dublin stood firm. La République une et indivisible! *The Gaeltacht held onto the gains it had made, mainly through the four years or so of militancy in South Conamara which came to be known as Réabhlóid na Gaeltachta (The Gaeltacht Revolution). A few years later, an Irish-language television station situated in Iarchonnacht was added to Raidió na Gaeltachta. But the language shift from Irish to English in the Gaeltacht continued, partly, I came to realise, because the 'modernisations' seemed to suggest speaking English as yet another one!*

Meanwhile, in a field behind the house in Maoinis I grew twenty-two kinds of vegetables. In the field in front of the house I dug drains feeding a pond on which I placed two rubber barrels in which the children, one in each, liked to spend time, even to eat meals. The 1970s had brought us a second daughter, Sorcha, in 1970 and a third (our last child), Kate, in 1972. For their births Mary with good reason went again to her chosen doctor in Limerick, leaving a local girl to help in the house. Such absences, so unlike the situation in Dublin when our first-born Oisín was being born, saddened me, made me feel left out. Our relationship was in trouble; Mary and I had grown apart. She had bouts of lethargy which depressed me. The doctor she consulted said it was caused by anaemia, a deficiency of red cells in her blood, and took measures to mend that but without lasting effect. Now I know in retrospect that the friction was mainly due to my absorption in public activities and in writing Beyond Nationalism,

*sometimes going away for periods to work on it, and the fact that we had
not taken enough time together away from Maoinis and the children.*

*With the income from my column gone and four, then five children
to support (while Mary continued teaching) I needed to find paid work.
The managing director of Údarás na Gaeltacht told me that with the high
profile I had acquired through public activity I had become unemployable.
I edited a series of parish history talks for Raidió na Gaeltachta. For two
years I lectured in the Politics Department of University College Galway,
my chosen subjects being the politics of peripheral regions and the Yugoslav
socialist constitution. (Yugoslav because, on the five occasions when I was
invited to the annual Croatian Writers' Congress in Zagreb, I had informed myself there about Yugoslav socialism and found its application of
Marxist principles attractive.) In the History Department, at the request of
Gearóid Ó Tuathaigh, I tutored European intellectual history. When this
UCG work required it, I stayed sometimes with my friend Tony Christ-
ofides who taught mathematics in the College and his wife, Bridie. During
the Gaeltacht revolution their house had been a* point de rencontre *for
the seditious, including besides those I have mentioned Michael D. Higgins,
the future President, who was also a lecturer in UCG. During that time
Brian Arkins, professor of Classics at UCG, and his wife, Jo, befriended
me and remained good friends afterwards: Brian to this day, Jo till her
death in 2011.*

*In 1979 we celebrated en famille my 50ʰ birthday with dinner in
the Zetland Hotel on the fringe of North Conamara. In the course of the
evening I noticed sadly that Mary's deference to me as husband had shifted
to Oisín as eldest son. That autumn the whole family, with Cilian resisting strongly, moved first to Bearna near Galway and six months later to
Galway city where Mary had secured a teaching job in the Jesuit secondary
school. In 1980 my column in the* Sunday Press *resumed.*

*During the Gaeltacht revolution, our two boys had been growing up.
From 12 years on Oisín worked with builder Jackie Dowd and learned
formal story-telling from traditional Gaelic storytellers, in particular Cóilín
Mháirtín Sheáinín. Cilian, storing away for future inspiration his en-*

counter with the Story idea, worked from 9 on with Pádraig Casey, a top
Maoinis fisherman who also built boats, and acquired a currach of his own.
It was an apprenticeship which would lead him from 14 on to fishing from
Cleggan and Rosaveal in Conamara, from Killibegs in Donegal and for
three seasons in his twenties off the New England coast. After the move
to Galway Oisín started a science degree in UCG and decided two years
later that because university study involved writing at length it was not
for him. His forte was still the spoken word, and to that side of college
life—debating, dramatics, politics—he took like a fish to water. He left
UCG and worked for four years for a Breton fish-dealer called Breizon
on the Conamara side of Galway Bay, where he began to learn French. In
the mid-1980s Cilian took a UCG degree in Marine Zoology and after
a few fishing trips to the Grand Banks of Newfoundland left fishing and
turned to sailing in Galway Bay.

In 1980 my column in the Sunday Press *resumed. In that same year*
I travelled to Glasgow to read a paper to the First International Confer-
ence on Minority Languages. At the conference I met Dr Sture Ureland,
a Swede teaching at Mannheim University, Germany, who subsequently
would invite me to many conferences of his Euroling group and become a
dear family friend.

The Glasgow conference had assembled academics and activists who
were interested in the fate of minority, mainly shrinking, languages. My
paper was influenced by my recent observation that after the efforts and
substantial gains of the Gaeltacht Revolution—the gains had resulted
mainly from actions by the Dublin Government in response to agitation
by a small number of Gaeltacht activists and a few Irish-language-loving
outsiders—the ordinary people of the South Conamara Gaeltacht, in
particular the young, were continuing their long-standing and instinctively
desired shift from Irish to English speech. My paper elicited a combination
of shock and thoughtfulness from the audience.

❖

CAN A SHRINKING MINORITY LANGUAGE BE SAVED? LESSONS FROM THE IRISH EXPERIENCE

Final summarising paragraphs: The attempt by the Irish State to save the dwindling Irish-speaking minority, and the failure of this attempt, offer valuable experience and lessons to all who would embark on such an enterprise. The Irish example serves to clarify certain things which were not clear beforehand.

A shrinking language minority is shrinking because its members predominantly want to switch to the dominant language. It cannot be saved by the actions of well-wishers who do not belong to the minority in question. In particular, its shrinking cannot be halted by the action, however benevolent and intelligent, of a modern centralised state. It can be saved only by itself; and then only if its members acquire the will to stop it shrinking, acquire the institutions and financial means to take appropriate measures, and take them.

The basic prerequisite is that they acquire the will to stop their disappearance as a linguistic community, and they can acquire this through the agency of a prophetic individual or group who either arises among themselves or comes to them from outside, lives with them, and identifies with them. Having acquired the will to save themselves, they will almost inevitably—human nature being what it is—acquire the institutional and financial means to take appropriate measures, unless they are forcibly prevented from so doing. Consequently, we can say, in summary, that a shrinking linguistic minority can be saved from extinction only by itself; and on condition that it acquires the will to save itself, and is not prevented from taking appropriate measures but assisted in doing so.

PART 2:
THE EVOLUTION OF A DISSIDENT: 1980-1995

In 1982 we were living in a rented house in Galway. Things had not improved between Mary and me and I disliked the children witnessing our dissension. Mary's mother, Kathleen Troy, decided when her sister died to move to Galway. Mary and she found a house near the sea which had a flat attached where Kathleen could live. As for myself, an offer of a lecturing job in Dublin beckoned. When Mary was on a trip to Spain I moved my chattels to Dublin and took the post as lecturer in communications (essentially English writing) in the College of Commerce, Rathmines. (I held it until retirement in 1993.) On a visit back to Galway I suggested to Mary that we all move to Dublin and 'start again'. But she said too much water had gone under the bridge. I contributed to the household expenses and the children came on regular visits to Dublin for me to buy them clothes and shoes. I was sad to be separated from Mary who had soldiered through so much with me. With my agreement she sold our house in Maoinis.

POST-COLONIAL DENATIONALISATION *

IN THE 1950s the Irish economy was stagnant or declining. During the previous decade, masses of people had migrated from the small farms and small towns of the West and South-West to Dublin and there had been a flow of emigration to England; now tens of thousands every year were leaving for England. The most pressing need, clearly, was for a great surge of industrialisation, a revitalisation of agriculture, and development of the neglected sea-fisheries; but above all the need was for industrialisation.

Since its foundation, the state had pursued the Sinn Féin economic policy of self-sufficiency, and this had been re-affirmed with emphasis by the republicanism of Fianna Faíl. Sinn Féin economics were a policy of national capitalism which depended, for its success, on the emergence of an Irish entrepreneurial class the equal of Norway's, say, in size, courage and ambition. By the 1950s it was clear that such a class had not emerged. If it had emerged and had provided the required industrialisation, and if the definition of national identity on which the state was founded had been developed and

* From *The State of the Nation: Ireland since the Sixties*, Ward River Press, Swords, 1983

reinterpreted to keep pace with and guide the economic and social transformations, then the Republic could have moved forward as a normal nation-state, a state identified with nation and retaining its sovereignty. Something like another spurt of 'modernisation' could have occurred, only different, because it was indigenously Irish and guided by different principles from what passed for modernisation in the power-centres of the capitalist world: something 'post-modern', perhaps, as the revolutionary humanists had intended when, in the early years of the century, they hoped for an Ireland that, by linking up with ancient values, would transcend the modern and make all things really new. But that was not to be.

The cluster of symbols of Irish nationality and sovereignty which de Valera's republic had gathered around it, and on which its fundamental legitimacy depended, was being undermined by the obvious failure of the system's economic principle. The state clothed in that symbolic array was simply not holding the people—not in the crudest physical sense, and decreasingly, therefore, in a spiritual and emotional sense. The latter was obvious in Dublin in the 1950s, which, as it happens, was the last great decade of Dublin as a cultural capital. Whether in the literary magazines (then so abundant), in the flourishing school of painting inspired by Paris, in the provocation of Church and State by several theatrical productions, in the poetry of Clarke and Kavanagh, or the determined and successful assault on book censorship, there was a straining against and away from a concept of Ireland that was felt, increasingly, to be imprisoning or illusory or both. Gael-linn, bringing a new style to the language revival and commissioning Ó Riada's *Mise Éire* and *Saoirse* music and Behan's play *An Giall*, and Sairséal agus Dill publishing Ó Ríordáin, Ó Cadhain and Ó Direáin, pointed another way. But that way was not to be.

The world was writing and talking of the 'vanishing Irish'. Not fundamental legitimacy, no such luxury, but contingent legitimacy—some elementary, conspicuous success—was now the Republic's imperative. Whitaker and Lemass realised that if the state was to hold its people in the crudest physical sense, it must be refounded on a new economic formula. Lemass did this by abandoning national capitalism and by refounding the state on the basis of foreign capitalism, and the industrialisation, jobs, and rising living standards, which it provided and promised to provide.

This was not how national sovereignty was supposed to render the nation prosperous. It was a confession of the failure of sovereignty to deliver the predicted material goods. The new policy involved an implicit declaration of dependence on the international capitalist system headed by New York. It entailed a free-trade agreement with Britain, and a re-entry, in dependent condition—two-thirds of our exports went to Britain—and with a feeling of dependence, into a United Kingdom arena which was dominated by London to an even greater degree than previously.

In the period since the 1920s the North of England had lost its industrial power and pride. In 1960, as though to symbolise this, the *Manchester Guardian* removed 'Manchester' from its title and a few years later moved to London. The new industry was mostly in the South-East. Increasing regulation and intervention by central government had made London loom larger in the land, and television magnified it further. In those years, moreover, London was moving into its 'swinging' decade, when it would set the style, as a world capital, for a new consumerist and 'permissive' modernity and a fresh wave of modernisation, this time *a l'Américaine.*

In 1960 the victory of *Lady Chatterley's Lover* in the English law courts set the style of that modernisation in one respect. In 1963, Harold Wilson set it in another, when, in a famous speech that dwelt on the wonders of computers and the promise of science, he promised a New Britain 'forged in the white heat of a technological revolution'. Finally, London no longer radiated its own power only; it served now also as a transmission-centre for American uprooting ideological influence.

Consequently, the Republic's new course was, in effect, a return by nationalist Ireland in the Twenty-Six Counties both to the politics of 'modernisation' and to the dependent condition, in intensified form, in which it had practised those politics in the pre-revolutionary period. Small wonder that on this occasion, too, modernisation went hand in hand with cultural denationalisation. Now, however, it was not merely the living Gaelic language and the general cultural fabric, apart from religion, which our modernisers began to reject.

Now, by gradual stages, it was Catholicism, as the religion typifying Irishness, and the whole symbolic system signifying Irishness which the nation, led by the nationalist state, had sponsored and upheld. More particularly, it was all the symbols and institutions which had underpinned that image, ranging from the GAA ban on foreign games and the Christian Brothers (as a nationalist teaching order) to the nationalist history books, the Gaelic language revival policy, the cult of the heroes of 1916, and the celebration of the national freedom struggle. But this time the denationalisation was more than cultural, for there was more than culture there to denationalise. The nation had acquired the political form of a nation-state, and this political dimension was embodied in the Constitution. Consequently, the denationalisation also had a political aspect: it was a subversion and partial cancelling of the Constitution.

It subverted that part of Article 1 which declares that 'the Irish nation hereby affirms its inalienable, indefeasible, and sovereign right to...develop its life, political, economic, and cultural, *in accordance with its own genius and traditions*.' It sapped the claim to the entire national territory in Articles 2 and 3, and the intention implicitly expressed there to integrate the nation throughout that territory. By causing the *de facto* abandonment of the Gaelic revival, it mocked Article 8 which declares that 'the Irish language as the national language is the first official language'. Most graphically of all, it removed from the Constitution, by referendum, that vague and nominal identification of the nation with Catholicism which was expressed in Article 44: those sections, namely, which recognised, firstly, 'the special position of the Holy Catholic Apostolic and Roman Church as the guardian of the Faith professed by the great majority of the citizens', and then all the other Christian churches by name and the Jewish community.

Like all self-denationalisation, it was a two-sided process. It was not only a deletion of elements of the Irish cultural fabric and a partial cancelling of the Constitution, it was also a replacing of the deleted cultural elements and of the lost substance of the Constitution by alien culture and political influence. The Republic was pressed by the denationalising forces, without and within, into increasing conformity with London's latest norms of cultural modernity—

which were now not exclusively English, but Anglo-American in fact. After two decades of this process, the historian Professor F. S. L. Lyons of Trinity College wrote in 1979 (*The Listener*, 20 March):

> Both parts of the island are now so exposed to the dominant Anglo-American culture that I cannot see the process of absorption ever being held in check, unless the political arrangements of the future take a much more sensitive account of our complex of cultures than they have so far...It could very easily and quickly happen that Anglo-Americanism could extinguish what remains of our local and regional identities. The things we quarrel about now may in fact have disappeared in a generation.

Terence Brown has this passage in mind when, referring to the talk about pluralism in recent years in Ireland, he writes of the 'troubling superficiality' of those who have attempted to formulate it, and continues:

> These, almost without exception, have spoken of the various strands of Irish tradition without taking due account of the enormous changes that have taken place in Irish society in the last rwenty years. In seeking an accommodation between the differing strands of Irish life, to create a comprehensive Irish identity, in a manner Russell and O'Faolain had advised so frequently, such thinkers may be striving for amity, cooperation and synthesis between wraiths of the past. Those who propose pluralism as a concept to illumine contemporary and future Irish reality may in fact be ignoring how much Ireland as a whole, the Republic where Gaelic civilisation and the Irish language were once so ideologically esteemed, and Northern Ireland where two antagonistic versions of Irish identity have traditionally asserted their vitality, may be losing the social diversity it once had in the homogeneity of a consumer society. If this reductive process is in fact occurring, then social and cultural pluralism will be before long an entirely otiose concept in a signally pallid and diminishing Irish reality. (*Ireland: A Social and Cultural History 1922-79.*)

Similarly, from the early 1960s onwards, Irish sovereignty, as defined by the Constitution, was increasingly replaced by British, and behind it, American dominance. Neocolonialism is the simple word for it. The resulting situation was manifested, graphically, in its political aspect, when the North erupted and its war became a feature of Irish life. Throughout the 1970s and into the 1980s, Dublin waited passively for British 'initiatives' on the North without producing one of its own, and spent hundreds of millions of pounds combating the rebellion against British rule and guarding the border of Northern Ireland against armed incursions from the Republic. It was therefore entirely in accord with the general pattern of the situation that, in 1972, the Republic voted for a further alienation of sovereignty, this time to Brussels, on the grounds, as the then Taoiseach, Jack Lynch, put it, that 'since Britain is joining the EEC, we have no alternative but to join'.

Some who dispute that we have lost independence since the 1950s point to the fact that we now send only one-third of our exports to Britain, whereas previously we sent two-thirds; but it is difficult to take them seriously. Even leaving aside the obvious increases in our political and cultural dependency, anyone who reads the newspapers knows that the Irish pound's exchange rate with sterling is still regarded as its most important exchange rate, and as a major determining factor in the health of our economy. But anyhow our economic dependence on Britain is now merely part of a wider dependence on foreign capitalism generally.

In the early 1960s, during the first years of the new course, it was not obvious that it was a reactionary or anti-national course. On the contrary, as wealth visibly increased, and first Dublin, then other centres, experienced a new bustle and sense of movement, morale rose and it was a morale tinged with national pride. In retrospect, it seems that this was principally due to the fact that Lemass, with his impeccable Republican credentials, was at the helm, and that he presented the new course in patriotic and nationalist terms. 'The historical task of this generation,' he said, 'is to secure the economic foundation of independence.' Not merely, as he pointed out, would the new departure do *that*: it would also, by making the Republic prosperous, provide inducement to the North to join it. Consequently, when he went to Stormont to drink tea with Terence O'Neill, and the Northern premier returned the visit, these seemed to be steps forward in a new, dynamic approach to national reunification.

Appearances apart, moreover, it is also a fact that, in those early years, the new course was not intrinsically reactionary or anti-national. Just as Lenin's partial return to a private-enterprise economy, in the New Economic Policy of 1921, was necessary to gain a breathing-space for the Bolshevik Revolution, so was Lemass's turning to foreign enterprise necessary to rescue the Republic's economy. The state's initiative in seeking and encouraging outside intervention was, in the circumstances, its only available means of serving the nation as it needed to be served. When a boat is sinking, it is right and proper to throw weighty, precious things overboard. What made the new course reactionary and anti-national in the long run was that, unlike Lenin's New Economic Policy, it was allowed to continue indefinitely, to become the new norm, and thus to undermine the Revolution which it was ostensibly intended to serve.

For the new course really to 'secure the economic foundation of independence', it would have been necessary, after a few years of benefiting from it economically, to end it; or rather, it would have been necessary, from the start, to regard it as temporary, and to proceed with preparations for ending it and for using its gains as a base for autonomous development. The 'economic foundation of independence' cannot be built in a context of decreasing independence or continuing dependency. It can be built only in the context of a movement towards independence and, ultimately and decisively, only in an independent nation which is reliant primarily on itself, and not on outsiders, for producing its wealth. Whether it was decisive in this respect that Lemass retired in 1966, and was followed as Taoiseach by Lynch, is a matter for speculation. The fact is that the Republic's New Economic Policy continued, and generated a wave of comprehensive 'modernisation' which, because it occurred in conditions of dependence—and not, as in Norway, of substantial independence—was comprehensively denationalising.

Dublin as a social entity had changed greatly during my years in Conamara, most notably in its expansion outwards. The days when le tout

Dublin, *to use that snobbish phrase, were to be found at night in the pubs and restaurants of the centre were gone. Many of my friends now socialised in old or new well-accoutred suburbs.*

As I had already found in University College Galway, lecturing young Irish adults was entirely a different thing from teaching young Spanish children. I was happy in my job in the College of Commerce, Rathmines, especially with the journalism class with whom I was able to conduct a proper course both in good English and in contemporary literature. Among the novels we used as textbooks were Yukio Mishima's The Sailor Who Fell from Grace with the Sea *and Angela Carter's* Company of Wolves. *All or most of the students had part-time jobs with Dublin newspapers. I suffered at the thought of their free young minds and personal vocabulary being remoulded by the new developing orthodoxy of the Dublin media: American neoliberalism cum political correctness. Daughter Natasha was a student in the College for two years, studying public relations, which I did not teach, but we bumped into each other occasionally, which was a pleasure! When she had finished she continued her learning of the communications business with Carr Communications in Dublin.*

THE IMAGINATIVE, THOUGHTLESS CELTS? ★

THE AOSDÁNA SCHEME, as it affects Irish writers, is not just a matter of some kinds of creative writers getting public patronage while others don't. It raises the question of whether we are to continue accepting that our role in the world is to be 'imaginative' and 'poetic', while others do the world's thinking and we live off their thought. The notion that this is the natural order of things has its origin in the English racialist thinking of the nineteenth century about the Germanic and Celtic peoples. Matthew Arnold did a lot to popularise it, but he wasn't its only sponsor.

Nature, so the theory ran, had made the Celts a vivacious, fickle, sentimental people, endowed with high qualities of imagination and poetic vision. It had made the Germanic peoples stolid, reliable and

★ From *Nice People and Rednecks*, Gill and Macmillan, Dublin, 1986, a selection from my *Sunday Press* column.

rational, good at thinking, ordering and executing. The particular gift of the Germans proper was for plumbing vast metaphysical depths. The Anglo-Saxons, for their part, excelled in thought which had direct, practical application, especially to such matters as economics and politics. Locke, Smith, Bentham, Mill and so on were there to prove it.

As it happened, this 'natural' division of mental gifts among the peoples of the British Isles made it natural that the Anglo-Saxons should be the rulers. But it offered the Celtic peoples a more flattering role than they had been offered previously by those rulers. So Scottish Highlanders, Welsh and Irish seized on it and made the poetic, imaginative Celt, who despised mere thought, into part of their respective self-images.

None did this more avidly or more successfully than the Irish. The splendours of the Literary Renaissance showed that we were the Celts *par excellence,* and that even non-Celts—such as Yeats, AE and Synge—who identified with the Celtic thing acquired its gift for creating literary fictions and spirit worlds.

Some who participated in that great movement were not entirely convinced by the 'thoughtless' part of the Celtic programme. In Hyde's view, the Gaelic League was primarily an 'intellectual movement' aimed at re-creating the disintegrated Irish mind. Thomas McDonagh, at his court-martial, referred to the leaders of the Rising, collectively, as 'the intellect of Ireland'—not as its 'poetry' or some such. AE, in the 1920s, maintained that Ireland now had an adequate supply of fiction and poetry, and that its urgent need was rigorous intellectual endeavour.

By and large, however, in the decades after the Treaty, the Irish intelligentsia accepted that thought wasn't Ireland's role, and that creativity for us meant continuing to produce the same kinds of work (stories, plays and poems) as the Literary Renaissance. When the Arts Council was established in the 1960s, it endorsed this view. Its state patronage of writing was devoted entirely to encouraging the production of more stories, plays and poems. Moreover, when benevolent Irish Americans founded the American Irish Foundation and Eoin McKiernan the Irish American Cultural Institute, they saw no reason for departing from the established norm. Their awards and bursaries, too, went to stories, plays and poems.

In view of the inherited provincial bias of Irish thinking, it was hardly surprising that, in these circumstances, Irish thought in every sphere continued, by and large, to be derivative and unoriginal. The measures of public recognition and financial encouragement which might have countered the inherited bias were non-existent.

Then, early in 1981, Charles J. Haughey decided to institutionalise, in a highly formal manner, what was by now the customary Irish attitude and procedure. He founded Aosdána to give recognised status to 150 creative persons, and to pay an annuity of £4,000 to such of them as needed it. Its membership was to include writers, but *only* writers of 'fiction, poetry and drama'. Writers of any other kind, no matter how creative they might be, were not eligible.

Nor was that all. It was decided that, as part and parcel of the Aosdána scheme, the title *saoi* (meaning 'wise man' or 'scholar') would be conferred on outstandingly creative persons. But it was not—as in any normal culture—to be awarded to, among others, outstanding philosophers or scholars. On the assumption, subconscious or otherwise, that outstanding thinkers cannot occur in our Irish, Celtic culture, the title *saoi* is to be reserved to members of Aosdána; and that means to painters and sculptors, composers, photographers, film-makers, and writers of stories, poems and plays, exclusively.

Now, the question, as I said at the outset, is whether we shall continue to accept this situation whereby our role in the world is defined as that of a 'poetic, imaginative and thoughtless people, living off the thought of others'. Personally, I don't accept it. I put it to Mr Haughey, when he was Taoiseach, that there should be public recognition and state-financed patronage for writers of creative thought. I suggested to him that, as a first step in that direction, the regulations for Aosdána could be reformulated on the same lines as the regulations for another of his initiatives—the scheme for exempting writers and artists from income tax. These regulations do not discriminate against thought.

The relevant section of the Finance Act (1969) describes the work which qualifies for tax exemption as follows—'...an original and creative work...which falls into one of the following categories: a book or other writing, a play, a musical composition, a painting or other like picture, a sculpture'. There is every good reason for basing Aosdána on the same formula—with film, photography and video added. In other words, the membership regulations could be re-phrased as follows: 'An artist or writer seeking membership will have produced a body of works of merit which are original and creative. The works will be in one of the following forms: books or other writings; musical compositions; paintings or other like pictures; sculpture; photography, film or video.'

If the 'books or other writings' submitted fall outside the normal competence of the Arts Council, the council could do as the Revenue Commissioners do in such circumstances: ask panels of appropriate experts to say whether the works in question are original and creative.

I also put it to Eoin McKiernan that the Irish American Cultural Institute should subsidise Irish creative thought. When Bill Shannon was in Dublin as the United States ambassador—he is also chairman of the literary awards committee of the American Irish Foundation—I put the matter to him. In this column, on a former occasion, I put it to philanthropic Irish businessmen.

From none of these quarters so far have I received a positive response. Everyone seems afraid to interfere with the role which the English allocated to us. Everyone who could effectively encourage us to think for ourselves about the world shrinks from doing so. I wonder why; and I'm sure, now that I have put it to you, that you will wonder also.

Back in the 1960s when the Cold War was being waged and Soviet Russia was completing its Communist collectivist indoctrination of its East European satellites, America had begun countering it by propagating in its West European satellites its new, equally Godless, individualistic neoliberalism complete with its Political Correctness: converting first of all the mass media and through them their consumers, followed by the national

institutions and governments. 'Swinging' London raised the new banner in Europe; Ireland, led by The Irish Times *and RTÉ, gradually followed. Groups of converts pursuing what was called 'the liberal (meaning neoliberal) agenda' emerged and agitated for feminism, contraception, divorce and abortion. Given that in the early 1980s I was writing a weekly column for the* Sunday Press, *it was inevitable that I would write about some of these topics.*

WHAT ARE 'WOMEN'S INTERESTS'? *

A FUNNY THING happened me on New Year's Eve. I had got a new radio for Christmas and I was fiddling around with it after the 1.30pm news. I soon found myself alternating between 'Women Today' on RTÉ 1 and 'Woman's Hour' on BBC 4. Both were broadcasting a series of excerpts from their 1982 programmes.

On RTÉ 'Women Today' I heard:

a lesbian complaining about the difficulties of getting a mortgage, and how society's arrangements were stacked against unusual people like herself;

Dr Noel Browne talking about tuberculosis;

a woman complaining about not being able to get sterilised;

travelling women being encouraged to complain about the wrongs done to travelling people.

On BBC's 'Woman's Hour' I heard:

women doctors who had accompanied the troops to the Falklands campaign talking about their experiences on shipboard;

a woman regretting her daughter's decision to have an abortion and telling how it disturbed her close relationship with her;

a woman journalist, who had accompanied the Queen to the South Pacific, telling about her experiences;

a woman dying of cancer telling about her prayers and her temptations to suicide, and how her husband's love helped her;

---

* From *Nice People and Rednecks* 1986.

a man talking about the Guernsey dialect;

*a woman flautist talking (she plays the programme's signature tune, …
and the interview with her was followed by 'Now listen to the following
well-known BBC signature tunes and see can you recognise them.')*

I heard more items on the BBC programme because it was longer and because I became increasingly reluctant to turn back to RTÉ.
To do that was like moving from Upstairs to Downstairs, from the
mistresses to the slaves.

I formed a picture in my mind of 'Woman's Hour' as a group
of intelligent, experienced, spirited women sitting around a table
in a sunny verandah, talking about life. The RTÉ programme came
across like a group of wan women, in dressing gowns and with
unkempt hair, sitting around a table in a corner of a hospital ward
and talking about their pains and aches, their operations, their sick
auld fellas and their sick children. It was the old whining, Vale of
Tears crew, whom we have all encountered, but without any Blessed
Mother, Queen of Sorrows to console them—very definitely without that. The BBC programme lived up to its signature tune, 'The
Merry Wives of Windsor'. The RTÉ programme belied its own
tune, 'Sweet Touch', for it was sour.

I had heard both programmes before, of course, and my memories of both throughout the year are influencing my depiction of
them. But it was striking to find those memories completely confirmed by their respective choices from the year's output.

As it so happened, I celebrated the New Year that night with
an old friend, and out of the blue—like many men of some leisure
he listens to the 1.30 news and often hears something of the programme following it—he said, 'Did you ever hear 'Women Today'?
It's incredible.' Since he said that, and I'm writing this, it shows that
we don't believe women, or most women, are like that. We know
better from our experience of them, and I'm talking particularly
about Irish women. But 'Women Today' could give some men who
don't respect women a very negative idea of them indeed. For that
reason I believe that the Council for the Status of Women should
concern itself with this radio programme.

Granted, of course, that this sort of programme does suit and reflect a particular psychological type of woman. But the trouble is that, since it's the only 'women's programme' broadcast by RTÉ, it seems to characterise women generally as whiners, with large chips on their shoulders, and a very limited and philistine range of interests. If there were five women's programmes of different kinds on RTÉ, as there are five or more women's magazines available, it wouldn't matter so much.

My experience on New Year's Eve set me thinking about this whole matter of special programmes, magazines, and pages in newspapers, catering for 'women's interests'.

There is no such thing as defining 'women's interests' in the abstract. They are defined by putting a spirited woman, with a wide range of interests, in charge of the magazine, the women's page or the radio programme, and then by measuring circulation, readership, or (in the case of the radio programme) deliberate, as distinct from accidental, listenership. But one way of not finding out what women's interests are is to let life-hating feminists define them.

DIVORCE IS NEITHER HERE NOR THERE *

IF WE HAVE become, as we have indeed become, a people lacking any coherent set of values, one of the things which have made us so is our dissolution of the Christian social contract which bound us previously. I mean our abandonment of our tacit commitment to base our life together on the Christian norms, and to measure behaviour by them. No one can seriously maintain that such a commitment exists in the Republic today.

But neither have we agreed to base our life together on some other set of values. Many still adhere, more or less, to the Christian view and the Christian way, while others, many of them very influential, have rejected these, deliberately and consciously.

When we recognise that this is the case, it puts many things into perspective. Take, for example, the campaign for divorce and the question of whether we should have divorce facilities. The only reason why our laws prohibit divorce is that we became, in the course of our history, a Christian people, and agreed to base our common life on Christian principles as we perceived them. When a people is

* From *Nice People and Rednecks*, 1986.

committed in this manner to a definite system of morality, that morality is reflected in its laws, particularly in the matter of marriage. It is a preeminent Christian principle that marriage is indissoluble. Naturally, therefore, we prohibited divorce.

Now, however, that we are no longer in agreement about living by Christian principles, or accepting the Christian view of marriage, the basis for the legal prohibition of divorce is gone. Whether we introduce divorce or not is, morally speaking, neither here nor there. It is a matter of expediency; and even the Catholic bishops argue against divorce, not on moral grounds, but on grounds of expediency. Our decision to have divorce, or to continue not having it, won't alter the basic fact that we have dissolved our tacit contract to live by Christian norms, and consequently, our agreement to regard marriage as an indissoluble institution. 'We' no longer regard it as that: some do, some don't.

Naturally, it would be equitable, if we did permit divorce, that those who still wanted to commit themselves to indissoluble, Christian marriage would still be legally capable of doing so. That would be a truly pluralist solution in the correct meaning of that abused word. As it so happens, a specific arrangement on those lines was recommended by the Oireachtas Committee on the Constitution in the late 1960s. But there are various ways in which two kinds of marriage—legally dissoluble and legally indissoluble—could be made available. Pagan Ancient Rome had that.*

RECEPTION OF *BEYOND NATIONALISM* **

IN 1985 PHILIP McDermott of Ward River Press had the courage, commercially speaking, to publish *Beyond Nationalism*. Already, in 1983, he had published with success a short book, *The State of the Nation: Ireland since the Sixties,* which I wrote ten years after my re-

---

* Added 2014. I was later to realise that we were indeed, like most of Western Europe, adopting another, uniquely state-determined, morality—that of Godless American neoliberalism: a set of new precepts added to some inherited ones that had been devised by idealistic American intellectuals and adopted by the American state and American business because it seemed advantageous to them, both domestically and for imposition on America's European satellites. (Only 20% of US citizens were self-identified liberals.)

** From *The Turning Point: My Sweden Year and After*, Sanas Press, Dublin, 2001.

turn to Dublin. In its treatment of what had occurred in the western world in the 1960s and subsequently, it was a sort of updating addendum to the 'big book'.

Beyond Nationalism was extensively and on the whole sympathetically reviewed; in Ireland, that is to say, for it didn't circulate much abroad. But the reviews did not engage with it in depth, it did not sell well and, after a few weeks, sank into a pool of silence. But it had served the primary purpose I had in writing it.

Into the early 1990s, I rode, so to speak, on a wave of the restored relationship with the world that completing it had given me. But it had failed to produce the effect that I had hoped it would provoke: the re-emergence in Ireland of a community of freethinkers such as we had had in the revolutionary years and in which I could participate. I needed that—the conversation, the debate and the colleaguely challenge—as I needed bread.

The fact was that since the early 1960s, patriotism had been as much a motive in my work as the urge to remake for myself a satisfactory image of the age. I fell in love with the humanist project of the Irish Revolution. I was in devoted sympathy with its aim of restoring in Ireland, collectively and individually, that being, man, *der Mensch,* whom I had been at pains to get to know. Affected by the general sense of unlimited possibility that characterised the 1960s, I believed that our revolutionary project could be realised. Trying to contribute to it by dispelling accumulated mental cobwebs, opening up humanist vision, and sketching out humanising programmes, I allied myself with others, persons and groups, who seemed to have a similar purpose. At its most basic level, the purpose was the full realisation of Irish democracy and self-government: the Irish, as a community of communities, truly governing themselves, and as part of that, shaping their worldview and life distinctively, out of their own genius. Daniel Corkery had called it a 'normal' nation as opposed to a provincial or abnormal one. Given that it would include a class of creative freethinkers who would provide the nourishment I needed, my patriotism included that urgent personal motive. (I imagine that Seán O'Faolain, in his time, had had similarly mixed motives.)

❖

ABORTION AND THE MASSACRE MENTALITY *

IT IS TRUE, as many have remarked, that the referendum next Wednesday is not about abortion. It is about an anti-abortion amendment—the Eighth Amendment to the Constitution—which is intended to buttress the existing statute law. But the Yes vote and the No vote will not be seen and represented merely as votes for and against that amendment. Because the amendment is anti-abortion, the votes for and against it will be seen and represented as, on the one hand, a declaration against abortion and, on the other, a refusal to declare against it: that is, as a protest against abortion or a refusal to protest.

Consequently, a Yes majority will mean, in effect, a declaration by Ireland that it will not conform, in the matter of abortion, to the consumer capitalist empire which surrounds us, which we are part of, and which is pressing us continually to conform. A No majority will mean a declaration by us that we are not determined to resist, and that we may, given another push or two, conform with regard to abortion, as we have conformed already in other respects.

Obviously, then, it is very important that we vote Yes. But it is even more important than appears at first sight, and the significance of a Yes vote will be greater than even the pro-life people realise.

Legalised abortion ranks with nuclear armaments as one of the two key features of contemporary civilisation—using that word in its loosest sense.

Legalised abortion and nuclear armaments are intimately related. The first means, in effect, continuous and approved massacre—ten million babies in the USA in the last ten years and almost 150,000 annually in Great Britain. The second means even greater massacres in preparation, with the consent and approval of governments and citizens. Both point to a conviction that human life is by no means sacred, and that, if the mass killing of human beings seems necessary or useful, it is legitimate. This profoundly anti-human conviction, this mentality approving massacre, has spread through our civilisation in the present century. It is now established at its core and dooming it to self-destruction.

No conviction, no mentality, could be more at variance with the European moral tradition as we inherited it from the Middle Age.

* From *Nice People and Rednecks*, 1986,

Europe was created then on the conviction that all human life was sacred, including very especially that of weak, defenceless, unproductive or burdensome people. One of the features of European life as it turned from paganism to Christianity were the laws and ordinances which forbade the abandonment of the old, the sick, or infants, and the massacre of civilians in warfare. The principle was established and accepted that life could be taken, legitimately, only in narrowly defined circumstances, and the life of babies, born or unborn, never. Institutions for the care of foundlings were one of the distinctive Christian charities.

Naturally, warfare continued, but the constant labour of the Church through centuries was to limit the times of the year it could take place, the numbers who were killed in it and the circumstances when it was legitimate to kill. Anyone who sought sanctuary in a church could not be harmed. Mail-clad knights were given a role within the Christian scheme of things, not in order to bless warfare, but so that they, its chief instruments, could be hedged about with moral restrictions.

As Europe became secularised, the concern to restrict killing in warfare passed to lawyers, philosophers, and the professional military men. Meanwhile, every European state, no matter how secularised, treated abortion as a heinous crime and did not consider itself entitled to massacre its citizens on any grounds.

It was after the Bolshevik revolution that the new mentality began to emerge. The Soviet Union was the first state to legalise abortion—it was done for the express purpose of striking at the core of Christianity. Not surprisingly, it was also in the Soviet Union that the massacre of citizens first became institutionalised as a normal measure of state policy.

In Western Europe, during the Second World War, Germany and England took the lead. Just as Eichmann was given the job of killing as many Jews as possible, Bomber Harris was entrusted with the task of killing the maximum number of German workers, together with their wives and children. But it was the USA, with its breakthrough into atomic armaments and its development of rocket technology, which brought the technique of massacre to its present degree of perfection. And the American example was followed by Britain, France, Russia and other countries.

Since the 1960s, massacre by legalised abortion has become common practice in the West. Its role, in effect, in the general scheme of things is to inure us to the occurrence of massacre and to the notion that it can be legitimate. In particular, it serves to kill the idea that the life of weak and defenceless persons is especially sacred, especially to be protected, and that the massacre of such persons is an especially awful crime. For obviously, there are no weaker or more defenceless persons than unborn babies.

Moreover, while legalised abortion erases moral sensitivity in this regard, it is simultaneously soaking millions of women and thousands of men in debilitating, personal guilt, so that they become incapable of resisting, or even protesting against, the use of their taxes and of the profits on their consumption to prepare the general massacre of mankind.

There is another respect, too, in which massacre by legalised abortion is linked to all the other kinds of massacre, actual or projected, which characterise our time. In each case, the massacre mentality supplies a rationalisation to the effect that those who are being massacred are 'not really human'. They are merely kulaks or reactionaries, Jews or Nazis, Orientals, Commies or foetuses. So it is not really a matter of massacring human beings.

In the light of these considerations it must be amply evident that the Yes vote next Wednesday [in support of a Constitutional provision to safeguard equally the lives of the mother and the baby] will be a protest against more than at first appears. Rightly understood, it will be a protest against, and a rejection of, the contemporary mentality which legitimises and rationalises the massacre of human beings.

Some of those who refuse to join in this rejection have said, in recent months, that, if the amendment is carried the pro-life groups may well begin to campaign for other causes. If that should in fact come about, there is no cause they could more logically espouse than the abolition of nuclear armaments, at least in the West.

CYCLING THROUGH MAYO *

COMING FROM DUBLIN, I had been finding the Mayo culture strange. As it presented itself, kaleidoscopically, it seemed at first to be simply Irish-American culture extended into Ireland. Certainly it is more Irish-American than Dublin culture; the older English elements in it, which are common to all of Ireland, have been pushed into the background by its up-to-date American overlay. (Cycling through Ballina, and noticing no other cyclists except children or occasional Continental tourists, I recalled motorised America where only children ride bikes.)

When I did, finally, at the other end of a street, descry a man cycling, I actually took out my glasses, as on the sighting of a rare bird, to make sure that I was seeing right. Later, I'll admit, I did see some other adults cycling. But the strong living connections with England, and the fact that Mayo people at home are involved in Irish, not American, politics, make the description 'Irish-American' unsatisfactory. What Mayo culture is, in fact, I think—and the same may be true of other parts of the West, but I am talking about Mayo—an Irish/American/English amalgam which Mayo people have so shaped that it is both *their* culture, and one which they can have equally, and be at home in, in Chicago, Mayo or Lancashire. It is a culture, in other words, shaped to fit the facts of their life during the past hundred years.

Catholicism, country and western music, 'old-time and ballroom' dancing, the *cúpla focal* in Gaelic, all these play bonding roles in it; but its central institution, in which all its elements meet, and which contributes to the common culture its most strongly and distinctively *Irish* mark, is the GAA

I even heard how the GAA is facilitating the new wave of emigration: young men getting a place on a team visiting the US, and then staying on as 'illegals'. Certainly it would be a foolish Irish politician who would undertake anything in Mayo that was disapproved of by the GAA.

In Ballina, St Muireadach's Cathedral, begun by Archbishop MacHale and finished in 1893, is a tall cruciform neo-gothic church fronting onto the Moy between two bridges. Coming up to eleven

* From *A Connacht Journey,* Gill and Macmillan, 1987.

o'clock Mass on Sunday morning there were about 250 cars parked outside it. In the porch I read that there was a vigil Mass on Saturdays at 7.30pm and four Sunday Masses. The *Universe* and the *Irish Catholic* were on sale. Alongside notices about pilgrimages to Knock and Lourdes, and about centres in Ireland and Britain where emigrants could get assistance, there was a list of 'parish organisations': Parish Council, St Vincent de Paul Society, Legion of Mary, Catholic Boy Scouts, Catholic Marriage Advisory Council, and so on.

Inside, the cream and red running up the great ribbed pillars continued across the ribbed roof. All the windows were of stained glass. One, beside me, showed, surprisingly, Saints William, Henry, Elizabeth, and Francisca Romana—in memory of Francis Devanny. But, of course, I said to myself, the family Christian names. The confessional in carved wood bore an intimidating notice: The Bishop. He was saying Mass. There were some Mass-leaflets lying around, but most people were not following the readings, and the reader was only intermittently intelligible. A girl sang the antiphonal verses, responses included, while the people either remained silent or answered with ragged murmurs. The Bishop, reading the Gospel, could be clearly heard. He preached on the virtue of faith and its difficulties. At the Communion a young woman in a 'diaconal' garment came and stood beside the Bishop's box, distributing the hosts. Meanwhile a girl sang hymns from the lectern, very sweetly, sometimes attaining the heart-rending quality of a boy tenor. 'That I may be the channel of your peace'—those words, sung in her voice, I took away from that Mass with me. After the closing blessing and dismissal, spoken in Gaelic, we poured out towards the waiting collection-boxes of Fine Gael. Besides the Irish papers, most of the English Sunday papers were on sale, but especially *News of the World*, *Sunday Mirror* and *The People*.

The sun was shining as I cycled off along the Moy to get a good place at the jazz session in the Riverboat. Since my days in Galway, when Chris Dooley's All That Jazz played, first in the Great Southern, later in Twinks on the Salthill seafront, jazz on a Sunday morning is one of my delights. This too would be a waterfront. I passed the salmon-fishing stretch of river, a large children's playground, the municipal tennis courts 'presented by the Soroptimist Club, Ballina,

1968', and the sign pointing to the Golf Club. At the bridge across the Bunree, with the Downhill Hotel off to the right and the Boxing Club ahead, I turned left past the Anglers' Club and 'Boats for Hire' into the riverside village of Crocketstown that terminates in the Quay.

Jack Ruane and his boys were tuning up in the Riverboat. Who in Ireland, or in the Irish centres in England, in the 1950s and 1960s, hadn't heard of Jack Ruane's Orchestra? It was the first Irish dance-band to tour in the States. Jack is the father of Judd Ruane, owner of the Riverboat. Judd's wife introduced me to him, a white-haired, fine-featured, blue-eyed old man. 'You've spent a life-time in music,' I said. 'And loved every minute of it,' he answered. 'Oh, I was very despondent back in 1977 when the band broke up, but that only lasted till we started the jazz here.' One of his sons was with him in the jazz band. They played a mixture of dixieland and blues, with occasionally a bit of pop.

The upstairs lounge filled, the usual Sunday-morning family parties. I should have said something before now about the children, all those little people, who had been giving me their smiling, confident 'hellos' along country roads, by riversides, on village streets, or who played pool with me in the back-room of the pub in Belderrig. From the age of three or four upwards they stared at the jazzmen with wonder, and led the clapping. I watched Jack Ruane playing the clarinet, after fifty years in music; swaying into the music as he played, his devotion like that of a monk at the Divine Office. The brotherhood of music: anyone putting that tube to his lips to play a piece made well-known by other musicians is brother to them and knows it; he is playing to them, and for them, in his own mind.

I went out to the riverside wall to listen to the jazz with flowing water. Up river, beyond the town, Mount Nephin stood guard. Near at hand, on the quay, were old warehouses. A man standing at the wall told me the port, once a busy one, had been reopened the previous year for a man who imported coal from Germany; he brought in a load, then absconded. In the pub again, I got to talking with Judd Ruane's brother Harry who was on holiday from Galway where he worked with the American computer firm Digital. When I told him I was sorry to have missed Rosserk Friary, on the way into Ballina, he said he'd take me to it by boat that afternoon—he had been thinking of going fishing.

I went to lunch in the Downhill Hotel, which was full of family parties, many of them from the North and Dublin. One of the attractions seemed to be facilities for sports and games; it had everything from sauna and jacuzzi to squash courts and table tennis. In the dining-room, which looked out through big windows onto the Bunree river, I liked the flurry and abundance of the service staff and their liveried hierarchy. There were two women in red blouse and black skirt, several girls in striped blouse and mauve skirt, two in white blouse and black skirt, and a boy in striped shirt, violet waistcoat, bow-tie and short striped apron carrying a folded cloth on his arm.

According to their dress, they put down or took away plates, presented the bread basket, opened bottles and so on. I had avocado with ham and cheese. Coffee was served in the lounge by a boy in white shirt and black trousers, but I took my coffee in the new cool-coloured, split-level bar, looking out on the garden. This was Frogs Piano Bar, which I had heard about, and should have mentioned when I was talking about Ballina on a Saturday night.

Back at the Quay, Harry Ruane fixed an outboard engine on a boat and we set off baywards on the dead calm river, helped by a strong pull from the outgoing tide. Looking down on us were the mansions of Quay Road. After twenty minutes Rosserk showed up on the west shore, a square tower over peaked roofless walls. We tied up the boat at a seaweed-covered jut of stones which may well have been the friars' pier, and reached the friary after a short walk. It was almost intact except for the roof. There was a chart of the building in the cloister, which didn't have a covered walk as at Moyne. The chapel windows had graceful traceries, and there was a small sculpture of a round tower—that of Killala?—to the right of the altar. On the way back to the Quay we had some trouble from large pieces of rubble that had been washed down the river, Harry told me, by the flood waters.

On the afternoon of the following day I took a bus to Sligo in a thunderstorm.

THE SHED IN CARROWRAE *

SETTING OUT TO return to Boyle by car, I gave a lift to a man who wanted to go to Elphin. Just after we had turned off the Tulsk-Boyle road, heading for that town, I saw a large IRA memorial. Raised on a lofty plinth were three giant figures of republican guerrillas carrying rifles; two of them standing, the third on his knees. I recognised it as the work of my deceased friend, Garry Trimble. The inscription on the plinth, in Gaelic and English, read: 'In proud and loving memory of the Roscommon soldiers of the Irish Republican Army whose names are inscribed hereon, who made the supreme sacrifice in defence of the Republic proclaimed on Easter Monday 1916.' Underneath this: 'Ireland unfree shall never be at peace. P. H. Pearse' and about forty names in Gaelic. It reminded me of one Sam Cryan 'of Carrowrae, Carrick-on-Shannon, Co. Roscommon', whose trial I had been reading about in the papers a short time before. He had been jailed for having eighty-four Kalashnikov rifles in a shed near his house—arms destined for the IRA in the North, it seemed. I recalled at the time a man by the name of Cryan whom I had met once in Carrick after giving a lecture there. The road I was on was pointed towards Carrick, and I guessed from the 'Co. Roscommon' in the address that Carrowrae could not be far away. In Elphin I made enquiries and found I was only a few miles from the place.

The house was on the top of a hill on a back-road near lakes. The man standing beside a car in front of it said he was Dick Cryan. 'I'm calling because of Sam,' I said, 'to say I'm sorry for his trouble.' A boy of 16 and a girl of about 13 were with him. 'My niece and nephew,' he said. 'Come in for a cup of tea.' Dick, it turned out, was the brother who had lived with Sam. In the kitchen I met another brother, Pádraig, the father of the children, who had driven up from Carrick. He remembered me from the lecture fifteen years previously.

Dick and the girl disappeared and Pádraig made me tea. He was obviously the head of the family. 'I was a butcher in Carrick,' he said, 'until my eyesight gave. Since this happened to Sam, I come up here as much as I can to help with the farm.' He talked about the day Sam and Dick were taken to Carrick for questioning. 'Well,' he

---

* From *A Connacht Journey*..

said, 'the people around knew for days before that something was going on, only Sam didn't seem to know. Two men were seen on the hill over there, looking through binoculars. They said they were hunting. Then people down the road saw this van marked "Ordnance Survey" and two men working with an eye-level and acting as if they were measuring the road. And when a woman who lives there spoke to one of them, and he began to explain what they were doing, the other called him over and shut him up. And there were these cars with a man and a woman in each of them passing along the road. They had brought detectives down from Dublin, and on the day they took Sam and Dick in, there were about a hundred of them around the house. A man called Hegarty in Derry was the informer. He disappeared the same day to England, and later when he came back he was shot.

'Dick,' he continued, 'was let go but Sam was taken to Dublin for trial. But in the court they had no evidence. Sam said he knew nothing and you'll see for yourself there's a separate entrance to the shed where they found the stuff. But then at the end of the trial, the sergeant handed a piece of paper to the judges and Sam was sentenced to seven years. Hegarty gave others away too—along the route, you might say. There was a man in Gurteen near Boyle and a man in Strandhill near Sligo. Besides, they *had* observed a van coming and going here and had followed it.'

We talked for a while about a four-province federal Ireland—the theme of my lecture—and how it would be a good thing and why it hadn't taken on. The boy had been listening all the time, and to bring him in I asked was he interested in politics.

'He knows the slogans, "Brits Out" and the like,' his father said, 'but his older brother has more of an intellectual grasp.'

'I must be going,' I said.

'But you must have a drink,' said Pádraig. 'They'll be back any minute.'

They came shortly after with whiskey, Dick and the girl, and Pádraig poured me a generous glass.

'It was the monument made me think of calling on you,' I said.

'Yes,' said Dick, 'our own crowd put you in jail now for doing what those ones did. When they got power, they got corrupted.'

'But doesn't that always happen?' I said. 'It's easy to be pure in your ideals when you haven't power.'

We thought and talked for a few minutes about power and its mysteries. Then Pádraig took me out and showed me the shed and its separate entrance. As we approached my car, the others were there before us and they moved towards us.

'So that's the famous shed,' I said to Dick.

'Yes,' he said, 'and who knows but one day it really will be famous. Ours is a strange history.'

He stood facing me. 'I'll tell Sam you called,' he said. 'He'll be very pleased.'

'It was the least I could do.'

'It was the most you could do.'

I saw that he was almost crying. I looked towards the girl, who was looking at her uncle, and saw with a shock that, like all young girls, although she had said nothing, she had taken everything in, felt everything, knew everything, and she was trying not to cry. I shook hands abruptly with the men, got into the car, and drove off, waving to them; and I, too, staring blankly at the road, just managed to hold the tears back.

JOYCE'S STRANGE NON-ENCOUNTER WITH THE ADRIATIC *

APART FROM FIVE months spent in Paris in 1902-3, James Joyce's first period of residence outside his native Dublin was in Pula on Croatia's Adriatic coast, where he arrived in November 1904. Today, in the summer holiday season, there are direct weekly flights from Dublin to Pula. But Joyce, accompanied by Nora Barnacle, travelled by boat and train via London, Paris, Zurich and Trieste. He had not chosen or intended to live in Pula or anywhere on the Adriatic. Leaving Ireland because he felt he must leave it, he had been promised a job teaching English in the Berlitz school in Zurich; but the promise proved false. Recommended to the Berlitz in Trieste, he was again disappointed there. Finally he found a job in the newly-opened Berlitz in Pula. After spending four months there, he moved

* A paper read to the annual Croatian Writers' Congress which I attended five or six times in the 1970s and 80s. Published in *Most,* Zagreb, 1987.

to the Trieste school and, except for a brief period in Rome and three visits to Ireland, lived for ten years in that city. In 1915, after Italy had entered the First World War, he moved to Zurich.

Towards the end of Professor Ivo Vidan's paper on 'Joyce and the South Slavs', the author comments:

> Joyce lived for a time in South Slav territory, heard Slav languages spoken among his students, and admired an artist who tied his work with his philosophy of Yugoslav nationalism (Ivan Meštrović). But he never took any interest in the life and culture, and hardly at all in the language, of these little nations.

I think Prof. Vidan's explanation of this is accurate. On the one hand, he writes:

> Joyce was tired of the problems of a small country deprived of in-dependent statehood, dominated by a foreign power, and pouring its most vital energies into nationalist agitation...The disjunctions and moral crises within an oppressed community were particularly painful to [him]...Whatever he may have known of the Slavs must have put him off, and made him impervious rather than sympa-thetic.

I understand this from my own experience. The long agony of Northern Ireland in these past twenty years, and the shadow which this casts over life in all of Ireland, make me, and I think other Irish people, resentful and angry about how this is robbing us, for so long of the normal life which as human beings we feel we have the right to. If we travel abroad, we feel no urge to get involved in similar anguishes elsewhere—quite the opposite.

Similarly with the long, frustrating involvement which I have had, with some friends in the problems of our Gaelic language mi-nority: it has made us feel that we don't want, when we travel, to hear about similar problems elsewhere. We have heard it all before. If we go to live abroad, we want to experience 'normal' life, in a 'normal' nation. Indeed, many of us would choose the experience of self-assured metropolitan life—even if we regard the world me-tropolises as the enemies of our own small nationhood! When Joyce came to Pula, Paris, which he remembered with pleasure, was where he really wanted to be.

Secondly, as Prof. Vidan also says, the Italian side of his Adriatic experience was much closer to Joyce 'because of his education among the Jesuits, his literary sympathies from Dante to d'Annunzio, his love of Italian music, his knowledge of the Italian language.' Most of his important acquaintances and friendships in Pula and Trieste were Italian. In this respect, his encounter with the Adriatic was simply an extension and continuation of an already existing aspect of his intellectual make-up.

But his affinity with things Italian did not extend to the remains of ancient Rome—and this was another respect in which the Adriatic world brought nothing new to him. He ignored, as Prof. Vidan remarks, the splendid Roman remains in Pula though these are difficult to ignore; and his reaction, some years later, to the ancient ruins in Rome itself showed that this was no accident. He hated them and was depressed by them, because they were 'like an old cemetery'. For him that 'exquisite panorama' was made up of 'flowers of death, ruins, piles of bones and skeletons'. Again probably, his Irish background had something to do with his attitude. Ireland was a country of ruins—physical, cultural and social; some of them romantic perhaps, but ruins nevertheless. Joyce, like many other ambitious Irishmen of his generation, wanted at long last some positive and modern achievement to redeem and replace that broken past.

For my own part, however, as I read Joyce's letters from Pula and Trieste, and his works written in those years, it is another absence of response to his environment that strikes me most immediately. When, coming from Dublin two years ago, I dropped out of the sky into a May-morning Pula. I was struck immediately by the luminous quality of the light; I could not take my eyes of the shimmering blue sea; I felt keenly, first the balmy air, and then, as the sun rose, the deeply warming heat; I noticed the different, luxurious vegetation. It was the South. Sitting in the harbour, waiting for the train to Zagreb, I recalled those town-encrusted islands, like jewels in the sea, that I had seen on previous visits to the Adriatic.

Apart perhaps from those passages towards the end of *Ulysses* where Joyce has Molly Bloom recalling Gibraltar, there is no evi-

dence that any of this impinged directly on him or that he took
pleasure in it. His master Ibsen remembered in old age the moment
when, after passing through a dark Alpine tunnel, he suddenly encountered at Miramare near Trieste 'the beauty of the South, a wonderful soft brightness'. Joyce had no such sensual encounter.

Insofar as this was a lack of visual response, I think it was due primarily to this short-sightedness and his generally bad eyesight—in
the course of his life he had eleven operations on his eyes; but also,
though the two things were probably connected, to his obsession
with city life and mental life and his corresponding lack of sensitivity for country life and the beauty of nature. As for the heat of the
sun, which draws so many northerners to the South, Joyce noticed
this but did not welcome it. In Trieste, in the autumn of 1905, he
wrote to his brother, Stanislaus: 'I went out yesterday for a walk in a
big wood near Trieste. The damned monotonous summer was over
and the rain and soft air made me think of the beautiful (I am serious) climate of Ireland. I hate a damn silly sun that makes men into
butter.' I must say that I understand that feeling about continuous
hot sun—I share it with Joyce and some other Irish people; but
most people in Ireland would disagree with me.

The point, however, is that these reactions and non-reactions of
Joyce to his Adriatic environment combine with those we have previously noted to illustrate his extreme introspection from his early
manhood onwards: the extreme degree to which he carried with
him to the Adriatic his Dublin experience and cast of mind, and remained enclosed in these imperviously. Add to what we have noted
already the fact that Joyce never showed any interest in the Adriatic
or in the civilisation specific to it—never for example, during those
ten years in Trieste, visited Venice or Ravenna.

Was there, then, any real encounter at all—in the sense of a meeting which influenced his personality, his work or both—between
Joyce and his Adriatic environment? Richard Ellmann, in his biog-
raphy of Joyce, voices a view on the matter. He tells us that what Ibsen said of his encounter at Miramare with 'the beauty of the South,
a wonderful soft brightness' that it 'was destined to set its stamp on
all my later production' was true also of Joyce. Ellmann continues:

It had a similar effect on Joyce; slowly, in spite of many flare-ups, his anger cooled; his political ideas, at first assertive, almost vanished; his literary aim shifted imperceptibly from exposure to revelation of his countrymen; he applied himself to creating a subtle and elaborate art, less incriminating, more urbane than the chapters of *Stephen Hero* or the early stories of *Dubliners*. He brought, in the person of Ulysses, the bright though unsentimentalised Mediterranean world to sombre Dublin.

Ellmann cannot mean that the physical reality of the South impinged on Joyce sensually and pleasurably, as it did on Ibsen, for that was not the case. I take him to mean that the South somehow set its stamp on Joyce's work after 1904-5, as it did on Ibsen's later production. In support of this, he argues that a general softening occurred in Joyce's work and political ideas, and that the Ulysses theme, as used by him, was an influence from the 'bright Mediterranean'.

I find this unconvincing. It is true that Joyce's attitude towards Dublin and Ireland, and his style of writing about them, softened in the manner which Ellmann describes. But to attribute this mellowing to the supposed 'softness' of the South is unsustainable. In the first place, it is merely Ellmann's view, though not unique to him, that the South is essentially softness; with equal validity it can be said to be characterised by hard clarity or fierce passion. Secondly, in the absence of any evidence that Joyce himself viewed or experienced the South as soft, it seems much more credible to attribute his mellowing to other factors: affection for the homeland arising from his exile; his experience of love and (effective) marriage with Nora Barnacle; his experience of fatherhood; and the relativising perspective on Ireland and its foibles which he gained from his wider experience of the world in the Trieste years.

But this mellowing did not extend in a blanket manner to Joyce's political ideals, as Ellmann suggests. While his socialism, never very well-informed or serious, disintegrated, his aversion to nationalism lessened, and he became an adherent of the Irish economic and political nationalism then being propagated by Arthur Griffith and Sinn Féin. As for Ulysses being an influence from the 'bright Mediterranean', this is true only in an objective and intellectual sense, not because Joyce lived in Trieste. His interest in ancient Greek tales dated from his schooldays in Ireland, and already, in his first novel,

Stephen Hero, he had given the hero a surname, Dedalus, derived from one such tale.

All in all, then, it seems that Joyce's encounter with the Adriatic was a non-encounter in the sense that this human and physical environment—which he had not chosen, but where he found himself by accident—did not impinge on him in any formative way. Of course, I am speaking of that environment as a whole; many details and individuals from Joyce's years in Trieste found a place in his work, and his friend Ettore Schmitz, a Jewish businessman, was one of the principal models for Leopold Bloom and an important source of Joyce's knowledge of Jewish matters.

Trieste, as a city, did play a significant role in his life inasmuch as it provided continuance for two factors in his mental makeup which he had brought with him from Dublin. One, as we have seen, was his *penchant* for Italian culture; the other was his experience of provinciality, that central modern phenomenon which Joyce had first noticed in Dublin and which was very much in his mind as he wrote *Dubliners* and later, *Ulysses*. Indeed, not only as an embodiment of provincial and marginal life, but also as a port city where a nationalist irredentism (Italian) declaimed against an empire, Trieste—and this did not escape Joyce—was in some important respects a second Dublin.

Taking up where I had left off with Sketches of the New Ireland, *I persuaded Tom Barrington, Raymond Crotty, Roy Johnston, Michael O'Flanagan, John Robb (then an appointed Senator) and John Roden to join with me in founding the Constitution Club in October 1986, with printer Michael O'Flanagan as its recording secretary. At its monthly public meetings of up to thirty people in Buswell's Hotel we heard and discussed papers on various aspects and possible reforms of Irish government. Dónal Ó Brolcháin, a civil servant who had worked for years on such matters, contributed his working papers. Except from June to August, the club met monthly until 1988.*

While still in my Joyce phase, in 1988 I walked Leopold Bloom's path, step by step, through Dublin and wrote a book about it, which was published in 1990 by Ward River Press as Bloomsway: A Day in the Life of Dublin.

For a time I gave a drinks party for a number of friends on Saturday afternoons in my flat on Palmerstown Rd. At night I occasionally frequented Joys night club, the best part of that being the late-night-early morning sessions with such as Vincent Browne, Shane Ross and Eamon Dunphy. Sometimes, when we were the last guests, the owner Frank Conway would leave and, pointing to the fridge, say, 'Help yourselves.' On Saturdays it was often lunch in the Unicorn restaurant, sometimes with daughter Natasha, and with a number of regulars at other tables such as Adrian Hardiman and Michael McDowell, followed by an adjournment to Doheny and Nesbitt's pub across the street. In the latter part of the decade I met Fergal Tobin, commissioning editor at Gill and Macmillan, every Friday in Neary's for good talk. I was disappointed that his firm published no more of my books after Connacht Journey *(which, by the way, I had wanted to name 'The Meadowsweet Month: My Connacht Journey' because that flower was blooming during my journey. But his commercial department decided otherwise.*

In 1990 I applied for a D. Litt. Degree (Doctor of Literature) to the National University of Ireland by submitting for judgment the books I had written, and was awarded the degree. In that same year I moved from the furnished flat on Palmerstown Road to a cottage down a lane in Portobello which I furnished myself. It had a small fenced front garden with perennial shrubs, which even if I couldn't use it for growing vegetables, like my field in Maoinis, I liked because it contained growing things.

❖

HOW LONDON AND VENDLER
MADE HEANEY'S REPUTATION *

IN ORDER TO get to the top today in poetry, transatlantically, there are three prerequisites which a poet must fulfil, and Heaney has fulfilled all of them. The first is to write only or mainly lyrics, and prefer- ably fairly short ones. The idea has been put around that the lyric is what poetry essentially is, and that narrative, satirical, philosophical or dramatic poetry, and long poetic works generally, while they may continue to exist and sometimes to merit praise, are not necessary for the health of poetry. Poetry is now generally written about as if it were synonymous with lyrics, and the two words are often used interchangeably. Lyrics, moreover, are the kind of poetry suitable for printing in newspapers and magazines, and for reading on television.

When people go to a poetry-reading, it is lyrics they expect to hear. Secondly, the poet must actively manage his career with par- ticular attention to the fact that we live, as we are so often told, in an age of public relations and mass communications, and in a free market economy. Heaney has done this well. Unlike many poets, he has regarded poetry as a career to be taken as seriously as any other, and has used his intelligence and personal charm accordingly. He has noted and responded to the signals of his socially chang- ing and geographically shifting audience. Though living in Dublin, he has been careful to maintain his Northern Ireland persona. Ac- cused by some of condoning Irish republican violence, he 'balanced' with a poem to mark the assassination of the British Ambassador. In choosing the poems for selected editions, he has been guided by political as well as aesthetic considerations. Above all, he has been an assiduous communicator about his work, thereby ensuring that critical writing about it is interspersed with critical comments and explanations of his own.

* From *Whatever You Say, Say Nothing: Why Seamus Heaney Is No. 1*, Elo Publications, Dub- lin, 1991. For this large-format pamphlet and my following book *Dreams of Oranges*, my artist friend Robert Ballagh kindly supplied the cover designs. For the pamphlet, Heaney- lovers gave me a bad time in the letters columns of *The Irish Times* while phone-callers and private letter-writers told me, 'About time!' The pamphlet's full text was republished under the original title in *Stand Magazine*, Newcastle upon Tyne, UK, Autumn 1991 and by Milestone Press ,Little Rock, AR, USA, 1994.

The third prerequisite is hinted at by the poet and critic Martin Bell, writing in the *American Poetry Review* (May-June 1990): 'Much of our [American] official criticism grows on the East Coast, and looks to the Old World, perhaps unconsciously, for cultural signals.' He adds: 'Puritanism may apply: it seems to be flourishing . . .', but of that more anon. To get to the top, transatlantically, in poetry, you must reach the top first in London. Heaney accomplished this.

Heaney's Path to the Top via London

To begin with, along with Mahon, Paulin and others, he was one of the 'Northern Ireland poets' who, from the late 1960s onwards, were being hailed in London as the rising hope of British poetry. They were hailed as that because Northern Ireland is British and they were publishing in London; their matter was new to many there; and their vigour and quality stood out in the tired British poetry scene, where the muted post-war epoch was fizzling to a close. Heaney, who won prizes in London with his first book, *Death of a Naturalist*, emerged as their leader. In Faber, he had, to quote a London poet acquaintance, 'the only poetry publisher who has got his act together'. From 1969 onwards, when the violence in Northern Ireland put the province daily in the news, it came to seem the most exciting, because embattled, place for a poet to be. In 1972 Heaney moved south to near Dublin. His reputation had not been enhanced by his second book, and he had begun to be typed, even caricatured, as a rustic bard of farmyards and country lanes. But his stock rose again in 1972 with *Wintering Out*, which offered fresh, vibrant language and a couple of hints of Northern violence. Finally, with *North* in 1975, he delivered the 'war book' that London was waiting for, and which made him top poet in Britain. Blake Morrison, in the essay I referred to, 'Speech and reticence: Seamus Heaney's *North*', writes:

> The book had barely come back from the printers before various funding bodies were rushing to cast their cheques at Heaney's feet. *North* was made the Poetry Book Society choice; it won the Duff Cooper Memorial Prize and the £1,500 W. H. Smith Memorial Prize; it was gushed over on television and radio...A sceptical observer might have suspected that there was rather more to the

acclaim for *North* than appreciation of the book's literary merits…
For some years, in a new version of the old cry 'Where are the war
poets?', critics had been calling for a poetry that would 'deal with'
the Northern Ireland 'problem', and in the reviews of *North* there
is an almost audible sigh of relief that at last a poetry of stature had
emerged from the 'troubles'.

'A poetry of stature' not least because two of its most striking
characteristics, its 'nothing-saying' and its poverty of meaning, were
prized poetic qualities in London critical circles. Dr Morrison continues:

> At the same time it was noticeable that…hardly anyone seemed
> interested in what it was that Heaney had to 'say' about Northern
> Ireland. Indeed the suggestion seemed to be that while it was good
> to have a poet like Heaney 'involve himself in' the Ulster troubles,
> *his poetry was valuable insofar as it could not be seen to be making state-*
> *ments: poetry, after all, should not mean but be* [Italics mine].

Perhaps Morrison's citation of Archibald Macleish's dictum is
not without a shade of irony—he himself is critical of this view
of *North*—but what matters for our purpose is his account of the
prevailing view. Somewhat further on, in a sentence which sums
up neatly the two main currents that had joined to make Heaney's
poetic, he explicitly integrates Heaney into the post-war English
mainstream of poetic 'reticence':

> Having grown up in a community, the Catholic minority in Ulster,
> where to speak openly is a dangerous activity ('whatever you say,
> say nothing', as one of his poems has it), *and belonging as he does to*
> *a modern poetic tradition which distrusts poetry that too explicitly 'states'*,
> Heaney is loth to wear the mantle of the political poet…[Italics
> mine]

Morrison is inexact when he suggests that the English 'reticent'
tradition shrank from 'too explicitly stating': it shrank, generally,
from explicit statements about large or general things, not about
the self and small, particular things. But the point of what he says
is that, in Heaney, the poetically adapted speech behaviour of Co.
Derry Catholics fused, happily, with the similarly adapted speech

culture of the English military-administrative caste. Thomas Foster, in his book, remarking on the 'terseness' of an early Heaney poem, says that 'it recalls a characteristic tone in contemporary British and Irish verse: defensive, tight-lipped, understated'. From 'characteristic' subtract 'Irish'; the operative word is 'British', and more precisely, English. Foster continues:

> One thinks of a similar hard edge in Jon Silkin's 'Death of a Son' or any number of poems by Philip Larkin, Charles Tomlinson, Geoffrey Hill, Roy Fuller, Kavanagh, and Hughes. While the British may have learned that pose and attitude from Thomas Hardy, Edward Thomas and the Georgian poets, as well as, according to Larkin, the privations of World War II, Heaney and the…Ulster Irish have learned to hold their tongues from extraliterary affairs…

Actually, the special virtue of Heaney that was sensed, rather than identified in London, was that he went one further than reticence by practising 'nothing-saying' or effective silence. Larkin, for all his reticence, had occasionally allowed himself clear statements about the human condition. In that respect Heaney trumped him, just as, in his poems reflecting the Northern Ireland conflict, he trumped the other English top player, Hughes, who had strongly influenced his early poetry. Where Hughes, deviating from the genteel English mainstream, had offered sinister violence, imaginatively, in his animal poems, Heaney provided it, not in animal, but in human form, and not imagined, but actual—as actual as the television news. To crown it all, and to speed the transatlantic crossing, Robert Lowell, then the reigning poet of the American academy, but living for some time in England, described Heaney in *The Observer* as 'the best Irish poet since W. B. Yeats'.

Heaney in America

The upshot was that *North* was rocketed to New York with the labels 'The Best That Britain Can Offer' and 'According to Lowell, the Best since Yeats'. Heaney had a certain reputation in the US based on his early bucolic poems and their Frostian echoes. 'Digging', with its present-participle title recalling Frost's 'Mowing', 'Mending Wall' and so on, became, and has remained, his best-known poem there. People were grateful to him for 'bringing the theme back into poetry', something that had never been noticed in Ireland or Britain where the 'theme' had never disappeared. Already, before *North*, his reputation in London had helped: now that book's triumph there ensured that it was received enthusiastically in most of the American journals, mainly academic ones, that review poetry. Henceforth Heaney was up front in the East Coast poetry stakes. But *North* did not bring him to the top there, let alone in the US generally—that would not be until the 1980s. He rose to that eminence partly because of his continuing British reputation, his teaching in Harvard, and the gratuitous advantage of being a foreign poet. 'You know the four great poets in this country in recent years?' an American poet said to me ironically. 'Heaney, Brodsky, Miłosz, Walcott.' More decisive, however, was the fact that Heaney's work was congenial to the American poetry establishment—particularly to its queen, Helen Vendler—and that he worked, successfully, to make it more so.

Given that poetic modernism in English was pioneered by Americans, it is not surprising that, by comparison with Britain where there is little, and Ireland where there is none, poetic theory plays a big role there. In this respect, and with various groups of poets practising different *isms*, the American poetry scene is more like Central Europe than the British Isles. To a degree which must have surprised Heaney, this world of theory, especially on the East Coast, accommodated his kind of poetry. If it wanted Puritanism, the cool chastity, emotional restraint and guilty introspection of his work supplied it. Macleish's 'A poem should not mean/But be', which had eased the way for him in London, had even more force in Macleish's home country. Since the 1950s the most celebrated American poets had been writing a downbeat, cerebral, hermetic (though often loquacious) poetry that literally meant little or nothing to the great majority of literate Americans, so that 'meaning little or nothing' had become, effectively, a defining attribute of contemporary poetry, and the doctrine that this was how poetry should be, a justification of the reality. As for 'silence', had not Macleish, in that same *Ars Poetica*, said:

A poem should be palpable and mute
As a globed fruit,

Dumb

As old medallions to the thumb,

Silent as the sleeve-worn stone

Of casement ledges where the moss has grown—

Pulsing through the American academic-poetic world, since Pound and Williams, Ransom and Jarrell had successively asserted and developed it, was a poetic theory that made particulars, for their own sake, the core of poetic creation: poetry was about 'concrete particulars', the purpose of literature was 'the knowledge of particulars'. The composer John Cage had got himself into the dictionaries of quotations, under the heading 'Poetry', by writing, in a book called *Silence*: 'I have nothing to say and I'm saying it and that is poetry.' More to the point: 'Vendler doesn't like poems that *say* something,' wrote Bruce Bawer, in 1989, in a long critique of *The Music of What Happens* in the *Hudson Review*. Even if he then added, '—or, more accurately, she's very strict about the ways in which she thinks it is proper for a poem to say something', he had conveyed, with the first statement, the impression she gives.

Field Work, Heaney's next collection after *North*, was recognised by the critics as 'Heaney Lowellising', and it contained an elegy to Robert Lowell. In the year it appeared, 1979, Heaney taught for a term in Harvard, and the following year his selected poems and selected prose were published. In 1981 Helen Vendler came out strongly for both in the *New Yorker*, one of the few general magazines that reviews poetry. Plath, Berryman and Lowell had created a vogue for painful, personal 'confession' in verse, and Heaney's keenly-felt soul-searching had fitted well with this. Now, in 1985, in *Station Island*, he supplied a full, penitential session of it, perhaps not so keenly felt. Again, in the *New Yorker*, Vendler approved. Then, after *The Haw Lantern*, she presented her ultimate accolade by using a Heaney verse as the title of her new book (her previous book title was from Wallace Stevens).

Bruce Bawer calls Vendler 'the colossus of contemporary American poetry criticism...[she] looms hugely over the ever-shrinking landscape'. But the full significance of her wholehearted acclaim for Heaney is not apparent from her *New Yorker* articles. Probably because these were for the general public, they confine themselves to

explaining background, summarising, commenting lightly and praising highly, without discoursing on poetry as such or her own ideas
about it. There are a few significant indications in some expectable
phrases: 'evil, violence and our individual helplessness in history'; 'a
barer, "adult" aesthetic'; 'things founded clean on their own shapes';
'ritual sacrifices, of which the Ulster murders on both sides are simply recurrences, are tribal customs defeating all individual reason or
endeavour'; 'free from a superficial piety'; 'another source of fracture
and culpability'; 'thorns of conscience and apprehension and moral
revulsion'; 'to devote himself rather to the ardours than the pleasures of verse'; 'extraordinary descriptive powers—dangerous ones';
'Heaney's lines [are] not corrupted by pure linguistic revel'. There
are hints there, but we are not given a rounded picture of the kind
of poetry Vendler likes, the kind she values most highly and why, and
therefore, the kind of contemporary poetic elite she was receiving
Heaney into. Only when we know that, as she reveals it in her fully
professional writing, can we understand what being a top poet in
America means, and how well Heaney, especially in his later books,
qualifies as one. But Vendler's poetic has an additional interest. During the 1980s, as poet, professor and critic, Heaney adopted Vendler's
view of poetry, and developed it, and this has been influencing both
his poetry and his apologia for it.

Helen Vendler's Poetics

In *The Music of What Happens* Vendler writes about John Ashbery.
Because he is her favourite living American poet, her opening description of his work is interesting:

> It seems time to write about John Ashbery's subject matter. It is
> Ashbery's style that has obsessed reviewers, as they alternately wres-
> tle with its elusive impermeability and praise its power of linguistic
> synthesis. There have been able descriptions of its fluid syntax, its
> insinuating momentum, its generality of reference, its incorporation
> of vocabulary from all the arts and all the sciences. But it is popular-
> ly believed, *with some reason*, that the style itself is impenetrable, that
> it is impossible to say what an Ashbery poem is 'about'. An alterna-
> tive view says that every Ashbery poem is about poetry—literally
> self-reflective, like his 'Self-Portrait in a Convex Mirror'. *Though this*

may in part be true, it sounds thin in the telling, and it is of some help to remember that in the code language of criticism when a poem is said to be about poetry the word 'poetry' is often used to mean many things: how people construct an intelligibility out of the randomness they experience; how people choose what they love; how people integrate loss and again...[Italics mine]

Poetry that has doubtfully a subject is like abstract painting: words added to it tend to thrash about and flounder. Here, and in the following seventeen pages of Vendler on Ashbery, I am back in the 1960s, reading one of those French art critics who could surround the work of a voguish abstract painter with a volume of very similar prose.

However, if that passage merely suggests Vendler's idea of good poetry, another essay in the same book deals directly with the matter. She is discussing the views of three American writers who want poetry to have 'a strongly mimetic and a strongly communicative value'. In addition, one of them, Robert von Hallberg, wants 'a directly civic value,' while the others want 'an ethical value'. 'But I myself', she writes, 'think aesthetic value, properly understood, quite enough to claim for a poem'. (Clearly, here and in what follows, she is equating poetry and 'a poem'—from Homer, Lucretius and Juvenal to Dante, Shakespeare, Goethe, Dryden and Yeats—with lyric poetry.) She writes:

What [a poem] represents, ultimately, is its author's sensibility and temperament rather than the 'outside world'—but of course that sensibility and temperament have been shaped by the historical possibilities of the author's era. Thus, in representing a sensibility, the poem does represent a particular historical moment. The poem ingests, it is true, the outside world (which it uses for its images, its symbols, and its language), but it does so, as Marvell said, in order to color everything with the mind's color, reducing to zero ('annihilating' said Marvell) the entire creation into its own mentality.

The mind, that ocean where each kind
Doth straight its own resemblance find;
Yet it creates, transcending these,

Far other worlds and other seas,
Annihilating all that's made
To a green thought in a green shade.

As is evident from the text, Marvell did not say that a poem does
that, but that the mind does it; in a garden, to be precise. It is note-
worthy that Vendler here equates 'a poem' with a mind. She goes on
to explain that, of course, 'all kinds of ethical and civic topics turn
up in poetry, as do trees and flowers and ladies' eyes; but they are
all material for the transformation into green'. Granted that what
she means to say is that a poem is similar to, and represents, a mind
at work on its environment, this might seem to imply that a poem
is like any thoughtful discourse. But elsewhere she makes clear that
she does not favour a poetry of ideas—that would mean 'saying
something'—and Bawer writes of her, 'Time and again in Vendler's essays, language-as-action wins the day.' In sum, her ideal poem
might be described as 'conclusionless thinking in active language',
or a vigorously verbal musing. As for communicative value:

> Because language is the medium of poetry, and language cannot,
> when used according to any of the possible rules of its coding, not
> communicate, there is, it seems to me, no need to worry about po
> etry's 'communicating' itself. All poems grow easier with time, even
> *The Waste Land*. And there is no need to worry about 'universality'
> or speaking for everyone.

In her previous book, *Part of Nature, Part of Us*, published in
1980—the year before her first article about Heaney—Vendler tells
us more about the notion of poetry that is adumbrated in the above.
In an essay on Robert Lowell, she describes what poetry is when it
is 'grown-up', and therefore, presumably, most truly poetry. Lowell,
she writes, began with the youthful belief that poetry needs religious
vision, the poet as questing pilgrim, resonant Hebraic denunciations
and the well-made poem. But in his late poetry, which is 'seemingly
mused rather than written, ruminating not spontaneous', he came
to a better understanding and practice. Vendler lists the characteristics of this 'musing' poetry, beginning with 'profoundly irreligious'
and ending with 'exempt from the tyranny of the well-made poem'.
Around the middle are these two: 'addressed not homiletically to an

audience, but painfully to the self' and 'private rather than public'. She concludes: 'It is in this sense Chekhovian. In fact, reading the complete Lowell is rather like seeing Dostoevsky grow up to be Chekhov.'

'A private musing addressed, painfully, to the self, and expressed in active language.' That seems to be the core notion of really good poetry which runs through Vendler's discourse. And it seems to me that we have here another instance of justification after the event. Certain persons, by getting their verses published, rank as poets; and some of these, judged very good or the best by the academic-poetic complex, are producing quantities of verse which mean little or nothing to ordinary literate people: they are obviously not speaking to them, nor trying to. *Ergo*, poetry, at its best, is not public speech, but private musing addressed to the self. As a delivered product, it is *published* private musing. Since the verse in question was, presumably, written for publication, this is a fiction; but it is a useful fiction because it explains everything. No one expects somebody's musing to himself to mean much to others; it has its private syntax, its own unique and personal way of connecting meanings and words. Logically, moreover, if a number of poets are at it, it needs Vendlers, hundreds of them, to interpret it and 'teach' it. In short, the poet *par excellence* becomes a sort of ruminating, groaning shaman, delivering oracles which his academic acolytes interpret to the students within the temple and the heedless multitude beyond the gates.

Heaney qualified in Vendler's terms, and he worked to qualify better. Obviously he had the 'active language' and the 'pain'. For the rest, it was a matter of how you conceptualised and described poetry which, though published to wide audiences, said nothing about general matters, and therefore cancelled itself as genuine public speech. For Vendler it was musing directed to the self, and, as such, poetry at its best. Quite early in his career, Heaney had hinted in his poem 'Thatcher' that poetry was a work of rumination and measuring. Neil Corcoran, in his book, finds in some poems in *Wintering Out* and *North* that 'the poet's "I" is detached from ordinary social circumstance, withdrawn to solipsistic meditation, ruminatively entranced . . .' The fact is that much of Heaney's poetry in the 1970s could be regarded as private musing or meditation—with any intrusive general views censored out—rather than as public speech which, in the Co. Derry manner, 'said nothing'. But Heaney, with long Irish and English traditions of poetry as public speech behind him, had hesitated to commit himself to the 'private meditation' concept. Now, in response to Vendler's high valuation of such poetry, he did so, and the result can be noticed in the increased self-absorption and indifference to readers in *Station Island* and *The Haw Lantern*. Significantly, the first blurb of a Heaney collection to describe his work as 'meditative' is that of *Station Island*. Since then he has been consciously not speaking to us, even to 'say nothing'.

I wrote the following in 1990 after attending a strategy meeting of the Potsdam branch of the SPD (West German Socialist Party) while the election campaign centred on German reunification was in full swing. GDR stands for German Democratic Republic i.e. Communist East Germany; CDU for the West German Christian Democratic Union. PDS for the new, successor party to the East German Communists.

HOW THE LEFT/RIGHT MYTH KILLED SOCIALISM *

AT THE SPD meeting tonight, I felt that the party was writhing to establish a distinct position for itself between the Christian Democrats and the new PDS [Party of Democratic Socialism], successor to the Communist ruling party; writhing but not succeeding well.

The main difference between it and its two main opponents is that, while the campaign stances of the latter are based on conviction and tactics, that of the SPD is almost entirely tactical. When the SPD man from Bonn suggested, obliquely, to his audience that the SPD West had 'not abandoned' socialism, he was being untruthful. Like the other West European social-democratic and labour parties, the SPD has for several decades not been aiming at socialism, in any sense. Socialism, whatever else it can mean, does mean, irrefutably, a different socio-economic and political system than what we call, for short, 'capitalism'; meaning individualistic, pluralistic, liberal capital-

---

* From *Dreams of Oranges: An Eyewitness Account of the Fall of Communist East Germany*, Sanas Press, Dublin, 1996.

ism, and by that again, a system which, to a greater or lesser degree, has responded to the socialist critique by paying workers decent wages and subsidising the poor.

The SPD is an integral part of West German capitalism and aspires simply to manage it. But in this electoral context it seemed tactically useful to pretend to be something else; hence their statement in the early days of this campaign that they were for 'democratic socialism'. But as became pretty obvious tonight, the SPD is substantially committed to the West German Constitution, and fully committed to the social market economy and the social provisions of the Federal Republic—partly because it has helped to shape both. But it has seemed useful, in the GDR electoral context, to dilute this commitment: to propose talks about a new constitution, and to advocate a circumspect approach to reunification. By this combination of tactical devices, the SPD hopes to appeal both to those who want the D-Mark, the market economy and union with the Federal Republic, and to GDR patriots who value socialism. Judging by tonight, it has ceded GDR socialists to the new, ex-communist PDF.

What, then, does the SPD really stand for? For capitalism (and all that goes with it, including NATO), yes and no. Like other social democratic parties, it stands for a critical attitude within capitalism: a qualified yes, a partial no. Thus it is precluded from crusading for the West German capitalist package *in toto*, as the CDU and its sister party DSU are doing in this election; it is compelled to criticise their approach, and to urge a different one. But more important for SPD people than their partial no to capitalism is their total no to 'the blacks' i.e. 'the clericals', 'the right', 'conservatives'—an interlocking continuum of concepts, which can be simplified as the Right. In this context, the SPD stands for anti-clericalism and an emphatic secularism, as distinct from the muffled secularism of the 'Christian' parties. Moreover, in the SPD tradition and for many SPD people, the blacks and clericals are *par excellence* the Catholic Church and Catholics, and support for the SPD a way of saying no, specifically, to these.

There was a hint of that tonight in Herr Beck of the SPD's account of where CDU support was located in the GDR. He mentioned Catholics in the first instance, although, as I understand it,

Catholics are not numerous enough in the GDR to be a major political factor. For someone imbued with SPD tradition—and despite, for example, the historical fact that it was the votes of Protestant liberals that brought the Nazis to power, Catholics have to be at the core of all 'conservative' or 'right-wing' phenomena. Similarly, the opposite religious extreme, 'atheism'—as in Herr Beck's reference to Chemnitz as an 'atheistic and Marxist' city—is a positive concept, assumed to be equivalent to 'red' or 'left' politics. What we have, then, at the emotional core of the SPD, is a quasi-religious enthusiasm, based on a nineteenth-century, mythical and Manichean view of the world. The Right, the enemy of man—everything old, religious, dark, backward, tyrannous—is at war with the Left, the good of man—everything modern, non-religious, enlightened, progressive and free. Opposition to the Right and victory over it is the meaning and purpose of history.

Originally, this was a myth of modernising Liberal capitalism in Western Europe, with the notable exception of Britain and Ireland. Created by the French bourgeoisie of the Revolution, it was adopted by Liberals in neighbouring countries.* Even the anti-Liberal conservatives accepted the myth, but with reversed values. The Right, which they embodied, included the Catholic Church, conservative Protestantism, traditional monarchists and aristocrats, and the military castes and rural populations who were attached to these. But as time passed, the old-style monarchists and aristocrats exited from practical politics. Liberalism absorbed the bulk of residual conservatism and divided into right and left wings. When socialism challenged capitalism, the left-Liberals adopted some socialist language, and the socialists joined them in articulating the Left idea. The Right which they jointly opposed was, in the first place, the Catholic Church—as the principal and most uncompromising embodiment of Christianity—together with all that was culturally rooted and 'unmodern'; and secondarily, right-Liberals, as the conservative ideologues of untrammelled capitalism.

* Only in the decades following the moral endorsement of Hiroshima and the other American aerial massacres in the Second World War was the Left of the Left/Right myth, with its quasi-religious, anti-Christian ardour—its radical opposition to the inherited civilisation—widely adopted in the English-speaking countries, first in the US, then in Britain and Ireland. On this and related matters see my *Uncertain Dawn,* Sanas Press, Dublin 1996.

Granted, capitalism weakened socialism by making pre-emptive adjustments in its own practice. But it destroyed it by persuading the majority of West European socialists that Left loyalty, in the cosmic struggle of the Left against the Right, must be their *primary value;* that the issue of socialist society versus capitalist society was, accordingly, of secondary importance; and that the overriding indicator of Left loyalty was Left *language,* whether left-liberal-social-democratic or plain socialist. The agents of capitalism in this persuasive process were the semi-socialist-talking left-liberals. Their success, as recruiters for the solidarity of the cosmic Left at all costs, led to the suicide of socialism in two stages. (Literally, and with fatal consequences, they drove socialism to *distraction.*)

First, the great majority of West European socialists, hooked on the Left/Right myth, became emotionally committed to the Left struggle primarily, and lost awareness of what they were really about. (James Connolly warned trenchantly against this.) Without fully re-alising it, and believing they were still 'true to the faith'—they were, to the Left faith, and still hated black and wore red—they became 'left-wing' adherents and managers of capitalism, and gave up the struggle to replace it.

Second, when a Muscovite tyranny speaking extreme socialist language established itself in the USSR, and similar tyrannies later appeared in east-central Europe as far as Berlin, the great vocal bulk of the West European Left (left-liberals and nominal socialists) spoke of these regimes, and treated them, at least with critical respect, at most with admiring enthusiasm. Because speaking Left language was what identified the Left, Left loyalty required that. Even when these regimes denied the Liberal freedoms, ran secret-police states, sent millions to concentration camps, persecuted Jews and Christians, confiscated all property, shot citizens for engaging in business, and formed under Moscow an empire of subject peoples, Left loyalty required that those in the West who spoke for left-liberalism and socialism must recognise them as 'really existing socialism' and as 'socialist countries'. The solidarity of the Left forbade rejection of them as fascistic, oligarchic despotisms that mocked socialism's historic aim and promise.

If the socialist-talking West had done that, if it had rejected and decried them, the good name of socialism would have been saved and a future held open for it; but that would have meant agreeing with what the Right was saying about Soviet Communism if not precisely in the same terms; so it was impossible for Left loyalists. And then, in 1989, the people came out on the streets and shouted that 'really existing socialism' was everything the Right had been saying and worse. And the Marxist–Leninist regimes fell in ignominy. The net result? On top of the accomplished demise of socialism in West European practical politics, a worldwide smearing of the concept 'socialism', disgrace for those who had given critical respect or more to 'really existing socialism', the anti-communist Right proved right, the general collapse, barring waffle, of the 200-year-old socialist project—and capitalism, winged as heretofore, flying triumphantly on.

THE EVENING BEFORE THE END *

DESCENDING THE STEPS to the Pergamon museum's next room, I guess from the blue tiles I see through the open door that it contains the Ishtar Gate of Babylon. On entering the room, I must turn around to look up at the gate itself done in tiles of two colours: patterns of light yellow—with bulls and dragons in the same colour—set off against ethereal blue. The scale-model nearby shows that this castellated gate-arch, lofty though it is, was the lower of two gate-arches standing close together, the other towered higher still. The Processional Way has been reconstructed to just over half its width and only parts of its sides have the original tiled facing. It was used at the New Year Festival, when rulers and people entered the city by this route from the festival house outside the walls. Walking along it I emerge into rooms filled with remains of the ancient Middle Eastern empires: Hittite, Assyrian, Babylonian. There are inscribed steles, tablets of cuneiform writing, heads of rulers; a statue of a lady with her maid, the death meal between them, the winged sun-god above them. There is a fine display explaining the evolution of cuneiform writing from hieroglyphs: how it was simplified to three basic signs which were then combined in different numbers and directions to represent syllables. Many of the steles list the deeds of kings. Look-

* From *Dreams of Oranges.*.

ing up I see that some of the rooms have ancient decorative patterns around the walls.

There is a time to stop when visiting a museum or a large art gallery, and it is before blurring and fatigue set in. I recross the foot-bridge and set off along the canal bank towards Marx-Engels-Platz. It is a balmy twilight going on for six o'clock. Soon the white and brown Palace of the Republic comes into view, and the vans and lorries of the television companies parked beside it on the Platz, some of them with satellite dishes mounted. Tomorrow night the Palace, built to symbolise this Republic, will be the headquarters of the election count that ends it. My head full of Nebuchadnezzar and the rising and falling of states and empires, I think: this is the last evening of the Marxist-Leninist GDR, the last time the sun goes down on it. I wonder what Erich Honecker [Communist de facto Head of State] is thinking. Crowds are still strolling along Karl-Liebknecht-Strasse. As I cross Marx-Engels-Platz, where the massed thousands proclaimed their loyalty to the regime, the fawn Television Tower stands out against the blue Hotel Stadt Berlin and the neon signs are coming on singly. By the time I reach the other side, the cars on Werderstrasse have their lights on. Police have gathered behind the Palace, presumably to protect the election headquarters.

Unsure what to do after Berlin, I flew from Shannon to Minsk, capital of the former Soviet republic Belarus. Bob Quinn's wife, Miriam Allen, Director of the Galway Film Fleadh, had arranged that I could stay a month there in the care of Natasha Borochik, whom she had got to know at the Berlin Film Festival. I wrote a book about that month which remained unpublished.

GETTING TO KNOW DUBLIN 4 *

DUBLINERS REGARD THEIR city as being divided principally into a northside and a southside, with the river Liffey as the rough dividing line. The southside, particularly when taken to include the borough of Dún Laoghaire which extends from it southwards, is

* From *Heresy: The Battle of Ideas in Modern Ireland*, The Blackstaff Press, Belfast, 1993.

on the whole much more affluent than the northside. Moreover, it contains many important institutions: the Dáil and Senate, government buildings, the Republic's two biggest universities, the national television and radio service (RTÉ), most of the newspapers and big hotels, and the headquarters of many important companies and banks. The southside jokes 'Why did the Southside woman go to the Northside? To get her handbag back.' 'What is a Northsider in a suit? A bus conductor.'

Since the early to mid-eighties, the name of a postal district in the heart of the southside, Dublin 4, has come to signify a powerful force in Irish politics. This symbolic usage was invented by the Mayo journalist John Healy in his column in *The Irish Times* during the FitzGerald government of 1982-87. The literal Dublin 4 is characterised by old, leafy suburban roads and contains, besides a number of embassies, the Royal Dublin Society showgrounds, RTÉ, University College Dublin, some research institutes and the Chester Beatty Library. But Dublin 4, in the political sense, is understood to include a much wider area of southside life. It is perceived as a powerful social group with a characteristic mentality and agenda, which is located in South Dublin, exists largely outside parliament and the government of the day, but includes varying proportions of both.

So far, Dublin 4 has escaped analysis by political scientists and has been described only in impressionistic terms. Healy, writing from a West of Ireland perspective, depicted the FitzGerald-led Dublin 4 of the mid-eighties as a smug and inward-looking coterie, unsympathetic and inimical to the values and welfare of the rural West, and of rural and small-town Ireland generally. Healy died in January 1991. Towards the end of that year, *Jiving at the Crossroads*, a best-selling book by a young Roscommon journalist, John Waters, treated Dublin 4 at some length. Once again, the basic perspective is Western. The author, who grew up in the small town of Castlerea, Co. Roscommon, first encountered what he was later to recognise as 'Dublin 4' in the guise of RTÉ radio voices.

> At some point in the late seventies or early eighties, when we in the West of Ireland became conscious for the first time that the voices on the radio and the television were not our voices, we automatically began to think of them as Dublin voices. What we really felt

was that they were not saying things with which we could sympathise, and they certainly did not seem to sympathise with us. They lambasted us for our conservatism, for our backward notions of politics, for our profligacy with public money.

Later, in the mid-eighties, when Waters came to Dublin to work for a rock magazine, he realised that there were two Dublins: the 'real' Dublin, on the northside, which was 'a visual and human wasteland', and 'official Dublin', on the southside, known by the name of 'Dublin 4'. It was in the latter, he discovered, that most of the people he had heard on the radio belonged. On the last page of his book, Waters describes the RTÉ television election studio as situated 'in the geographical as well as the spiritual heart of Dublin 4'.* But before that he has had a stab at giving body to 'this something real but nebulous in the language of modern Irish politics'. Writing of his first encounters with it, he says:

> There were as many definitions of 'Dublin 4' as there were perceptions of it. Its most general usage, however, was as a pejorative term to describe what was effectively a new class of people, whose principal characteristic was perceived as a stridently professed aversion to unreconstructed forms of Catholicism and nationalism, but in particular to Fianna Fáil, and most especially to Charles J. Haughey.

By 'nationalism' there, Waters means Irish nationalism. At the time, he and his family were Fine Gael supporters, but they would later switch to Fianna Fáil—by far the largest of the political parties, with support from all social classes but especially the less well-off.

Dublin 4, writes Waters, could also be seen as synonymous with the people who frequented certain pubs and restaurants between the Shelbourne Hotel and Jury's Hotel, 'the equivalent of what in London were known as "the chattering classes": people who, through their jobs in the media, the civil service and the professions, were in a position to influence the direction of society in an intravenous manner'. Dublin 4 had 'many of the qualities of a country village' but without the disadvantage of a village hierarchy to put you in

---

* Added 2014: In the 1980s after the evening news bulletin RTÉ television broadcast a programme of provincial news. I forget its name but the boys and girls who worked on it called it 'Redneck Roundup'.

your place. As such it was initially attractive to this young man from a small town. He continues:

> There were those who held that the term defined a class of people who regarded themselves as the social and intellectual élite of modern Ireland, but who ideally would have liked to have been born somewhere else. Others saw 'Dublin 4' as a new bourgeoisie, a class of people who had transcended their own class and background, who were out to culturally colonise the country...

On the one hand, it was 'an attitude of mind'; on the other, 'a generation that had been reared to the promise of an Ireland free from the grip of history and religion', and for whom 'rural Ireland' was 'a darkness on the edge of town'. To an extent the Ireland that Dublin 4 wanted 'had already been brought about in its imagination. All that was required was for the rest of the population to agree to lie down and die.'

While angrily rejecting Dublin 4's view of the Republic outside Dublin as a dark, priest-ridden place peopled by stunted halfwits, Waters concludes his main treatment of the subject on a mellow note:

> But ultimately, if we were honest, 'Dublin 4' was a part of all of us: the part of our brains that wanted Ireland to be different, better. We all needed some escape from reality, but in the creation of a whole section of society that had allowed this tendency to dominate its thinking, there was scope for seriously deluding ourselves.

As a Dubliner who grew up on the northside, lives on the southside, and does not belong to 'Dublin 4' but knows it well, I recognise Waters's images of it. But its precise nature, in social, political and ideological terms, remains to be defined.

I became interested in the matter while working on two articles about Ireland and the Maastricht Treaty and at the same time reading Waters's book. In my analysis of European Community politics in Ireland, I came to the conclusion that there was a class of people in Dublin, but predominately on the southside, whose present and future interests were bound up with Ireland's being and remaining a member of the European Community, or Union as it was now to become. Using a term that I had come across in the analysis of black African states, I called this class the 'state class'. Moreover, I argued, in view of the Republic's bad experience in the EC hitherto, and our worse prospects in the Union, there was a divorce between the interests of this state class and those of Ireland generally. During our membership of the EC, since 1972, our general economic condition had deteriorated: 40,000 fewer people were employed; we had acquired a crippling public debt; economic emigration was heavy during the 1980s until recession abroad stopped it; and by early 1992 our unemployment rate had reached 20% of the workforce and was still rising. Maastricht, I believed, on top of this, would be disastrous for us as a society. While writing these articles, I concluded with some surprise that the 'state class' I had identified was identical with 'Dublin 4'.

The main political event around this period was the final resignation, after many battles for survival, of Charles Haughey as leader of Fianna Fáil and Taoiseach. On 8 February Paul Gillespie, the *Irish Times* foreign editor, enumerated the features that had made Fianna Fáil something of a 'populist' party: ⋆

> It may be seen in the attempt by Fianna Fáil to combine tradition with modernisation; in the belief that it is possible for the periphery to control the modernisation process; in its anti-intellectualism (an attitude apparent more with the media than with the artistic and literary intelligentsia during the Haughey years); in its appeal to 'the people' against the establishment—Dublin 4—which was certainly reciprocated so far as Mr Haughey was concerned.

Here we find Dublin 4 equated with 'the establishment'. This is unsatisfactory on two counts. The word 'establishment', which is little used in contemporary Ireland, denoted in its original, English usage a powerful group of people who, among other things, epitomised Englishness or Britishness; and the same is suggested,

---

⋆ *Added 2016:* The word 'populist' was Gilllespie's. Its dictionary meaning is 'a party which seeks to represent the interests of ordinary people'. Its use here is an early instance of a usage now commonplace in English-language political commentary to describe a party which the journalist disapproves of. As such, it reflects the sharp divergence that has come about between the neoliberal-state-and-media-class and 'ordinary people', which was evident in the English Brexit referendum and the American presidential election of 2016.

mutatis mutandis, when the term is applied in say a French context. But Dublin 4, far from epitomising Irishness, is in conflict with this concept and even with the word. (To cite a simple verbal example: in the language of Dublin 4, 'an Irish solution to an Irish problem' is a cant phrase meaning 'a remedy that is intrinsically undesirable and reprehensible and which should not be attempted'.) Furthermore, whilst Dublin 4 does include much or most of what might, in more normal circumstances, be called the Irish establishment, a fair number of people who belong in that category are not part of Dublin 4.

Nuala O'Faolain, writing a week before Gillespie, depicted the anti-Haughey element in Dublin in more explicit terms. A northsider who moved to the southside, she is generally a staunch exponent of the Dublin 4 line, but departs from orthodoxy in having a soft spot for Haughey personally as distinct from politically. In the special article she was recalling the reactions she had got from certain people when, a couple of years previously, in her account of an interview with Mr Haughey, she had described his cultural interests:

> What kind of a fool was I, to be taken in by his fine talk? What kind of journalist, to let him off the hook? And above all, how could I give any credence to his pathetic cultural pretensions? The implication was that I'm as much a vulgarian as he is. 'But then, you're both from the Northside,' one man said to me.

Appearing between O'Faolain and Gillespie, my articles on Maastricht suggested that Dublin 4 could be seen as the 'state class', which I described as follows:

> It is a class in the sense that it comprises people who feel they share—and actually do share—values, and a common interest, that distinguishes them from the nation generally. It includes a growing majority of the political class—higher civil servants, government advisers, MEPs, Brussels lobbyists, top party officials, and the majority of Oireachtas members in all parties except Fianna Fáil; also people who derive substantial income or status from the institutional appurtenances of a typical modern state, whether in the 'national' television and radio stations, the 'national' airline, press, university system or art gallery, the 'national' banking and courts

systems, or in the provision of 'essential national services' such as electricity, telephones and road-building.

I went on to remark that the state class, or Dublin 4, 'functions, politically, as a party, both inside and outside the Oireachtas, and has the national media as its "party press".' During the past twenty years or so, the Dublin media have shed the political and ideological pluralism that once characterised them, and have developed a single Dublin media line on all major issues, domestic and foreign. Their priority issues, their advocacy and deprecation, derive from what is called the 'liberal agenda'. It is therefore plausible to see these media, with minor exceptions (the *Sunday Business Post* occasionally, the fortnightly *Phoenix* regularly), as the voice and propaganda of a single group or class.

A state class is different from a national establishment in two ways. It consists only of people who service or are nurtured by the state, and it is not organically connected with the nation or society it commands but floats above it, exists apart from it. On reflection, I think it possible that the Irish state class, as I have defined it, may not be exactly identical with Dublin 4, may still include some people who do not belong to Dublin 4. But it is a matter of 'still', for Dublin 4 is an upwardly mobile and growing group. Moreover, there can be no doubt that it relates to the state rather than to the nation.

'The state', conceived of as an intrinsically secular, non-religious and therefore benign being, has always been a god-term in Dublin 4 diction. Dublin 4 people speak as if the state belongs to them as of right, shares their nature mentally and morally, and is illegitimately possessed by Fianna Fáil—or at least Fianna Fáil as it has been hitherto. They urge it to be influenced in its laws and actions by themselves, by their 'liberal opinion', and by all who abroad and in Northern Ireland think like them, rather than by the Catholic Church, or rich Irish businessmen, or what some call the nation. In particular they warn it against the Catholic Church, which embraces the great majority of the nation. Assiduous in discovering and playing up 'Church-State conflicts', they always cheer on the state to win. Their extreme elements want our pluralist education system (Catholic, Protestant, Jewish and interdenominational, under the Department of Education) to be replaced by a single-ethos, secular state system. And until recent events in Eastern Europe, and even more recent scandals in the state-connected business sector, Dublin 4 exhibited a vaguely leftish tendency in favour of state-sponsored commercial enterprise (of which RTÉ is one instance).

A week after my *Irish Times* articles, on 11 February, the newspaper published a somewhat jokey letter from a reader in the depths of South Dublin. Not disputing the identification of state class and Dublin 4, the reader, Mr Tom Doorley, said:

> It is quite clear that the State Class or Dublin 4 Class comprises all those who are not the Plain People of Ireland. So, quite clearly, the State Class comprises a tiny group. Mr Fennell is a little coy about spelling out the State Class's identifying characteristics—or perhaps he regards these as being too obvious to mention,.

I had in fact been explicit about its occupational characteristics. What Mr Doorley meant is its ideological identikit, which he went on to supply, obliquely, by sketching the 'Plain People of Ireland':

> The PPI are noted for their firm stand against foreign games such as soccer, their aversions to foreign filth (much of James Joyce's canon was written on the Continent) and foreign soap operas. They are for the most part daily communicants and attend confession weekly. They are happy to agree that sex is for procreation and certainly not for enjoyment (even simultaneously and at the same time). They have a tendency to dance at the crossroads and have a wonderful facility with the Irish language.
>
> Not so the State Class. I'm worried, though, by Mr Fennell's strong implication that this State Class may be infiltrating the more progressive elements in Fianna Fáil.

If I had not directly made that last point, I certainly insinuated it: the state class, alias Dublin 4, has been making progress in detaching, or winning over, leading members of Fianna Fáil. Moreover, Mr Haughey himself was paralysed by his attempt to embody the 'plain people' *and* to placate Dublin 4. But the main interest of that letter is that, in its jokey way, it describes the two groups into which Dublin 4 sees the Republic divided. On the one hand, the great, ordinary mass: fans of the Gaelic Athletic Association or GAA (the largest sports organisation by far), xenophobic, painfully religious, Victorian in matters sexual, rurally traditional, and enthusiasts of the Irish language. On the other hand there are themselves, Dublin 4 people, who are proud to be none of those things. The unspoken subtext of this reactive and negative self-definition is that they, Dublin 4 people, are like normal, modern, consumerist people in London and the Western world generally.

What is reflected there, by means of a grotesque caricature of most people in Ireland today, is the mental set of those middle-class Dubliners who since the sixties have defined themselves as liberals, and who in the early seventies became known as 'Dublin liberals'. The word had not been a term in Irish politics since the British Liberal Party ceased to function in the country. For the great majority of Irish people for 150 years, the democratic Catholic Liberalism of mainstream nationalism, of the new state and the Irish Constitution, had been as natural as the air they breathed and consequently not remarked on. In the Free State and then in the Republic the ideological differences had occurred almost entirely within this Liberal consensus, and had expressed various degrees of commitment to the nationalist and socially redistributive objectives of the Revolution. This new, unqualified 'liberalism' of the sixties was a confluence of two currents: on the one hand, the new American brand of left liberalism in the Western world generally—secularist, social democratic, consumerist, extending the 'rights of the individual' to the removal of all restrictions on consensual sexual behaviour; on the other hand, and partly arising from the economic failure of the fifties, scepticism towards the political and cultural heritage of the Revolution, and consequently towards Irish nationalism.

The neoliberals redefined the ideological division in the Republic in terms of the Gilbert and Sullivan song: whoever was not a liberal had to be a conservative. But the difference from nineteenth-century English usage and similar usage elsewhere was that the people described as 'conservative'—they included all upholders of the previous Liberal consensus, of the Revolution and of the Constitution—had not chosen the description, either as a party name or ideologically. The neoliberals simply imposed it on them, fleshed it out with 'traditionalist' and 'reactionary', and through their growing ascendancy in the national media made it an exclusively pejorative label in the public discourse. 'Irish society', thus tagged, became 'a bad thing'. The few in the Republic who insisted they were socialists were reckoned by the neoliberals to be 'liberals' at heart, and generally were. Indeed, the small Marxist-Leninist Workers' Party, known colloquially as 'Stickies', made it their business to infiltrate the media, and were popularly regarded as providing the well-drilled core of 'liberal' hardliners in RTÉ and *The Irish Times*

By the eighties, when Dublin liberalism had become the Dublin 4 syndrome, it was pursuing a well-advertised programme called the 'liberal agenda'. Under the influence of the right-liberal economic policies of British Prime Minister Margaret Thatcher and US President Reagan, it acquired, in economic matters, a right wing which, in 1985, produced a party, the Progressive Democrats, formed by dissidents from Fianna Fáil.

The 'liberal agenda' is a proposition as well as an agenda. It is the proposition that progress for the Republic of Ireland means removing every taint of Catholicism and of Irish nationalism from its public life and institutions and accommodating itself to Britain, the Northern unionists and EC Europe, while retaining a state apparatus in Dublin. In a shorthand that anyone in the Republic in recent years would understand, this boiled down to divorce, more condoms, easy on abortion; support the EC, unionist demands, British policy in the North and revisionist history-writing; bash Charles Haughey, Fianna Fáil, the Catholic Church, the Constitution, the IRA, Sinn Féin, the GAA, Irish Americans, and all those ignorant, deluded people in northside Dublin and 'rural Ireland' (the rest of the Republic) who support that sinister man or one of those benighted organisations. It was the agenda, to requote John Waters, of 'a class of people who ideally would have liked to be born somewhere else'. Of late, there has also been a tendency to bash corrupt big businessmen, with particular attention to rich businessmen connected with Fianna Fáil. Haughey's conspicuous wealth and the suggestion that it was the result of shady dealings have formed part of the motivation for the Dublin 4 vendetta against him.

I think that Dublin 4 is now in focus. From the start, Dublin liberalism has had adherents, including some prominent politicians, throughout the city and the Republic. But by far the largest and for obvious reasons the most powerful concentration of them is in South Dublin. Moreover, it is from there and by them, via the national media, that the 'party line' is set and promulgated. 'Dublin 4' denotes this socio-ideological group.

Despite its pretensions, the neo-liberal agenda is anything but progressive. It opposes the 150-year-old endeavour to achieve and maintain the intellectual, cultural and political autonomy of the Irish nation in all of Ireland. In place of the self-definition of independent Ireland which it rejects, it proposes no new independent identity, but rather a renewed general merging with British wishes and cultural norms, and blind obedience to what they term 'Europe'. Thus it reneges on the Revolution and regresses to provincialism.

Postscript 1

Micromania. Strange, perhaps, that I should mention it as a postscript, when it has been a notable feature of Dublin 4 since the sect's earliest emergence. Micromania: the pursuit of smallness as a psychic imperative. It comes from their so desperately wanting Ireland and the Irish to be like them—in everything, even size. At the start of the 1960s, as for a hundred years before that, a Dubliner viewing the world from South Dublin still saw Ireland and Irishness as vast. 'Ireland's spiritual empire', as it was called in the public discourse, embraced the Irish communities in Scotland, Wales and England, the far-flung Irish millions in the USA and Australia, the Irish in Argentina, the thousands on the mission frontiers in Africa and Asia. Within the span of this Irish world, where the sun never set, but rose on churches called St Patrick's, even Dubliners, though they supplied fewer of the emigrants than other parts, felt a particularly vivid and grateful closeness to 'our Irish-American cousins'. And within the island thus conceived of as 'mother country' to many millions, Dubliners saw Irish everywhere from Antrim to Kerry, called the Northern nationalists 'our people in the North' and regarded the unionists as ours potentially—if they would come to their senses.

The Dublin 4 sect intensely disliked this spaciousness of Irish being—so unlike them, so threatening to their enterprise—and set about demolishing it. The first to fall was the great framework, the

'spiritual empire'. Mawkish talk, they said, and, inasmuch as it referred to exiles who were mainly Catholic, sectarian to boot. With
our compliance they erased the phrase from public discourse, and
we lost its consciousness. Then when the North boiled over and 'our
people' there were in rebellion against oppression, the sect, grown
more powerful, rapped us again. 'The unionists are "our people"
too,' they said, 'they are all, all "our people".' So both they and we
stopped calling any people in the North our own. Then it was our
transatlantic cousins. Foolish, ignorant people, the sect pronounced,
people with mad ideas about Ireland and, worse, supporters of the
IRA and therefore enemies of Ireland. So in Dublin we stopped
cherishing them, lost our sense of kinship with them, even learned
to feel ashamed of them. The sect, who held the stage and micro-
phone, could do these things.

'Rural Ireland,' they intoned liturgically—meaning the Republic
outside Dublin—'We can do without rural Ireland and everything
it stands for. Rednecks! Ugh!' Articles Two and Three,* they are now
saying, 'must go because the unionists say so, and say so with good
reason. It is provocative for Dublin to lay claim to Ireland beyond
the border.'

Postscript 2.

For long after the February 1992 hysteria, abortion, and the legal
and political tangle surrounding it, continued to figure prominently
in the 'national' media. The divide between the priorities of Dublin 4 and those of the Republic generally, as well as the illusions of
the former about the latter, are vividly illustrated by the opening
sentences of a new weekly column on the provincial newspapers
introduced by *The Irish Times* on 13 April.

Like a traveller reporting home on a fabled foreign country,
the columnist, Kathryn Holmquist, an American resident in South
Dublin, writes thus: 'The prevailing view that the moral outrage of
the public [about the abortion issue] stems from rural Ireland was
revealed to be a myth on reading the latest issues of local newspapers. The bank strike and other job-related issues dominated the
headlines in eleven cases. There was not one lead story on the abor-

---

* i.e. of the Constitution, which lays claim to the North.

tion issue in the sixteen local newspapers reviewed and only three news stories on the subject.'

In 1993 I retired from my lecturing post in the College of Commerce, Rathmines, where I had worked happily. I decided to take a holiday—a holiday with no writing strings attached. My friend Bill Ryan, who lived in a small town in the state of Washington, USA, invited me to visit him. I flew to New York and on to Seattle, where Bill met me at the airport. I stayed with him four weeks, travelled by train to Chicago, stayed there a few days, and took the train to New York. My holiday—though it turned out to be much more than that and gave a new focus to my life and thinking—lasted just over six weeks.

WHAT I REALISED IN NEW YORK★

> We must consider that we shall be a City upon a Hill. The eyes of all people are upon us.—John Winthrop, first governor of Massachussets Colony, 1680.

> Modern man is obsolete....It should not be necessary to prove that on August 6, 1945, a new age is born. Nor should it be necessary to prove the saturating effect of the new age, permeating every aspect of man's activities, from machines to morals, from physics to philosophy, from politics to poetry.—Norman Cousins, *The Saturday Review of Literature* (New York) August 18 1945.

NEW YORK, 13 May 1994: Estrangement is a finding strange of something that previously seemed and felt familiar; but what is 'found strange' is, to begin with, not the thing itself, but one's unexamined image and sense of it. Seeing now what is afoot in America, what contemporary America really is, I have discarded the images and feelings that blinded me to it. I was blinded by the unreflectingly 'familiar' way I have regarded this country, by its manner of repre-

---

★ From *Uncertain Dawn: Hiroshima and the Beginning of Post-Western Civilisation*, Sanas Press, Dublin, 1996,

senting itself to the world during my lifetime, and by the false notions which are implicit in much rhetoric about the contemporary 'West'. Unreflectingly, as an English-speaking European, as an Irishman, and despite America's obvious cultural hegemony over Europe since Hiroshima, I still regarded it as an exotic outreach of Europe, an exotic home from home. There was so much cultural and racial affinity among the exotica that it was easy for me to do that. The United States, for its part, encouraged my illusion by so often representing itself, through its spokesmen, as the bastion of western values against all that was alien to these. And I again, for my part, listened uncritically to the grandiose talk, beloved of European intellectuals and politicians, about the modern or postmodern 'West'; talk which thoughtlessly suggests that Western Europe and the US uphold the 'western values' of Goethe, Plato and Dante, and are continuing to develop, though in strange, new forms, the ancient civilisation of Europe. Semi-credible until you think about it. Estranged now for a week or more, from all those images, I have been looking sharply, and with excitement, at what has become for me a strange land. And I am seeing meaning, and a pattern of meaning, which I didn't see before.

Just beyond the radiation experiments,* in the background, are the Hiroshima and Nagasaki bombs and their sensational massacres. That, I now realise, was the symbolic break with the old order and start of the new, President Truman's Edict of Milan, the unnoticed fanfare. Logically, the radiation experi ments followed it; Latin melted from the curriculum; figures from Greek mythology and Roman history faded out of the common culture;** and, in 1963, a Supreme Court ruling ended organised Christian prayer in the nation's schools. In a flurry of moral re-ordering covering the next twenty years, various actions which Christianity called sins were taken, authoritatively, off the sin list, and new sins (or names for

---

* A few months previously the US Government had revealed that,, in the 30 years following the war. state-sponsored scientists had conducted experiments with high levels of radiation on about 800 persons—terminally ill patients, disabled prisoners in a jail, etc.

** It occurs to me that Caesar has survived in the popular 'Caesar salad', but Icarus, Prometheus, Medusa, the Gorgon, Augustus, Maecenas, Cato and the rest have missed out on culinary embodiment.

sins) invented, but without calling them sins: anti–Semitism, racism, McCarthyism, censorship, sexism, fundamentalism, homophobia, sexual harassment, fatness, earth abuse, smoking, pollution, unsafe sex, species murder; in certain sects, lookism, ableism, heterosexism, flesh-eating, ageism. For this re-ordering of American morality and religious expression, justification was found in feelings, science, and liberal principle, and in the parts of the Constitution that dealt with religion, equality and personal liberty. For most of it, the people's consent, or at least indifference, has been forthcoming. The exceptions had to do with abortion, school prayer and environmental protection. Considerable numbers of citizens remain in simmering revolt against the denial of rights to babies in the womb and the permission given to kill them. Many parents and students still resent the prohibition of prayer in their schools. Farmers, businesspeople and local communities often oppose what looks like the rulers preferring animals and wild nature over people. But the new direction has got strong support in the academy, with academics making their own, theoretical contributions. From the 1970s onwards, especially in Eng. Lit., Women's Studies, and African-American departments, thousands gave courses, or wrote papers, which excoriated European humanism as an oppressive force in European, American and world history. DWEMs, meaning the Dead White European Males who created that humanism, became a term of contempt on many campuses. Thousands of courses and essays, scores of books, taught young Americans to find inspiration elsewhere—in the cultures and civilisations of the druidic Celts and American Indians, in black Africa and spiritual Asia. Commerce, getting the Hiroshima message, promoted popular music with jungle-beats and anti-melodic raucousness. Street and trendy culture, reaching to socialites and celebrities, followed through with 'primitive' hairstyles, elaborate tattoos, and pierced body-parts suspending metal rings and bars.

But to return to the start. A central and distinguishing feature of European humanism was its persistent and moderately successful effort to limit war and civilise warriors. Pursued assiduously through the Christian Middle Age, disrupted by Renaissance cynicism and the religious wars, resuming in secular dress in the eighteenth and nineteenth centuries, it continued, with American collaboration,

through the early twentieth. For this entire western humanist tradition, massacre was grossly immoral because it spat in the face of
Europe's conceptions of man, of civilised treatment of man, and
consequently, of civilisation. Not least, perhaps most, it offended European men's valuation of women and children as sacrosanct. That's
why I see the Hiroshima bomb as the symbol of the new departure.
The symbol, because the actual break and fresh start occurred after
the Nagasaki bomb.

For at least a year before Hiroshima, in Germany and Japan, and
with increasing deliberateness, the US air force had been using the
destruction of residential areas and the mass killing of civilians as a
routine method of warfare aimed at 'undermining enemy morale'.
In Japan, in the first half of 1945, firebomb attacks on scores of cities incinerated a million people. Alone in the big fire-raid on Tokyo
in March, when B-29s, flying low, dropping gelled-petrol bombs
on wooden houses while crews smelt the roasting human flesh, a
hundred thousand women, children and men perished. (A holocaust
is a 'wholly burnt animal sacrifice', but wasn't there a special word
for sacrifice of many animals burnt together?) Hiroshima, in August,
where seventy thousand were killed outright, was different only in
that one bomb sufficed, and that tens of thousands more died of its
delayed effects. Hiroshima was a continuation of an existing practice
by more efficient technology. But it wasn't, despite its sensational
nature, a decision that massacre was moral. Of itself, therefore, it
was neither a definitive break with the old humanism nor the com-
mencement of the *novus ordo*. It came to stand for both, symbolically,
by virtue of what followed and what did not, as the American government and people made their momentous moral choice. Would
they let Hiroshima be an immoral and uncivilised assault on the
Japanese people, and repent, as did the Germans of their assault on
the Jewish people; or would they, by standing over it and all their
other massacres, make it a rejection of western civilisation?

Nagasaki followed. The President and leading Americans declared
the nuclear massacres justified. The first rule of the new morality
was implicitly promulgated: 'If, in a war, it is believed that killing any
number of women, children and men in their homes will shorten
the war or prevent deaths of American soldiers in battle, it is right

to kill the people; wrong not to.' Put differently, killing women and children to save soldiers or shorten a war was declared the first virtue of the new order. No apology was made to anyone. The rare calls for national repentance were ignored or rebuked. When Nazi leaders were tried and condemned at Nuremberg for killing civilians by various means, doing so by aerial bombardment was deliberately omitted. As confirmation that the United States was committed to the new morality, its government ordered more nuclear bombs, President Truman called for a hydrogen bomb, and the production of nuclear weapons became a routine part of US industry.

To justify this overthrow of the inherited American humanism, or at least to paralyse troubled consciences, Communism, at home and abroad, was powerfully represented as an evil so diabolical and threatening that civilisation and Christianity were morally obliged to fight it by any and every means. The end justified the means. In 1948, during the crisis with the Soviet Union over Berlin, plans were made to atom-bomb scores of Soviet cities. Dissent, on moral or other grounds, was never sufficiently strong to be politically effective. The corporations and the people paid their taxes, the elected representatives voted the funding. As an ultimate expression of popular consent, the angry exclamation 'Nuke them!' passed into the American vernacular. (The word I wanted above is 'hecatomb'.)

It was these subsequent omissions and actions that stamped the symbolism of moral break and new departure on the fateful fraction of a second in August 1945. But the effect wasn't only retroactive; those years of yes-saying to massacre reach forward to the present to found the American presence in the world, and contemporary American humanism, on a rejection of western humanism made concrete in the thousands of ready-for-action nuclear missiles.

That six-week holiday, most of it spent as the guest of Bill Ryan in a small town in Washington state, constituted a big advance and a new departure in my understanding of what had been taking place in the Western world, Ireland centrally included. Among other things, I now understood why official America felt a new morality—the Godless neoliberal one—

was needed. As I realised, walking along a New York street, that America, pulling us in its wake, had left European civilisation, the historian in me skipped a few celebratory steps along the footpath. I had lived to witness this momentous event! After a brief return to Ireland I decided to spend some time in Seattle to study and research the phenomenon on its home ground. I spent more than a year there completing Uncertain Dawn: Hiroshima and the Beginning of Post-western Civilisation. *At that time, I saw the new American regime as a new civilisation emerging in the wake of Europe's. Later, as I pondered on that new departure and the similar seventy-year departure of its recently ended Soviet Russian counterpart—both of them with indoctrinated satellite nations—I would cease to regard it as such. A civilisation makes sense to its people.*

Before I returned to Ireland, the book had been refused by two Irish academic publishers. I published it through the Sanas Press founded by John Minahane and that I now shared with him; gave an article summarising its conclusions to the Dublin Jesuit journal Studies; *and delivered a lecture on the theme to an Arts faculty seminar in University College Galway. Son Cilian was now working in television and was producer of the Late Late Show. He invited me on the show with my book. There was the usual studio audience and also a panel of about six people. After some questions from the host Gay Byrne, the panel got its say and a male member of it started shouting uncontrollably. I think that that was remembered rather than my strange, important message.*

I felt I had still had a lot to think about. Apartness was needed. So in 1997 I sold my cottage in Portobello, Dublin and travelled much of Western Europe by train, reconnoitring between Munich and Vienna, in the Vienna suburbs, in Languedoc, and landing finally in Anguillara, a town of about 15,000 people on a great lake 35 kilometres north of Rome. I went there because my late friend the poet Desmond O'Grady had recommended I speak to an Italian countess who lived there. She put me in touch with a Russian woman who had a furnished flat for rent in the higher part of the town. I took it and unpacked.

PART 3:
CONCLUSIONS: 1996-2016

1997-8

AUTUMN DAY

Translation of 'Herbsttag' by Rainer Maria Rilke★

Lord, it is time. The summer was immense.
Lay your shadow on the sun-dials
and on the plains release the winds.

Command the last fruits to fill themselves;
grant them two more temperate days,
urge them to completeness and chase
the last sweetness into the heavy wine.

Who now is homeless builds himself no house.
Who is alone now will long remain so,
will stay awake, and read, and write long letters,
and in the avenues, when the leaves are drifting,
wander anxiously.

NO REPENTANCE★★

THE CONTEMPORARY WEST is built, not on Auschwitz and Treblinka, to which we have said 'No', but on Hiroshima and Nagasaki to which we have said 'Yes'.

US Secretary of Commerce Henry Wallace kept a diary. In the entry for 10 August 1945, the day after the nuclear attack on Nagasaki, Wallace wrote that at a cabinet meeting President Truman 'said he had given orders to stop atomic bombing. He said the thought

---

★ Published in *The Irish Times*, 18 October 1997, shortly after my arrival in Anguillara, Italy.

★★ Written in Anguillara 1997-8, published in *The Postwestern Condition: Between Chaos and Civilisation,* Minerva Press, London,1999. Living in Italy, assuming that after the refusal of *Uncertain Dawn: The Beginning of Postwestern Civilisation* by two Irish academic publishers, this new book had no hope of publication in Ireland, and not having an agent in Britain, I got London's publish-for-payment Minerva Press to publish it. Later, on a visit to Ireland, and meeting my favourite Irish poet Derek Mahon, I was very pleased to hear that he had found it and appreciated it.

of wiping out another 100,000 innocent people was too horrible. He didn't like the idea of killing, as he said, 'all those kids'.

If the question of Truman's 'repenting' for ordering the atomic bombings had not been raised during his lifetime, we could say only that 'he did not repent'. But because the question was raised on at least three occasions, two of them directly personal, we can say that he 'refused to repent'. In March 1946, the US Federal Council of Churches issued a report signed by twenty-two Protestant religious leaders. (Truman was a church-going Protestant. In a radio address to the nation after the dropping of the bombs, he had said of the new weapon: 'We thank God it has come to us instead of to our enemies. May He guide us to use it in His ways and for His purposes.') 'We would begin,' the churchmen stated, 'with an act of contrition.' They continued:

> As American Christians, we are deeply penitent for the irresponsible use already made of the atomic bomb. We are agreed that, whatever one's judgment of war in principle, the surprise bombings of Hiroshima and Nagasaki are morally indefensible. They repeated in ghastly form the indiscriminate slaughter of non-combatants that has become familiar during World War II...As the nation that first used the weapon, we have sinned grievously against the laws of God and against the people of Japan.

The report also condemned as immoral the massive firebomb attacks on Japanese cities which had preceded the atomic bombings. It urged Americans to offer a 'convincing expression' of repentance, to help rebuild Hiroshima and Nagasaki, and to cease production of atomic weapons. Truman did not respond. Twelve years later, in 1958, when he was no longer president, the Hiroshima city council sent him a resolution it had passed. The resolution protested 'in deep indignation' against a statement of Truman's that he had felt 'no compunction whatever' about ordering the dropping of the atomic bombs and that 'hydrogen bombs would be put to use in the future in case of emergency'.

Truman, in his reply, ignored the implicit demand to withdraw his statement of 'no compunction'. He pointed out to the councillors that the Japanese themselves were responsible for the bombings.

'The need for such a fateful decision...never would have arisen... had we not been shot in the back by Japan at Pearl Harbour.' The American ultimatum from Potsdam in 1945 had 'evoked only a very curt and discourteous reply...The sacrifice of Hiroshima and Nagasaki was urgent and necessary for the prospective welfare of both Japan and the Allies.'*

Finally, at a Columbia University symposium in 1959, Truman was asked whether he had any regrets about any of the great decisions he had made while in office and in particular about his decision to use the atomic bomb. He replied: 'The atom bomb was no "great decision"...It was merely another weapon in the arsenal of righteousness...'

Truman refused to repent because he did not believe he had done wrong; he believed he had done right. He had acted out of two closely intertwined motives which he believed were right. The first of them is hinted at in his replies to the Hiroshima councillors and the Columbia university students; he was the agent of righteousness punishing wicked, beastly aggression. (In a private letter two days after Hiroshima, Truman wrote, 'When you have to deal with a beast, you treat him as a beast.') Moreover, the nature of the weapon used had given the act of punishment a mystical, quasi-divine quality. Not only was it something to thank God for and therefore, in a sense, a gift from Him; it was also, as Truman said in his statement announcing the bombing, 'a harnessing of the basic power of the universe, the force from which the sun draws its powers'. Truman could feel that he had exercised the punishing power of a Protestant Yahweh.

At the same time, more mundanely—this was his other, intertwined motive—he believed that by obliterating the two Japanese cities he had served the immediate interest of his primary earthly value. This was righteous American power and what it stood for: the Christian liberal-capitalist West facing atheistic Communist Russia. He had served the interests of that power by displaying in punishing action, and thereby establishing, warningly, American superpower

However, it was one thing to believe that he had acted virtuously, another to persuade his people and the western world that

---

* A remarkable harking back to the very early human motive for human sacrifice.

this was the case. He settled for giving reasons for his action which he believed that ordinary people would find cogent and morally adequate. The bombs had shortened the war, had saved an (ever-increasing!) number of American soldiers' lives.

His first public use of this theme, 9 August 1945, cited 'thousands of American lives'. By December it was 'a quarter of a million' lives actually saved. In 1948, in Toledo, Ohio, it was 'a quarter of a million young Americans' and 'an equal number of Japanese young men'. By 1959, in Columbia University, it was 'millions of lives.★

He worked hard at believing these had been his real motives—they had influenced him at most peripherally—and were of themselves sufficient. His fellow rulers, his nation and Europe accepted them as justification for the massacres in question, and by implication as justification for all similar acts in future by American rulers or their allies. In this way, Harry Truman became the founder of our post-western ethical system.

A ruler whose lot it is to overthrow a time-honoured sacredness and thus set in motion a great historical change cannot, by definition, repent. Constantine could not repent his blatant betrayal for the Christian man-god of *mos maiorum,* the 'ancestral ways', and Jupiter Best and Greatest whose temple had crowned Rome for nearly a thousand years and received home its triumphant generals. That great change, like the change ushered in by the endorsement of Hiroshima, had been in preparation long before. It was a matter of reaching the ripe moment and the ruler who would serve as agent—and not repent.

Five more excerpts from The Postwestern Condtion:

JOVE'S THUNDERBOLT

THE NOTION OF the atomic bomb as an instrument of divine justice first cropped up a few hours before the Hiroshima bomber crew departed on their mission. Their chaplain, William Downey, read a prayer on their behalf addressed to a hybrid God of the Old and

---

★ The advance estimates of the American military of fatal casualties in a full-scale invasion of Japan varied between 20,000 and 63,000 men, with 46,000 being the most accepted estimate.

New Testaments. It began:

> Almighty Father, who wilt hear the prayer of them that love thee,
> we pray thee to be with those who brave the heights of thy heaven
> and who carry the battle to our enemies…May they, as well as we,
> know thy strength and power, and armed with thy might may they
> bring this war to a rapid end.

And it concluded: 'In the Name of Jesus Christ. Amen'.

THE 'PAPAL' ASPECT OF 'SUPERPOWER'

THE 'PAPAL' ROLE which accrued to Truman when his redefinition
of the ethics of massacre was accepted by the West was thenceforth
an attribute of American superpower. US rulers and official preachers became, apart from Rome, the only centre from which ethical
principles and instructions on how to behave were issued to the
West generally. Naturally, in a West that had accepted Superpower's
overthrow of God's law, the teaching of New York-Washington carried far more weight than Rome's.

THE RISE OF 'SUPERPOWER'

ON 21 DECEMBER 1947, David Lilienthal, chairman of the US
Atomic Energy Commission, wrote in his diary: 'The fences are
gone. And it was we, the civilised, who have pushed standardless
conduct to its ultimate.' In the landscape cleared of the old moral
fences, Superpower arose and flourished. The word, an American
coinage, had originally referred to electricity supply. Now it was
used to describe the power born in August 1945: a power greater
than any that had been known in western civilisation. 'Great Power'
had been the previous designation of maximal political power. Superpower was greater in every way—bulk, capacity, reach, function.
Whereas 'Great Power' had denoted, essentially, the military power
of a strong state, Superpower was a composite of politico-military
power with that of financial and marketing organisations and mass
media of communication.

Moreover, in the aftermath of World War II, each of these components was greater in bulk, capacity, reach and function than it had

ever been; each was growing still greater; and they were much more closely interlocked than in the preceding age.

Tom Wolfe in his novel *The Bonfire of the Vanities*, set in New York of the 1980s, calls the phenomenon simply 'the Power'. It was empire, domestic and external, of an unprecedented degree and scope. Branches were established, progressively, in the West European satellites, and in each of these, heedful of its sponsor, a proxy superpower went to work.

Superpower took to itself the entire sphere of moral teaching and of rules for right behaviour and right thought. Mocking and undermining the authority of clergy, parents and adults, of schoolteachers, men, social custom, and local communities, and of the books of western wisdom, Superpower asserted its overriding competence as arbiter of good and evil. Its message, implicit and explicit, went something like this:

> See, how we have done or assented to what the West called savage and unchristian, and by refusing to repent, redefined civilisation. Learn from this that the old restraints—barring exceptions we will spell out to you—hold no more. Anything you feel like doing or choose to do, and can do, in contravention of them is right—unless we who have liberated you and made you the Free World, forbid it in our new, pro-human rules.★ Learn that to ignore the old morality and to accept our new emerging one is freedom, virtue, maturity and the good life. Money admits you to its full enjoyment. Make it, get it, borrow it—middle-class women and teenagers as well as men. If you cannot get it, we, as benevolent rulers, will give you some. We want everyone to have the power it gives. We want you all by spending money, and by spending sexually at will, to become superpowerful individuals, casting away the chains of the ages. We will help by showering you with new rights.

The rulers allowed this message fifteen years to filter through the West's collective consciousness before spelling it out in stark terms in the famous Sixties. Then, the time being ripe, 'IS GOD DEAD?' was blazoned on the cover of *Time* magazine.

★ They turned out to be Godless neoliberalism.

PERCEIVED BUT NOT UTTERED?

PERHAPS THE POSTWESTERN condition was indeed perceived, but failed to get successfully uttered, such was the determination of the 'postmodernists' to protect their academic honeypot and the coerciveness of 'Western' Cold War solidarity.

THE FIRST FEMINISTS?

THE MERCILESS BOMBERS pioneered the radical feminist assault on the West's discrimination between the sexes. Not only did they treat women no differently than men, they made them indistinguishable from men. Tokyo Radio reported this of the log-like burnt corpses.

I had settled in happily into Anguillara, first for six months in the Russian woman's flat high up in the town. My landlady turned out to be a bossy, new-rich woman who every month came to collect her rent and to stalk about her property inspecting and correcting my housekeeping. Hearing of a small house for sale at an affordable price near the adjacent huge lake, Lago di Bracciano, I bought it from its Italian owners, moved there and found my Anguillara home. I liked that in front it had a rectangular tiled terrace enclosed by a black railing that supported rectangular flower pots in which I was able to grow flowers to my heart's content. Every morning, walking down a short, cobble-stoned lane beside the house, I greeted the lake with 'Buon giorno, Lago!'

Interfering as usual in existing arrangements, I had got the Comune (town council) to reschedule the little bus that met the commuter train from Rome so that, instead of going to the station any old time, it went there at the times the train stopped there. And having taken that train to Rome, I noticed there that the English version of the explanatory historical notice in front of the Baths of Diocletian was full of mistakes and got the Directress of the Baths to produce a fully literate version!

A short time after settling in Anguillara I learned that daughter Kate had gone to Istanbul and was living there. After finishing her degree in

Russian and Classical Studies in Trinity College Dublin she had spent a year living with Mary in Galway, doing some work in radio and television, often visiting Galway's Café du Journal to read its supply of newspapers. Now her interest in Byzantine art had taken her to Istanbul. I had formed the impression she was at a loss about what to do with her life. Her flight to Istanbul came across to me as an escape from that dilemma. I flew there from Rome and she put me up in the apartment where she was staying. On that first evening she took me to a café on the shore of the Bosphorus and I looked across the water as the lights came on on the Asian side. Unforgettable! I told Kate that I wanted her to return to Dublin and within a month to have a job, a flat and if possible a car. I stayed maybe two days, did a little sightseeing and flew back to Rome. Kate did what I had asked her to do—she got work with a Dublin film company, Liberty Films. I was very glad. When she had been studying Russian at Trinity College, Russia had become her favourite world abroad and she spent long periods there. I was not to know until later that after that first visit to Turkey, it would replace Russia in that favoured role.

All my Anguillara neighbours were friendly and my Italian progressed rapidly with much help from Harvey in whose restaurant I often lunched. Every Friday evening I met special friends at Harvey's for a pizza— Enrico, Enrica, Scottish Christine and her husband Carlo Pepe, German Barbara and occasionally Greek-German Gabi. The first from Ireland to visit me was my good schoolteacher friend Miriam Duggan, followed by son Oisín with his daughter Sorcha Óg. Miriam came thereafter for most of her school holidays and was a regular at the Friday pizza sessions.

For Christmas 1998 she and I, accompanied by Kate, went for the first of what would be several Christmas visits to the snowy Dolomites in the Austrian-Italian South Tyrol, this first time to the village of Welschnofen. After a couple of Christmases we would take to staying instead in the nearby big town and capital of the South Tyrol which honours the medieval poet Walther von der Vogelweide in its main square on the grounds that he was born nearby. (I had written a paper about him when at UCD.) In due course, daughters Natasha and Sorcha and son Cilian would visit me in

Anguillara, all the family except Mary. In 1998 I heard that she had been in Trinity College taking a further course in Hebrew and Arabic, had gone to visit Natasha in Australia and backpacked with her there and in Indonesia and Thailand. She was now at the Ratisbon Institute in Jerusalem pursuing Jewish medieval religious studies.

AN ABNORMAL PASSION*

Cleansing Irish Literature of Irishness

I GOT THE idea for this essay from an article by a Frenchwoman, Maggie Pernot, in the Tralee literary journal *Asylum* (Winter 1997). Madame Pernot was writing about the short stories of Neil Jordan in the late 1970s, of which 'Night in Tunisia' was and is the best known. In particular, she was exploring a programmatic decision of Jordan's as reflected in these stories. I quote from her second paragraph:

> From the outset Neil Jordan had chosen to move away from tradition and to write about aspects of everyday life that would not immediately be identified as Irish. The smell of boiled cabbage is conspicuously absent from his stories as are the whitewashed cottages, the rain-drenched winding lanes or the Dublin pubs with their roaring drunkards, to give just a few examples. In the same way, references to the past, or to Irish war, are either non-existent or alluded to briefly and then, only as memories rather than experience.

Mme Pernot explains this decision partly by the fact that Jordan was born in 1950 and had no experience of the major historical events in Ireland in the early part of the century. But there was more to it than that. Jordan had told her that in his stories he was consciously 'not referring to ideas of national identity' but 'expressing another reality, everyday facts, ordinary facts...something mundane, contemporary...So, recent Irish history and ideas of national identity were out.'

One of his stories made clear that the 'recent Irish history' which was not relevant included even mid-century de Valera and what he stood for. Moreover, Maggie Pernot, quoting further—this time

---

* From *Incognito* journal, Vol. 2, Dublin 1997

from an interview with Jordan by Richard Kearney—shows that the great works of Anglo-Irish literature were also out. Jordan had told Kearney:

> When I started writing I felt very pressured by the question: how do I cope…with the notion of Irishness? It meant almost nothing to me. I was, of course, profoundly moved by the Irish literature I encountered as a student—Yeats and Joyce. But how was I to write about the experience I knew, as someone born in Sligo and growing up in the suburban streets of Dublin in the sixties? The great books of Anglo-Irish literature had very little to do with this, they had no real resonance at this level. My most acute dilemma was how to write stories about contemporary urban life in Ireland without being swamped in the language and mythology of Joyce… The only identity, at a cultural level, that I could forge was one that came from the worlds of television, popular music and cinema which I was experiencing daily.

Note, in passing, that these *'worlds'*, and the East Coast urban teenagers who dwelt in them and who figured centrally in Jordan's stories, were actually part of contemporary Irishness: a non-distinctive, largely British and American part of it. So it could be said that Jordan, as compared with most of his predecessors, was simply shifting the focus within Irish life. He was directing it to a previously neglected class of characters—suburban, middle-class Dublin teenagers—and to aspects of Irishness that were internationally shared rather than distinctive. But that is not what he said or what he conceived himself to be doing: he conceived it in much more dramatic terms, as a turning away from Irishness, whether historical, literary or lived, towards a contemporary, non-Irish reality, shared with non-Irish people.

Mme Pernot then proceeds to check out the stories in detail to see whether Jordan has indeed fulfilled his intention of writing 'un-Irish' literature, which she takes to mean, reasonably enough, literature that is 'simply human'. That can mean having human significance of a contemporary kind or, more broadly, of a perennial nature; here it is a matter of 'contemporarily Anglo-American Western'. As the checking-out proceeds, item by item, it becomes unintentionally amusing. The teenagers of many of the stories are into pop culture: there is nothing distinctively Irish about that. The same goes for their interest in girls and sex: that is how boys are today anywhere. True, the placenames and some other details suggest an Irish *setting*, but 'that in itself would not be enough to prove their specific Irishness, especially as the seaside resorts of the east coast of Ireland, with their beaches, amusement arcades and tennis courts, could just as well be situated on the other side of the Irish Sea and the two Dublin street names [that occur] are to be found in many British towns.'

No, where Jordan's stories, in Pernot's judgment, do backslide into betraying their Irishness is not so much 'in the geographical landscape, as in the spiritual landscape'. There are many indications that the setting is a Catholic country. Moreover, in the treatment of the adult characters there are clear signs that they are people who have absorbed not only Catholicism, but the general Christian and religious scheme of things. That, I would comment in passing, does not seem a very convincing indication that the stories are specifically Irish. Rather is it an indication that they are not British or American; or simply, that they are situated in a Catholic and religious country. At all events, Mme Pernot meticulously lists the references and phrases that indicate a Catholic and generally religious ambience.

As I remarked, this meticulous checking-out becomes amusing. But there is also, on the face of it, something amusing in the reported endeavour of an author of fiction to eradicate any trace of his national milieu from his stories. Clearly, a passion was at work here, a passion as distinct from a reasonable purpose, and it was a strange passion. The distinctively native thing, which is present one way or another in most of the world's literature, was felt to be something that would thwart, sully or diminish the art. To keep it out as much as possible would result in a cleaner, purer, more genuinely human art; a more real art that would more really reflect the contemporary human condition in Ireland or the West generally.

As we focus in on the passion in this manner, it ceases to be amusing and becomes familiarly sad. It is recognisable as an instance of the psychological dermatitis that afflicts deeply colonised people in successive bouts. Literally or metaphorically, they sense that the skin they were born with and grew up in, and which distinguishes them, comes between them and being real persons living a real human life in the world. So, afflicted with angst about their condition in the world and hoping to right it, they try to get rid of their skin, or rather, to change it, literally or metaphorically. In a succession of efforts, and with the dermatitis always returning to spur them on, they change their faces as much as they can, abandon their distinctive dress or food, their laws and customs, their language, their literary models; finally, with great difficulty, their religion. And the norm of humanity that they pursue in all this, and that they strive to adopt, is the norm of the imperial power—singular or hybrid—that is colonising them. As everyone knows, a fresh bout of this psychological dermatitis hit the Irish of the Republic in the 1960s and intensified in the 1970s. The norm of proper humanity to which it aspired was the package of new norms proclaimed in those years by New York-London.

Jordan was not alone in his endeavour. In Irish literary circles it was in the air. The year after his collection *Night in Tunisia* was published, an American, William Vorm, who had noticed a change in Irish fiction, especially among the young writers, published a collection of new Irish short stories called *Paddy No More*. A more programmatic title would be difficult to imagine. The book included, besides two stories by Jordan, stories by Dermot Healy, Lucille Redmond, John Montague, Desmond Hogan and Juanita Casey. However, the belief that divorcing Irish fiction from Irishness was a good thing and attempts to do this did not first emerge at this time, in the late 1970s. Both entered general literary consciousness in these years, but they had surfaced earlier.

Besides writing stories, set in Ireland, which avoided a distinctively Irish flavour, another way for Irish authors to achieve 'non-Irishness' in their work was to set the stories in foreign milieus. Although this is a commonplace in Gaelic Irish fiction since the Gaelic *Voyage of Maeldun*, it had rarely been done in Irish fiction in English before Aidan Higgins published his collection of stories *Felo de Se* in 1960. The foreign-language title, the fact that Berlin and other European parts figured in a few of the stories, and the sprinkling of foreign languages and names—all this caused some pleasurable excitement. A sign of the times, this 'Continental' quality had a significance not evoked by the few previous forays abroad of English Irish fiction, mainly to Spain.

However, in the early 1960s, the feeling was not so much that Higgins had (largely) excluded Irishness as that Irish writing was breaking out, conquering new terrain. Higgins had, after all, been living on the Continent. I am unaware whether, apart from that, he had any programmatic intention, even when—still living mainly abroad—he followed up with a travel-book, *Images of Africa* (1971), and a novel, *Balcony of Europe* (1972). But it *looked* like it.

John Banville certainly had the intention of breaking with recognisably Irish writing when in 1971, and while living in Ireland, he published *Nightspawn*, set in Greece, and, after touching down in Ireland with *Birchwood*, followed with *Doctor Copernicus* (1976) and *Kepler* (1981). Banville gave an interview this year to the *European English Messenger* (Spring 1997, Vol VI/1), at the end of which he said as follows:

> The only direct statement I've ever made in any book that I have written is at the end of *Birchwood* where the protagonist says: 'I'll stay in this house and I'll live a life different from any the house has known' (p. 174). And that is my statement. I stay in this country but I'm not going to be an Irish writer. I'm not going to do the Irish thing.

In that, clearly, Banville was speaking not only for himself, but for quite a number of the younger Irish writers of his generation.

However, in the matter of an Irish author excising Irishness from his writing, the great forerunner of the period was, of course, Samuel Beckett. Beginning in the 1930s, his fiction moved from Irish settings and characters to English settings with some vaguely Irish characters, to a merely nominal Irish character (Molloy, Malone) in an undefined environment. Then, in his plays, from *Waiting for Godot* onwards, he proceeded to achieve a complete cleansing of Irishness. True, for those in the know, private memories of Irish circumstances, and the occasional Irish turn of phrase, could still be detected; but that was inevitable. It took nothing from the abstract purity of the works for his international public, and even for most Irish people, who were unacquainted with his biographical details.

Let us turn now to the situation today, twenty years after *Paddy No More*, and examine what has been the net effect on English Irish fiction of what might be called the Paddy No More movement. Very little it seems. The overall situation appears much the same as it was in the 1960s. In the first place, even in the newest writing, the old themes predominate. In the Dublin *Sunday Tribune*, of 20 July 1997, a new collection of short stories, *Phoenix Irish Short Stories 1997*, edited by David Marcus, was reviewed. The reviewer, Colin Lacy, writes as follows:

> Assuming that 'Ireland' is the subject of this collection [*note this continuing assumption*], one wonders what a reader coming to this nation's literature for the first time since, say, the 1960s would make of us. Emigration looms large. Over the 16 stories included here, so does the Catholic Church, sex, alcohol and various forms of physical and cultural displacement—hardy perennials all. Shaping up as an annual state of the nation report on Irish short fiction, David Marcus's second Phoenix collection suggests that the themes that have teased Irish writers since the days when the Celtic Tiger was a malnourished cub are still the themes that bind.

Where the reviewer calls emigration, the Catholic Church, sex, alcohol and various forms of physical and cultural displacement 'perennials all', I think we can fairly take it that he is not referring to those themes individually—for individually they can be found in many national literatures—but to their conjunction and joint recurrence in an Irish setting and with a fairly predictable treatment. In the literary context, in the present century, that is very perennially 'Irish' indeed.

Second, English Irish prose fiction continues, as in the lifetime of most of us, to make no notable contribution to the depiction of the contemporary human condition. By 'notable' depiction, I mean the creation of fictional worlds or characters which become representative icons of the contemporary in the English-speaking literate consciousness, our own included. Joyce created such a world in *Dubliners* and *Ulysses*, and such characters in Leopold Bloom and Stephen

Dedalus. (His Molly Bloom went beyond the merely contemporary to become an icon of *perennial* woman.) But since Joyce, no Irish writer of prose fiction has done either. Beckett, alone among Irish writers, contributed icons of the contemporary, not in his prose fiction, but in his plays of the 1950s and 1960s. All the other fictional worlds and characters that have lodged, as icons, in the consciousness of literate, English-speaking people, including ourselves, have come from English or American fiction.

For example, and in no particular order: the 'Greene world' of Graham Greene and the characters of Pinkie, Scobie, the Mexican whiskey-priest, the 'Quiet American'; George Orwell's *Nineteen-Eighty-Four* and *Animal Farm* and the character Big Brother; John Updike's contemporary everyman Rabbit, the car salesman; Aldous Huxley's *Brave New World*; Evelyn Waugh's *Brideshead Revisited* and the character Sebastian Flyte; Raymond Chandler's world, the character Philip Marlowe, and the image of 'the mean streets'; the worlds and principal characters of Hemingway and Scott Fitzgerald; Saul Bellow's *Herzog*; the world of John Le Carré's novels, the title and images of *The Spy Who Came in from the Cold*, and the character Smiley; J.P. Donleavy's *The Ginger Man*; the Agatha Christie world; Kingsley Amis's *Lucky Jim*; the woman's world of Doris Lessing's *The Golden Notebook*.

As you will have noticed, quite a number of those titles, worlds and characters have passed into everyday language. Casting the mind over that random list, it seems that, apart from notable representational skill and subtle insight, what qualifies fictional writing to be notably contemporary by the measure I am using is its contemporary adult theme. By that I mean, roughly, *a recognisably contemporary adult person (or persons) involved in typically contemporary preoccupations and activities.* Given that most English speakers, in Ireland as elsewhere, are such people, this is a theme-category central to the consciousness and interest of our times. (True, I am using the word 'adult' to refer to something more than mere age, without troubling to define exactly what more. But it is interesting to note that Neil Jordan's attempt at the contemporary focused on teenagers.)

Finally, what Irish writing continues to be notable for, and most valued for, both abroad and in Ireland, is its occasional, strong depiction of life that is sub-adult, sub-literate, offbeat, weird, poor, and possessed of a naive, occasionally hilarious, charm. Life, in short, which is an attractive marginal oddity. This is, of course, an age-old stereotype of Irishness in the English-speaking world.

I am thinking, most immediately, of the recent, simultaneous success abroad—and by derivation in Ireland—of the novelist Roddy Doyle, the memoirist Frank McCourt and the playwright Martin McDonagh.

Frank McCourt, whose remembered depiction of life in Limerick slums, and of those awful Catholic priests and nuns, was extracted, prior to publication, in the *New Yorker*, went on to win the Pulitzer Prize, and is being advertised in London—I saw the posters—with this quote from a review: 'Out Roddy Doyles Roddy Doyle...It is amazing.' London Irishman Martin McDonagh, launched by the Druid Theatre in Galway with his play *The Beauty Queen of Connemara*, who went on to scale the heights in London, and who will soon be big in New York with plays entitled *A Skull in Connemara*, *The Lonesome West*, *The Cripple of Inishmaan*. The titles adequately reflect the content. But I am also thinking—in terms of theme only, let me stress—of the other Irish novels and plays that have drawn most hype and acclaim in recent years in Britain, or in Britain and America, and of course, therefore, in Ireland: Dermot Healy's *A Goat's Song*, with its trumpeted bucolic title and mainly West of Ireland setting, where the narrator's central concerns when lonesome without his woman or despairing in her company are whether something alcoholic is left over from the night before, and which pub is the best one to begin the day's drinking in; Patrick McCabe's *The Butcher Boy*, about a curious, violent, idiot-boy, seeing visions of the Virgin, begorrah, and other marvels in a moronic Border town; John McGahern's *Amongst Women*, about the dour peasant Moran patriarching his womenfolk in a time warp Irish rural scene, set in timeless Irish amber; fascinating book-at-bedtime reading— *'really quite remarkable people, the Irish, and what beautiful writing!'*—for the folk jaded with contemporaneity who listen to BBC Radio 4; and for good measure, Brian Friel, with his tales of Ballybeg peasants, and above all his greatest international success, *Dancing at Lughnasa*, where those Donegal wenches get up and jig like mad on the kitchen table and chairs to the music from the ould steam radio.

These are the sort of fictional works for which Ireland remains notable. All of them are valued by the contemporary English-speaking world as icons of *Irishness*, which define by their contrast the adult normality of that world. For this reason, they are fussed over for a time before being dropped from the general consciousness.

So what went wrong? Nothing went wrong because in the Paddy No More movement there was nothing that could have gone right. The notion that there was an intrinsic opposition between being Irish and the contemporary, and that the way to depict the 'contemporarily human' successfully was to avoid the distinctively native, was a delusion. No such literary rule exists.

Joyce's fiction of Dublin was steeped in the distinctively native and it proved contemporary to an iconic degree. Beckett achieved the same in an abstract, unfeatured setting, as did Kafka. Whether Graham Greene set a story in Brighton or in Mexico, in both cases he drew on the distinctively native—this does not have to mean the distinctively native of the author's own land. Nothing more French than Flaubert's *Madame Bovary*, and yet the story and the woman have become representative icons for all time: not only contemporarily human, but perennially human also.

Quite a number of Irish prose writers since Joyce have created fiction with a contemporary dimension. Some have attained the perennially human; the work of others has exuded no significant human radiance of either kind. But what has decided the matter has not been the presence or absence of distinctively Irish content. John Broderick, setting his novels in a recognisably Irish town (Athlone), and in a middle-class milieu, achieved some general human dimension. In the unmistakably Irish tales of Seamus O'Kelly, Mary Lavin, Kate O'Brien, and Sean O'Faolain at his best, the perennially human is present. In John Banville's novels, because a voice rather than a person is central and the brilliances are mainly verbal and intellectual, little of human significance is exuded, regardless of whether the settings are non-Irish or Irish. Maeve Binchy's stories, set in Ireland and with a casual, unstereotyped Irish ambience, have contemporary meaning for the English-speaking world and beyond. Valerie Mulkern's novel *Very Like a Whale*, situated in contemporary, middle-class Dublin, Brian Friel's *The Faith Healer* set in England, or a Hugo Hamilton novel moving through present-day Berlin, all these have a contemporary edge and, in Friel's play, perennial meaning also.

If, nevertheless, it remains true that no Irish prose fiction since Joyce has supplied a notable depiction of the human condition, contemporary or timeless, the impeding factor, clearly, was not a recognisably Irish colouring. That was not the case in Neil Jordan's youth nor has it been the case since then.

In 2001 Bob Quinn's son Toner, who was employed by the Dublin publisher Veritas, published a book of essays about me called Desmond Fennell: His Life and Work. *On the back cover Toner had quoted Ruth Dudley Edwards:*

> I respect Desmond Fennell's moral courage in being a dissenting and often unpopular voice who has said much to try to make us reflect as a people—something we are very bad at doing.

Toner continued:

> To many in Ireland Desmond Fennell was a familiar voice in the 60s, 70s and 80s. His challenging newspaper columns from that era are often recalled, but few seem aware of his work beyond that. He has been described as one of Ireland's most creative thinkers and yet today most of his work is out of print. He is rarely quoted and almost never publicly discussed.

All of the contributors selected by Toner were friends of mine or at least well-disposed: Brian Arkins, John Waters, Nollaig Ó Gadhra, Joe Lee, Risteárd Ó Glaisne, Mary Cullen and Bob Quinn. Far from endorsing every word I had written, some were vigorously argumentative. Carrie Crowley of RTÉ contributed a radio interview she had done with me. I was grateful to Toner for having organised the book.

During a visit to Ireland in 2002, after giving a lecture in Co. Cork, I met Eileen Murphy from Cork city. In the course of conversation I told her I had written a book, The Revision of European History, *and was trying to find a publisher. She suggested Athol Books, the book-publishing arm of a group led by Brendan Clifford and Jack Lane, both from Co. Cork, and Brendan's wife Angela, a Palestinian. The group had begun as the British and Irish Communist Organisation and in the context of the Northern Ireland conflict launched the 'two-nation theory'. Now located in London, it called itself the Irish Political Review Group after its monthly journal of that name. I offered my book to them and they published it. It was the first of my three Athol Books. A disadvantage was that they paid no royalties! I became an occasional contributor to their* Irish Political Review; *they publish several other journals, most notably* Church and State.

2001

THE SILENCE TONER QUINN REFERRED TO*

I HAD A thick skin and I did a lot of shrugging. Colm Ó hEocha didn't want me full-time in University College Galway? The worse for him and for UCG! Some supercilious brush-offs from politicians and civil servants? Sad, so hidebound, so colonised! Because in those decades I had exposed myself more continuously than any other freethinker except Conor Cruise O'Brien, I had incurred the sullen, pub-talk hostility of Dublin journalists, who now formed a homogenised tribe. But from the late 1960s to the 1990s, the most active continuous hostility came from RTÉ producers in three or four departments, most of whom I never met. The thing began when, between 1969 and 1972, I was publicly developing a new approach to the Northern question that deviated from orthodox nationalism. They expressed what amounted to hatred by a total boycott. Subsequently, in the 1980s, when I had returned to Dublin from Conamara, it became routine for them to invite me onto a programme with feigned interest in something I had written, and then to use the occasion to charge me with thought crime and to have

* From the closing section of *The Turning Point: My Sweden Year and After,* Sanas Press, Dublin, 2001, dealing mostly with the 1970s to 1990s.

me squashed by a chorus of right-thinkers! 'Let that be a lesson to deviants!' was, I suppose, the suggestion that went out. RTÉ listeners and viewers of those years will recognise the technique, of which I was by no means the only victim: the new thought controllers used public-service broadcasting as their Star Chamber.

As the 1990s began, I decided that enough was enough. *In Heresy: The Battle of Ideas in Modern Ireland* (1993) I rendered a final, summary account of my battling against the tide. 'Silence' with regard to my writings had amounted either simply to that or it had gone further to become a kind of *silencing* by means of writing me out of the record. This has happened, for example, in books or articles by Irish authors on themes to which I had contributed, there would be none to my relevant work.★ But this 'silencing' has also, occasionally, taken the active form of curt, dismissive misrepresentations of my positions or views. So it has seemed useful to me to set down, occasionally, a clear record of what I have been about and how and why. But with these accounts of my mental processes and my stratagems and struggles I have had another purpose in view. They are intended as a means—I have on occasion used more direct means—of encouraging other Irishmen and women, especially among the younger generation, to think freely for themselves. The message I intend to convey implicitly is: 'I speak from experience; this is how it's done, and be prepared for struggles, frustration and obstacles such as these!' It is a sort of home-made gloss and application of Kant's exhortation when he defines 'enlightenment' as 'the exit of man from a state of immaturity brought about by his own fault'. 'Immaturity,' he elucidates, 'is the incapacity to use one's mind without direction by another. It is immaturity brought about by one's own fault when its cause lies not in a lack of mind, but of the resolution and courage to use it without direction by another. *Sapere aude!* Dare to know!'

However, my sense of frustration was far from total. I was depressed, but not clinically so, and I hadn't a drink problem. I was gratefully conscious that, on a variety of minor fronts, my efforts had

★ Some instances have been so glaring as to cause me to write to the authors. Examples, where the letters sent may be found among my papers, are *Why Irish? Irish Identity and the Irish Language* by Hilary Tovey, Damien Hannan and Hal Abramson and (since I came to Italy) *Paths to a Settlement in Northern Ireland* by Seán Farren and Robert E. Mulvihill, London, 2000.

borne fruit or I had found collaboration. Writing, after all, had been my greatest effort, and a great deal of it had been done and a great deal published. A succession of editors and publishers from Douglas Gageby, Austin Flannery, Vincent Jennings and Mícheál Mac Craith to Richard Kearney★, Fergal Tobin and Declan Kiberd had provided space. From time to time, on the margins of Irish life, I had enjoyed intellectual give-and-take: in Irish in the Conamara Gaeltacht, on Northern matters with Protestants on both sides of the Border, and on a variety of themes with militant republicans.★★

Around the time I was winning acceptance for my 'new true images' of the Gaeltacht and the North, Cárna had, by my efforts, acquired an elected parish council, and St Macdara's chapel was not only restored but represented as an architectural treasure on an Irish postage stamp! The house I built with Mary on a height in Mao-inis—'Tigh Finnil' as it came to be called—provided a 'sea mark' for Cárna fishermen. The children we had reared there felt permanent-ly enriched by their Maoinis childhood. Some of the campaigns for Gaeltacht self-assertion in which I had worked with others—if not the main one, for self-government—had been successful. The response to my call for Irish-speakers with valuable skills to move into the Gael-tacht had helped those campaigns, while simultaneously enriching the lives of the immigrants and of many Gaeltacht people. In the wake of my pamphlet *Take the Faroes for Example,* emissaries from Conamara had visited those islands for inspiration, and partly to find a model for Gaeltacht television. The Gaelic League had at last issued a program-matic document, *Athréimniú an Duine in Éirinn* ('The Restoration of Man in Ireland'). It had got the message from my persistent recalling of the intention of its first president, Dubhghlas de híde.

In Galway, principally on the streets, there were marks of my three-year presence. After my memorandum to Joe Curley, president of the Chamber of Commerce, public maps of the city had been erected; the Oyster Festival had moved from Clarinbridge to the

★ The most enterprising Irish intellectual of his generation, he has emigrated to the US.

★★ It was the dead centre that thwarted me, that inert mass of the English-speaking, Catholic and post-Catholic intelligentsia who willy-nilly are the keepers of the nation's intellect. For these colonised minds, no new thought that is 'merely Irish'—not pre-stamped by London or New York as 'OK, discuss'—is worth attending to.

212 ABOUT BEING NORMAL: MY LIFE IN ABNORMAL CIRCUMSTANCES

city and, from having been an elite event, gone popular. After that night when Geraldine Quinn and I with four others—all masked and bearing torches and with Joe Steve Ó Neachtain proclaiming his *Dán na Féile*—had for the first time opened the Arts Festival with a street event, the masters in that genre, Macnas, had emerged and gone on to glory. Since those western years, Bob Quinn and Brian Arkins had remained friends who continually encouraged me.

On a quite different front, my critique in *The State of the Nation* of the eccentrically narrow definition of 'Irish literature' by the Arts Council and Aosdána had been heeded by Seamus Deane when he edited, splendidly, the *Field Day Anthology of Irish Writing.** In 1984 the Report of the New Ireland Forum had reflected the constant core of my restatement, since 1969, of Irish nationalism on the Northern problem; and the Report had since then been the basis for efforts to reach a settlement. Benedict Kiely and Francis Stuart, both of them *Saoithe* of Aosdána, had proposed me for membership of that body, and Jennifer Johnston joined in a second attempt. (The first application failed on a technical flaw, the second failed because I was a non-fiction writer.) Finally, in 1991, when on Pat Sheeran's suggestion I had submitted my written works to the National University for a Doctor of Literature degree, I had the satisfaction of receiving from fellow countrymen this formal recognition of my life's work thus far.

But these satisfactions could not outweigh the surrounding silence on the issue that centrally concerned me and the general stifling or ignoring of Irish original thought, my own included. Increasingly I felt bored and lonely. Going for a month to Minsk in Belarus, in 1993, was an expression of how desperately I wanted a change of air. Early retirement, in 1993, from my post as lecturer in Written English in the Dublin Institute of Technology, and a long holiday in the US, were other expressive gestures.

That holiday began my relaunch into the mainstream of my life's business. It led to fifteen months spent in Seattle in 1994-6 and to the book *Uncertain Dawn: Hiroshima and the Beginning of Post-western Civilisation,* which I published in Dublin towards the end of 1996.

In retrospect I realise that I was moving towards a decision to

---

* He has since emigrated to the USA.

leave Ireland for good. My 'Seattle book', which offered a very new but thoroughly discussible vision of the age got two reviews, both interested, in *Books Ireland* and *The Irish Times* and fell into a pool of silence. Shortly after it appeared, I published *Dreams of Oranges*, an eyewitness account of the fall of Communist East Germany. As with *Uncertain Dawn,* I did so by means of a publishing co-operative of bohemian intellectuals that John Minahane had founded.★ Irish commercial publishers, including the academic sort, had long taken the view that books on non-Irish themes lay outside their province. Denis Staunton, the *Irish Times* correspondent in Germany, reviewed *Dreams* very positively. But in nine months, in Connolly Books, the 'socialist bookshop' in Dublin's Temple Bar, the only Irish account of the fall of Communism sold one copy. And researchers will look in vain for references to it in the writings of Irish academics or the Irish 'Left'.

Rather than deciding 'to leave Ireland for good' I moved to Italy, to think about the American departure and to search for its roots in European history.

2003

THE DREAM OF POST-EUROPE★★

THE WEST'S BREAK with European civilisation has its deepest emotional and intellectual roots in the Italian Graeco-Roman revival of the fifteenth century. That movement which scorned Europe as it had developed until then, wanted to replace Italy, to begin with, with something like republican Rome in a contemporary Christian framework. More immediately, the present breakaway has its origin in the amalgam of ideas that supplied the ideology of the French Revolution and in part—along with English legal tradition—of the (First) American Revolution. Common to both revolutions were, on the one hand, the conviction that European civilisation had been an intolerable oppression and, on the other, the dream of founding another life, characterised by collective and individual sovereignty.

★ He has since emigrated to Slovakia.

★★ From *The Revision of European History, Athol Books 2003*. In those first years in Anguillara I studied European history searching for the background or roots of the American breakaway.

The French revolutionaries imagined the desired free life as a revived pre-European condition, which they described as natural or like republican Rome. In fact what they wanted was a Post-Europe that would be a negation of historical Europe. It would negate it by allowing nations and individuals the sovereignty which was theirs by nature but which Europe denied them. For the Americans this post-European condition would be a *Novus Ordo Seclorum* (the motto, meaning New Order of the World) on the reverse of the official US seal designed in 1782 and still legible on dollar bills. For the French Jacobins it was to be a radical new departure, beginning with their proclamation of Year One and the Reign of Reason.

Because of its influence on subsequent history, the most important event of those years was the emergence of the dream of Post-Europe and its settlement at the core of the western consciousness. Its adherents called it the 'progressive' vision and themselves in broad terms 'progressives'. They believed that, because human sovereignty was a supremely good thing, they, by working for it or simply desiring it, were rendered good persons and thereby entitled to it, while those who opposed or hindered them were ipso facto evil. The most successful progressives were the Liberals (in the original sense of that word) who were also moderately conservative. They pursued the dream by stages within inherited ethical limits as reason moderated by feeling seemed to indicate. For Post-Europe they substituted 'enlightened Europe', meaning themselves and how they ordered things. Flanking them, in a kaleidoscopic spectrum of individualism and collectivism, were the fundamentalists, the utopian absolutists. They strained for unmitigated sovereignty immediately, by violent overthrow if need be.

That first American attempt to implement a Post-Europe resulted in a constitution of society which fell far short of the absolutist goal. The Rousseauist rhetoric of the Declaration of Independence, the democratic Constitution and the location outside Europe seemed to the colonists a sufficient cancellation of their European past. They settled for the moderate sovereignty, collective and individual, of a Liberal-Protestant republic. Its rulers read the Bible, knew Latin and some Greek, and promoted liberty and equality within the limits set by reason, Protestant ethics, white skin and capitalist economics. An American semi-Europe, it lasted until World War II.

The French attempt at realising post-Europe was full-blown but short-lived. After less than two years of absolutist Utopia in 1793-4, it petered out in the reformed France and Europe of the brief Napoleonic empire and the nineteenth century. But the dream that had inspired it haunted Europe during that century and into the twentieth. Both in France and in other Latin nations there were recurrent lurches in the direction of the dream. Russia and Germany went for it wholesale and realised it for, respectively, seventy years and—omitting the terminal crisis of the German effort—ten. The Bolsheviks and Nazis, as the Jacobins before them, failed to make their Post-Europe last. In sum, before the second, this time full-blown American effort that we are still experiencing, the dream of Post-Europe spawned four major efforts to realise it, with none of them having more than temporary success.

Mary and I had not seen each other for more than twenty years. Our ways had diverged. Miriam during her latest school-holiday visit to Anguillara showed signs of staying and making a business of house property. We discussed marriage. In 2002 I proposed divorce to Mary, who readily agreed. We applied for divorce and in early 2003 it was granted in Galway. I didn't like that divorce was against my Catholic principles. I viewed it pragmatically as a regularisation of an existing false situation. Miriam did not in fact settle in Anguillara and stayed in Ireland for over a year involved in a scheme for establishing a Christmas market in Dublin. For me Mary remained dear! But whether in Dublin teaching or in Anguillara sharing my life, Miriam was now my dearly loved life-partner.

ENGAGING MODERNITY IN A HI-TECH CENTRE ★

I HAVE JUST reviewed a Celtic Tiger book by a bunch of academics and here comes another of them, *Engaging Modernity*, published by Veritas. You know the sort of thing, I let it speak for itself. '*Engaging*

★ *The Irish Times,* 28 May 2003.

*Modernity p*rovides a new appraisal of Ireland's engagement with the phenomenon of modernity. The path we have travelled from being a rural-based, religious, traditional, insular country, to a secular, highly prosperous economic hi-tech centre has brought in its wake both problems and advantages.'

Two things cry out for saying. The first has to do with the notion—ignorant but it's in vogue—that during the Celtic Tiger decade Ireland finally stopped being 'traditional' and became 'modern'. (That other book I have just reviewed, called *Reinventing Ireland*, went on about 'modernisation' as something that happened here in the 1990s.) I have taken down off the shelf, to check the title, Joseph Lee's book, *The Modernisation of Ireland 1848-1918*—and Lee writes as a professor of history and a careful user of language.

But I don't need any book to tell me that the Irish engaged with the French Revolution when that was the most modern thing around, and before that with the Protestant Reformation when that was, and centuries earlier encountered and adopted Norman stone castles, body armour and courtly love, and much longer ago, when these novelties first arrived from the Continent, iron swords and ploughs and pots and pans to replace the bronze ones. What is 'modernity' but the latest thing in vogue in the power centres, which subsequently spreads to the provinces and is eagerly adopted by the provincials, led by their fashionable élites?

'Modernisation' has been happening in Ireland since prehistory. Far from its being a case, now or ever, of 'modernity versus tradition', the Irish have a long tradition of modernisation; it is part of our traditional way of life. A more recent Irish tradition is that, in every generation since Daniel O'Connell, journalists and academics tell us that modernity has hit us, and discuss the pros and cons. The Celtic Tiger academics will be followed, in due course, by others who will tell us how Dublin is modernising when, in expensive London and New York restaurants, people are eating prime Al Qaeda Terrorist meat!

In short, with some historical awareness and care for language, Eamon Maher and Michael Böss, the editors of *Engaging Modernity*, might have added 'in the 1990s'. Granted, it would have sounded banal, but the truth often is.

The second thing that cries out to be said is, yes indeed, we have 'travelled from being a rural-based, religious country to being a hi-tech centre'; we have heard that before *ad nauseam*. But what happens now and who's discussing that? What do we do with our final achievement of that indistinguishableness from our neighbours which—with some deviation in the post-revolutionary decades—has been the aim of successive Irish elites for centuries?

Getting rid of 'rural-based' and 'religious'—actually 'Catholic' was the trouble—has been only the tail-end of a process which, again, is illuminated by history. It began in the sixteenth century when our top people, with the rest following later, began abandoning Irish law, dress and cuisine for English law, dress and cuisine (there was such a thing then). It continued two centuries later, when our new middle class, strong farmers and gombeen persons, feeling still too recognisably Irish because of the sounds that came out of their mouths, abandoned Irish language for English language, and the lower ranks, trailing as usual, followed suit.

Finally came the 1960s and 1970s, and a new bourgeoisie felt uncomfortable that their country, by being 'rural' and 'Catholic', still stuck out on the surrounding landscape. England wasn't rural or Catholic, nor was America. So those Paddy marks, too, were disposed of. Now at long last, the self-image we project abroad, and like looking at in the domestic mirror, is Ameranglian to a T and free of Paddy marks.

But, mission accomplished, we do not need to be told and told again, in self-congratulatory tones, that it has been accomplished and how free it makes us. Free for what?

Animals which change their natural colouring to adopt that of the surrounding vegetation have, so to speak, rational purposes. They wish to protect themselves from attack or to facilitate their own attacks. Have we such purposes in mind? Or was stripping ourselves of our distinguishing clothing our particular, very daring and desperate way of becoming a rich country? And if it was, how will it serve us if we cease to be rich? Have we a project in mind for our post-national future? If there existed in the Republic a serious cultural debate—but abnormally we lack even one journal of ideas—these are the issues our culture specialists would be attending to.

Europe, or at least its anthropologists, will be watching what we do next. For, ironically, in making ourselves indistinguishable from our Ameranglian surroundings we have made ourselves unique among European nations. In Ireland alone, modernisation—to return to the theme—took this nationally self-obliterating turn, and so resolutely that it continued after political independence.

Alone among the nations, we Irish had sufficient self-hatred and sufficient daring to transform our nation into a *tabula rasa* and post-Irish space on which something culturally quite new and post-European can be built. But only if we stop hating the notion of being different . . . Anthropologically speaking, we are an experiment.·

Postscript
In a letter to the Editor when this review appeared in *The Irish Times*, Jaime Hyland objected to some of it as 'not history but crude invective' against persons such as he who had 'chosen to live without religion', not as part of any Dublin middle-class fashion, but out of personal conviction. It was unworthy of me as a reputed 'humanist'. In a reply, I conceded that he had a point—that I had used 'shorthand'. I was sure that in each of the 'abandonments' I had referred to there was a minority who were not acting out of conformist angst but who had 'well thought-out reasons'. It was the 'overall pattern of national self-obliteration' that interested me—that, and what we would do with the result.

As I read the proofs of my book, Cutting to the Point, *in Anguillara, I was intrigued to hear that a book had been published by Manchester University Press called* The End of Irish History? *Good question, good title.*

THE AUTHOR AS A DUBLIN-LIBERAL PROBLEM*

IN THE PREFACE to this book personally to the reader and, in the subsequent pages, to a variety of publics, I have been speaking as I am;

---

* From *Cutting to the Point*, The Liffey Press, Dublin 2003.

that is, in real life. I have been talking to readers who are interested in what I have to say on things, or at least on some things. I have assumed that, from page to page, you were agreeing or disagreeing with me, or thinking critically about what I was saying. It has been, in other words, a normal writer–reader situation and relationship.

At the same time, most of you know that besides this real-life man who has been speaking to you with these assumptions, there exists a person to whom my name is attached. At the very least, you have bumped into some puzzling remarks or references that seemed to suggest his existence. He is an urban, more precisely Dublin, legend. In the last chapter of *Heresy* and in *The Turning Point*, I had something to say about his creation from the early 1970s onwards. Two years ago, John Waters wrote a penetrative essay on the necessity of creating him and on how his continuing existence is managed by his creators. That was in a collection of essays called *Desmond Fennell: His Life and Work*, edited by Toner Quinn.

Waters, in an essay entitled 'Desmond Fennell and the Politics of Error', pointed out that because of the dangerously subversive things I write in reasonable language, and my harmless-seeming, real-life character as a pipe-smoking, smiling, conversational fellow with a respectable education, I presented a problem to those in Dublin who control the public Truth. I was not fit material for a liberal Bogeyman. 'So to deal with the problem, in the public interest, they were obliged to tag his name with all the liberal booh-words, thus creating a straw figure who was by definition and quite obviously Wrong. And having thus established Fennell's Wrongness and immersion in Error, they took reasonable prophylactic measures lest his Error spread.'

Waters's account is literary art in an ironic vein. But the matter has become such that it demands more precise exposure than either he or I have hitherto given it. The impersonating mechanism set in motion by my influential opponents thirty years ago still comes between a substantial sector of the public and me; its workings mislead even some who find meat in my writings. Most seriously of all, those workings are now implanting biographical falsities about my life and work.

These are urgent and sufficient reasons for presenting the precise exposure that follows. By backtracking to trace the origin and nature of the mechanism, and by illustrating, from a few examples, how it has been working this very year, I want to enable people not only to identify it at work and to discount it, but also to suspect the possibility of its presence whenever there is a reference to me in Dublin journalism or in a footnote to an Irish academic work. Such, over a thirty-year period, has been the spread of the infection, and you will see presently that I do not exaggerate.

At the same time, I am aware that my experience of this illiberal phenomenon is part of the ideological and political history of Ireland since the 1970s. Its significance extends beyond my particular case. So my secondary motive is to provide a precise historical record for those who will wish to have a comprehensive understanding of what was happening in Ireland in this period.

In *Books Ireland*, January 2003, John Kirkaldy, an Irishman with whom I have never had any contact, reviewed two of my books. His review, while complimentary to me as a writer and thinker, was broadly disapproving of the views the books express. By a happy chance, his article serves several illustrative purposes at once: it indicates the background out of which the impersonation sprang and exemplifies some of its present workings. In his introductory paragraphs, having listed the variety of subjects on which I have written, Kirkaldy writes of me:

> Nearly all his comments and ideas have gone against the conventional norms of the dominant liberal [i.e. neoliberal!] ideology that has tended to set the agenda for debate. For years he has been the Man You Love to Hate of Dublin 4.

That is true, and I find the verb 'gone against'—rather than, say, 'opposed'—particularly apt. The fact is that, from the late 1960s into the 1970s, when it all began, the 'liberal agenda' in its broadest sense—including its centralist, anti-nationalist and London-directed aspects—was clashing with my own agenda, which was the completion of the Irish Revolution. An Ireland democratically self-governing in all its parts, economically self-sustaining, intellectually self-determining and culturally self-shaping has been my goal. In as much as Dublin liberalism was also then beginning its assault on the people's religion, I was irritated by this, but on national grounds mainly; for my own, actually Catholic reasons, I supported the proposal to remove the Catholic Church's 'special position' from the Constitution. All this is evident from the selection of *Sunday Press* articles I published in 1972 as *Build the Third Republic*—and indeed from that very title which once caused me trouble with British soldiers at the Border because I was carrying a copy of the book! From what I have said in the Preface about my subsequent writing and activities until the late 1980s, it will be clear that, first in Conamara, then in Dublin, the Dublin liberals impinged on my concerns mainly as a counter-force to my agenda; that is to say, as the Counter-revolution.

Be that as it may, from the Dublin liberals' point of view, I was clearly an opponent and a dangerous one, in part because my *Sunday Press* column had given me a large all-Ireland following. But some knowledge of the world, as well as mental agility not possessed by doctrinaires, were required to reply to me and eliminate me by argument. So instead, the tagging of my name with the liberal boohtags got under way. Essentially, it was a matter of pub-talk and party gossip in the RTÉ–UCD–*Irish Times* triangle and its dependencies in Dublin and elsewhere; in journalism, academe and publishing. Those who engaged in it were the middle-rankers, the liberal cadres; the kind of people who, in any party, form along with the footsoldiers the, so to speak, standing army. Non-practising Catholics who had found a new, imported faith which gave them self-esteem and a sense of being a cut above the ordinary Irish, they felt threatened by the articulateness with which I challenged those precious acquisitions. To choose the tags they hung on my name, no mental effort was required; or rather, as little as is required for anarchist demonstrators to call the police 'fascist bastards'. Sufficient for them to believe that they were the latest wave of enlightened progress; two centuries of such waves had supplied a stock nomenclature for opponents, and to hell with what the latter might actually be standing for, even if they were stating it in plain words. So this particular opponent got the conventional, mindless tagging treatment of self-imagined new-wave 'progressives'. And as 'nationalist' and 'Catholic' also became liberal scare-words, those tags, added, made him a proper sight to scare the liberal crows and their wavering converts.

In short, the aim, rather than to contest me and defeat me with argument, was to neuter or, so to speak, airbrush me. Once my pseudo-persona had been established by the tagged figure passed around, it went without saying that no self-respecting liberal—and liberals generally respect themselves—could publicly agree with me, or even publicly discuss anything I might say or write.' Thus I became, in pluralist, tolerant, diversity-respecting Dublin liberal circles, something not unlike Hiroshima in the public discourse of the contemporary West. By dint of the cadres' constant watchfulness to suppress my real existence, I acquired an importance for them which I have retained to this day.

Fast-forward through thirty years, during which the Fennell-impersonating mechanism did its work by nudge and whisper until word of the tagged impostor reached John Kirkaldy and lodged in his mind as 'conservative, old-fashioned bigot'. In two quite contrasting ways, his article shows this had happened. In the first instance, because he is writing after having read two books of mine, that implanted image dissolves and I come through more or less real. In the second, because Kirkaldy hasn't the relevant reading material to hand, the implanted image makes him write untruthful nonsense about me. In the first instance, because *Books Ireland* has asked him to review the two books and he has agreed to and read them, he writes:

> Conservative, old-fashioned and bigot—all are unfair or inadequate descriptions. He speaks several languages (including Irish); he has travelled widely and lived in several countries (he currently lives in Italy; and his writings and speech are littered with philosophical references (which, unlike some, he has obviously read). Although his views are very emphatic, they are usually delivered in a reasonable tone. At his best, he writes in a clear and well-argued fashion. There is a touch of Swift about him but also a little bit of Malvolio and Eeyore.

It is a curious feeling to read someone describing you, more or less factually, in a tone of surprise! (In passing, let me clarify that I do not accept the smearing connotation which our liberals have given to 'conservative' in Irish public language. If my own inclination has always been towards imaginative innovation—Seamus Deane once suggested 'pathologically so'—that does not prevent my being aware of the positive value of principled, selective resistance to it.)

In the second instance, because Kirkaldy has not checked my writings from the 1960s to the 1990s, the implanted image rules and he writes of me:

> He has gone against the stream on abortion, divorce, contraception, economics and the current political mores. He has opposed much of what has taken place in Christianity since the 1960s, especially in the Catholic Church.

It is deeply disturbing to read such a highly inaccurate 'biographical note' about yourself written with such confidence. If by 'against the stream' Kirkaldy means against neoliberal opinion, it's an odd choice of expression, but let's assume he means that. I cannot remember writing anything about liberalising the law on contraceptives in the 1970s—the issue as such never excited me and I had competing concerns in those western years. Regarding the liberal push for divorce legislation, in two newspapers I briefly suggested a pluralist solution: two available marriage contracts, one indissoluble, the other dissoluble, i.e. open to divorce, as in Ancient Rome. True enough, I have been repelled by the Dublin liberal campaign of winks and nods in favour of permissive legislation on abortion. I have written that to condone abortion is to condone the killing of a human being, and that if, in any country, the law in fact permits it, it should restrict it to the first three months of pregnancy and have strict limiting conditions. 'The liberal stream on economics and current political mores'? I'm not sure what is meant; but if the latter item is a reference to the investigative tribunals, I took almost no interest in them and was, anyhow, mainly abroad. As for the Catholic Church since the 1960s, in that decade, as many people can recall, I was editing *Herder Correspondence*, an international Catholic magazine known for its strong support of the reforming programme of the Second Vatican Council. That indicates the general line of my writing on Catholic Church matters then and since.

It's really pretty shocking, isn't it? But it also provides remarkable

evidence of the staying power of the 'liberal' implant which Kirkaldy
had received. After reading the two books, he seemed liberated from
it; but here he is on the same page giving a fictional account of
my working life that is inspired by it. The 'pig-headed conservative'
notion governs it. And unaware that my differences with the neoliberals were marginal to my concerns, he has me all wrought up about
their central concern, their 'liberal agenda' as they called it, on sexual
matters and abortion, and contesting it indiscriminately every inch
of the way. (It was their central concern because victory on those issues would signify victory over the Catholic clergy and replacement
of them by themselves.) And he has me continuing this absorption
with them right through to the 1990s and the tribunals! Mere assumption stated as fact runs right through it all, and I could fault
him severely for the carelessness and disrespect of this—he's dealing
with my life. But at the same time I see him as one among many
victims of the campaign of nudge and whisper directed against me
by the liberal hacks, the Correctors, and that softens my anger.

Let me add, to finish with the matter and because I have promised to be precise, that I have indeed protested against, and depicted
with scorn, the bullying methods and contemptuous tones with
which the Dublin media liberals have conducted their successive
campaigns, whether on their central agenda or on other matters. I
have done that as one who believes in representative democracy and
pluralism. In particular, I have come down hard on the liberal-spon-
sored 'Soviet-style' referenda of the 1980s and 1990s with all the
Dublin media taking the same line. But those referenda concerned
European Union matters as well as items of the 'liberal agenda'.
With regard to those 'agenda' items, my stated positions, when there
were any, have been as I wrote above…

Stepping a moment into the Internet, I find there an Irish-American whose father I knew, Mark Gauvreau Judge, writing about me
with a wide knowledge of what is written and said in my regard in
Ireland. Trying this way and that to fit me into the American and
Irish ideological schemes, and failing, he summarises: 'thoughtful,
full of surprises' and then, with a rebellious edge—for he is aware of
the tags—'impossible to categorize'. More to the point, he quotes
Irish Book reviewer Bill Sweeney calling me 'a staunch, if not always

lucid defender of his own personal take on the human condition'. That is stark rebellion: I am just, what in fact I happen to be, a thinking man! But to return to where we were: No, I am not suggesting there is no variety in the characterisation of me in print in Ireland. I am talking about the casual, cocksure, Dublin-liberal-indoctrinated commonplace, which, with a thirty-year tradition behind it, is pretty common.

Generously, and with the best intention, Kirkaldy writes:

> I should make clear that I am opposed to much of what Fennell stands for, but would argue that he has made a substantial contribution to discussion and argument. Life would be much duller without him!

Pray, Mr Kirkaldy, 'a contribution to discussion and argument' *where*? You are a normal man who believes that when a known intellectual publishes new, thought-through ideas on matters of general interest, his fellow intellectuals, in his own country, will grab at them and kick them around, uttering cheers, caveats and anathemas. It is what would happen, say, in England, or in Holland or Lithuania. But, Mr Kirkaldy, you live in a country where a thinking man can make all the 'contributions' he is capable of, and the *normal* does not happen!

I could give notable examples of this, beginning with Tom Barrington, Raymond Crotty and Ivor Browne. With regard to my own 'contributions', as you call them—the latest in *The Revision of European History*—Irish liberal party discipline has not been the only impediment. There are also the limiting, Ameranglian paradigms within which our academics toil. And there are other historical conditioning factors that I won't enlarge on, because I have dealt with them in the last chapter of my Sweden book, and in this present book in 'The Irish Problem with Thought'. In short, Mr Kirkaldy, if intellectual life in Ireland would be 'duller without me', it is in truth, for a combination of reasons, as dull as that.

I have always believed that in the matter of tagging people with regard to their worldview or partisan zeal, the same etiquette should apply as in the matter of tagging them with a nationality. In the latter case, by general agreement, one should do so only with the person's consent. One does not say 'she's Irish' or 'you're German', if the person in question, in the first instance, says she is British or, in the second, a Dane. To do otherwise is plain boorish, with an imperialistic taint. In the matter of the other kind of tagging, these niceties are often ignored; polemical passion or the desire to do down by name-calling often overrides. But I have stated my own principle on the matter, and I try to make it my practice. In these pages, for example, I have not called the Dublin liberals 'illiberals'. I have called them 'liberals' because that is what they call themselves and like being called. On one occasion, true, I called their operation with regard to me 'illiberal'; but that's a different matter, it's not personal, and it's patently true. Other, cruder terms would equally apply, but on the assumption that my readers possess an adequate vocabulary, I leave them unsaid.

As this book [*Cutting to the Point*] goes to press, *The Encyclopedia of Ireland* has appeared (General Editor Brian Lalor, publisher Gill and Macmillan). Apart from abundant information about Ireland and Irish persons from ancient times onwards, the *Encyclopedia* contains several hundred entries about persons who did something notable or something minor—usually in fictive writing or traditional music—during the past forty years. Unfortunately, in matters of thought, writing and politics, the selection of these contemporary entries reflects the liberal-revisionist ascendancy, including its intolerance of disagreement with it. That I am not mentioned goes without saying; but more interesting and instructive is the good company in which I find myself.

Two random examples of the selection pattern: Roy Foster is in, Joe Lee out; Fintan O'Toole is in, John Waters out. Succinctly put, all those are missing who have prominently pursued agendas which were at variance with the neoliberal-revisionist agenda—or who have notably opposed some facet of it. Further examples of the excluded are Raymond Crotty, Anthony Coughlan, Tom Barrington, William Binchy, Damien Kiberd, Ruairí Ó Brádaigh and John Robb. This general airbrushing of persons who have been notably in disaccord with the reigning ideology results in a picture of the Republic in the period 1965-2003 as a community of orthodox neoliberal believers, without intelligent or argued deviance. It is also, therefore, a serious misrepresentation of Irish intellectual history during this period.

❖

Daughter Sorcha works for the Irish Catholic humanitarian organisation Trócaire and was at this time on mission in Malawi with her Israeli husband, Ron, an irrigation expert whom she had met on her African travels, and their two children, Thal and Maya. In spring 2004 I flew from Rome to Lilongwe, capital of Malawi in southeast Africa, to visit them. It was my first visit to black Africa apart from a brief stop my cargo ship had made on the way to the Far East years previously. They were living in a fine bungalow on the outskirts of the city. On a drive with them to very big Lake Malawi we passed many men and women walking with bundles and baskets on their heads and many of their single-storey houses. Sorcha told me that before a man married he had to have three houses built for his wives. At Sunday Mass in Lilongwe I was charmed by the very African singing of a women's choir. One day I asked Sorcha (in Irish) how many aid organisations were working in Malawi which had a population of 11 million. 'Na céadta (hundreds),' she answered. Astonished, I said, 'Well, you mean eighty or a hundred.' 'No, Daidí, na céadta,' she repeated. I paused, thought of Irish history and said, 'But that prevents the Malawians from having their own history.' She replied simply, 'They're in need of many things we can give them, so we give them that.' That notion of excessive well-meant 'aid' from Europe depriving nations of making their own histories remained with me.

In June 2004 I returned to Ireland for the celebration of my 75ᵗʰ birthday organised by Natasha (who was finishing four years as chief fund-raiser for Fianna Fáil) in Zetland Hotel, Conamara. I met again some friends from Maoinis and Galway and fellow activists from the 'revolutionary' days in South Conamara: Máirín a' tSiopa, Nollaig Ó Gadhra, Seosamh Ó Cuaig, Pat Sheeran, Brian Arkins. Miriam had not been invited; aggrieved, she sent a big bunch of flowers from Malahide. Cilian, after occupying top jobs in the Irish-language TV channel TG4 and RTÉ's

'Late Late Show', was now a freelance TV producer. Oisín, after spending a couple of years as set constructor for Roger Corman Films in Conamara, had returned to building construction as project manager, first in Galway, then in Dublin and Liverpool.

From Conamara I went to Maynooth, stayed briefly with Sorcha and then rented a flat in Parson's Court. Miriam joined me there. I had the intention of 'giving Ireland a try' for employment, academic or journalistic. I was working on an essay, 'About Behaving Normally in Abnormal Circumstances'. Finished, I sent it to the French journal Études Irlandaises where it was published a couple of months later. (It would appear again in 2007 in an Athol book that bore that same title.)

That Christmas, Miriam and I went again to the Dolomites and after a brief stay in Anguillara I followed her back to Maynooth. I stayed there until February 2005 when, having found no employment that might induce me to stay longer, I returned to Anguillara. I had enjoyed Maynooth and meeting old friends there and in Dublin. I would remember walks on the canal bank with old friend Mary Cullen and with Mel (as I had taken to calling Miriam). And I had witnessed a long correspondence in The Irish Times about the Irish lack of business enterprise, to which I contributed a short letter adding lack of intellectual enterprise to the complaint.

2005

THE ENEMY NOW IS SENSELESSNESS*

IN AN ARTICLE in The Irish Times, 'Lost values in a land of riches' (31 January), Carol Coulter raised a matter of the first importance. She pointed out what needed to happen in Ireland, but did not happen, during the years when 'the authority of the Catholic Church and of other centres of traditional authority' was lessening. 'What we failed to do,' she wrote, 'was to develop instead any new unifying sense of citizenship and social solidarity that transcended religious adherence.' And later, arguing that what had not been done then could still be done, Ms Coulter stated: 'What we need to do now is

* From The Furrow, Maynooth, May 2005.

start a discussion on what values can be shared by all citizens, whatever their religious or non-religious beliefs, what responsibilities we owe to each other as fellow-citizens, what restraints society should impose on personal and corporate behaviour, and what values we should impart to our children.'

What I understand Ms Coulter to be saying is something like this. Up to the end of the 1960s in Ireland, we had a set of values, behavioural rules and habits, which were subscribed to by the rulers and the citizens, and which furthered social solidarity. These have since been largely, not entirely, replaced in the public teaching and in practice by a new, hybrid collection of values, rules and norms. Because this new formula for living is a haphazard combination of some old and much new, it is a chaotic mess. Offending reason by its incoherence and lack of hierarchy, and equity by its random injustices, it does not make for contented lives or social solidarity and well-guided children, it is urgently necessary to impose on this chaos some rational and ethical order.

To my mind, the most serious aspect of the matter is this. The old formula for living, because it was the well-weathered product of an ancient civilisation—Western civilisation in its modern Irish adaptation—made sense for those who lived by it. The new formula, because it is new and thrown together pell-mell to further consumption of goods and sex, does not. The fact that some of its values and rules, apart from serving consumerism, have noble ethical intentions, does not alter this. Good intentions do not suffice for sense.

Current theorizing about why growing numbers of our young people have taken to suicide, binge-drinking and drugs misses this simple insight: all three are ways by which sensitive youths, confronted by a life that appears senseless, opt out. Sense perceived in life is the human spirit's bread.

As I see it, then, what Ms Coulter is calling for is a hierarchical ordering of our new collection of values, interpersonal rules and capricious economic and political practices into an amalgam which is generally subscribed to by rulers and citizens because it makes sense to them collectively. Essentially, that is what a civilisation is; so she is talking about a new civilisation. That its principles must be largely acceptable to people 'whatever their religious or non-religious be-

liefs' follows from the fact that the new values and rules have rejected Christian values and morality as their inspiration or guide.
A new, ordered formula for living must therefore be grounded on
non-religious principles, and be such as religious and non-religious
rulers and citizens would subscribe to as a sensible and moral, even
if imperfect, whole.

As steps towards achieving this recivilizing formula, Ms Coulter
proposes, first, that the need for it be recognized; second, that a public discussion begin about the matters on which agreement must be
reached. She lists some of these in the passage that I have quoted.
Clearly, as with all discussions of broad scope, it would help if some
bold persons presented drafts for the sought-after comprehensive
formula or even for one of the themes which Coulter mentions:
'what responsibilities we owe to each other as fellow-citizens' or
'what restraints society should impose on personal and corporate
behaviour'.

In such work, Christian citizens, judging what good principles
might be feasible and what not, would bring their contributions
to the common good. They would contribute much as did early
Christians serving on imperial advisory committees in the pagan
Roman empire. They might even, given their Christian respect for
natural reason and just order, lead.

Is there any chance such a discussion will take place? Will our
philosophers, theologians and academics rise to it? When you propose an idea like this in Ireland, the usual response is a silence which
means 'that idea has not arrived from London or New York labelled
'OK to discuss!' Obviously, London, New York and the whole western world are involved in this matter. The 'post-western' chaos of values, rules and capricious practices which obtains in Ireland obtains
there too. But that is no valid reason for not starting to draft and discuss, for our part, what well-ordered formula for living might bring
the senseless chaos to an end.

Afterthoughts 2007: I wrote that Ms Coulter wants an amalgam
of values and rules 'generally subscribed to by rulers and citizens
because it makes sense to them collectively' and added 'Essentially,
that is what a civilisation is; so she is talking about a new civilisation'.
I think I have hit there on the core of the matter. Repeatedly in the

course of history a people has created for itself a life framework—a view of reality and a derived set of values and rules that made sense to them; satisfied rationally and intuitively the needs of their being. And that community was thenceforth what we call a civilisation. Consider the civilisations in history, one after another.

People need sense in life as much as they need food, and just as they are capable of finding or making food they are capable collectively of creating a life framework—a system of values and rules derived from a vision of reality that as a whole makes sense to them. And because the capability to create such a sense-making life framework is inherent in people collectively that is the *normal* way for human beings to live; and to live experiencing life as senseless, as people under the neoliberal regime must do, consciously or subconsciously, is to live in abnormal circumstances, as a paralysed man must also do and as I have been doing since the 1970s or since post-Hiroshima.

EUROPE DYING FOR LACK OF LOVE*

WHAT WE HAVE got used to calling 'Europe', meaning the European Union, is in trouble because, unloved by its citizens, it faces an America, a Japan, and a China, which are bonded and dynamised by love. Put differently, this 'Europe', lacking the unifying and dynamising force of a patriotism, is faced by powerful nations which possess that in good measure. To say this is to place 'Europe', with respect to patriotism, in a global geopolitical context.

But even ignoring that context, and viewing this 'Europe' simply as a human collectivity led by national elites and governed by a bureaucratic elite in Brussels, it is approaching ghostliness because the many millions who compose it do not love it.

There is, indeed, a Europe that is loved by many Europeans, but it is Museum-Europe: the Europe inherited from the European nations, collectively, that is visible audible or otherwise perceptible in its art, architecture, music and literature, its beautiful cities, its diversity of languages and customs, its lovingly tilled countrysides, its remembered great men and women, its variety of landscapes, house-styles and cuisines. But the love that exists for that inherited

* *Magill,* Dublin, Summer 2005; the journal *2000* (Rome), June 2006.

Europe does not extend to or connect with the 'Europe' of now: the institutionally and administratively united Europe that has been engineered during the past half-century, in the wake of World War. II

True, this engineered Europe is appreciated in various degrees and ways. In a gamut ranging from politicians and bureaucrats pursuing their careers to migrant workers, farmers, travellers spending money, and ideologues who are pleased by some of its decrees, this construct called Europe is judged advantageous or good. But that falls far short of the patriotic love which evokes, in citizens, disinterested desires to contribute to the collective wellbeing, preeminence or power, and willingness to suffer for the common good.

It was such love, a prideful and grateful love, directed from inside them towards individual European nations, which made the Europe of history—as it makes America now—leader and mistress of the world. Within each of the leading nations, a collective self-image constructed out of values which were held to define and to distinguish that nation, induced that dynamising love. (In recent years, under Putin's skilful guidance, we can see such construction under way in the Russia that is emerging from the wreck of the Soviet Union.)

Because in that historic Europe the arenas in which this image of construction, and consequent patriotism, occurred were nation-states; it was called nationalism. It was the European nationalisms, singly, together, and in emulating rivalry, that made Europe, until the middle of the last century, the world's main centre both of creativity and cultural radiation, and of economic, military and economic power.

Inasmuch as the united Europe that has been created in this last half-century sought concordant unity in place of competing or warring plurality, it was a negation of that historic Europe. It was for Europeans a novel, unaccustomed phenomenon. It was novel, too, inasmuch as, under American urging, it substituted for Europe's home-grown and basically Christian values and rules of interpersonal behaviour a new collection of post-European rules. It was therefore a case crying out for the classic operation by which a new human collectivity is welded into an emotionally bonded, creative and powerful community. But this work, namely, the construction and diffusion of a value-encrusted image of present-day Europe that would distinguish it, positively, in the eyes of its citizens, from all other world communities, was not done. (In the popular imagination the resulting vacuum was filled by the image 'Brussels', which has induced, much more commonly than any positive sentiment, emotions of hostility and contempt.)

I am not, as people often are when they write in this vein, arguing towards a recommendation or advice. I am merely, I hope, throwing some explanatory light on psychological factors which are impeding this new Europe in its bid to become, like the old Europe, a cultural force in the world. It is better to know how things stand than not to know.

On the face of it, it would seem likely that if people don't esteem or love a collectivity they belong to—in this case, the European Union—they will not esteem, let alone love, the life it presents: what we might call 'the surrounding set of circumstances' as viewed by them individually. And it is indeed the case that in this new Europe people take a poor view of the life they are involved in. Assessing it as to quality, they perceive, not stability or improvement, but deterioration.

By chance, I happened recently on concrete evidence of this in the Irish and British segment of the European Union. Returning to Ireland from Italy, where I live, I spent some hours of a weekend updating myself with a few Irish and a couple of British newspapers and magazines. Reading casually, but with attention, I gradually saw emerging a pattern of dislike of the surrounding circumstances or life.

A review of a carelessly researched and edited book ended as follows (I insert italics): 'This book tells us many things. But most of all it explains why *modern publishing is in such disarray.*'

A review of another book—on the collapse of the Irish Press group—ended: 'For anyone with a passing interest in the media and *how they came to be in the state they are today*, this book offers an entertaining dissection.' The italics, in both cases, indicate what struck me after I had read the two passages and begun to see the trend. Turning to a heading 'A society that's caring less', I read: 'The shocking scenes of neglect of the elderly in Lea Cross are signs of a wider problem in Irish society, where people are just too busy to look after each other. Children spend hours in childcare; teenagers are left to run rampant in private estates.' Evidently the writer saw those three negative social features as new phenomena, deteriorations from a recent past.

A review of current television programmes offered: 'Thanks to a judge who took time to watch a video and was then willing to put his foot on the accelerator', because as a result 'we got to see something that is rare these days—an important television programme.' Rare these days as distinct from previously, was the implication.

In a British newspaper a columnist was upset about manners. 'Good manners have become unfashionable. It's thought authoritarian to point out that someone's behaviour is bad, that there is a right and a wrong way to do things...In the last century we saw an explosion of personal freedom, which enriched our lives enormously. However, we have come to value individual freedom far above the collective good. As a result, we are in danger of having no manners at all.' Again, a decline from a previous better state.

In a report on this year's Cannes Film Festival, I read that 'Cannes has become a tattered relic of what was once a great film festival'. And just then, RTÉ Radio, discussing Dublin twenty years from now, did a vox pop. To the question, 'What do you think Dublin will be like twenty years from now?' five or six Dubliners answered, in a variety of wordings, 'Much the same as now, I suppose, only worse.'

Nothing unusual for our times in any of those views. It was a representative sample of what you would find in other segments of united Europe, certainly in its older, western half. Notably, in the decades preceding the outbreak, of World War I—the period significantly entitled the Belle Epoque—all of Europe was in agreement that the quality of life was improving. The last time life was seen thus in Western Europe was the 1950s and 1960s, with Ireland adhering to the general view in the latter decade. (I was there, I know.) Interestingly, those samples I encountered in my read-around of the press indicate that, contrary to the publicly proclaimed theory, people's judgment of the quality of life is not significantly determined by the quantity of money—whether more of it or less—that is available to them or that is being spent on works around them. Ireland famously, but Britain also, is rich.

The fact that, in Europe now, we see the quality of the collective life as deteriorating points also to two other things. First, how complete has been the Union's failure to construct and diffuse an image of European life imbued with distinctive, positive value, and consequently lovable. Second, that in the European Union, in inevitable response to a life seen as qualitatively worsening, a pervasive depression of soul underlies all surface gratifications and excitements. (All too often, as we Irish know, it leads to suicide.)

The newspapers and magazines I read that weekend offered countless antidotes for this depression. All of these were things which, in sharp contrast to the falling quality of life, were purchaseable improvements on what had gone before them. A Sony camcorder which 'puts all previous camcorders in the shade'. The New Range Rover Sport—'the car you have dreamt of, but never had. Go beyond!' 'L'OREAL's contouring innovation. First tightening treatment for Legs, Bums, Tums in a cream!' Pleated blinds which 'added to your conservatory will transform your room into a stylish, year-round living space.' 'No more constipation worries, Feenix will produce a regular flow.' And so on.

All of them were desirable things, obtainable with money, which would improve the quality of your personal life, while the life around you deteriorated. So money plus these improving things were what you needed to feel better! Obviously, alleviation of the underlying depression is often not the primary motive for purchases of the improving things. But it is always, when the required money is present, an operative factor; now a minor, now a major one, according as personal perceptions of the declining quality of life in this or that part of the European Union remain constant, lighten somewhat, or darken more.

Do economists, commenting on the ups and downs of 'consumer spending' in the European Union, take this always present, if variable factor, depression, into account?

❖

Towards the end of 2005 at the request of Sture Ureland I became en-
gaged in writing a paper, 'The Linguistic Conquest of the North Atlantic
and Its Rebound', which I delivered in September 2006 in the Humboldt
University Berlin at the 7ᵗʰ International Symposium on Eurolinguistics
(published in 2010 in Studies in Eurolinguistics Vol 7 *edited by Sture*
for Logos Verlag Berlin).

In late December 2006 Miriam and I flew from Rome to Amman for
a ten-day tour of Syria and Jordan. In Amman airport we saw about 200
white-robed Muslim men on their way to the Haj pilgrimage in Mecca. In
Damascus we ate splendid food, visited the beautiful Ummayad Mosque
and the Mausoleum of Saladin, and saw the house where the prophet
Ananias met St Paul (then called Saul). Continuing northwards by bus
we visited Malloula, a town where Aramaic, the language of Jesus, has
continued to be spoken. Then on through desert to, on Christmas Day, the
magnificent remains of Palmyra—the temple of Baal, the Roman amphi-
theatre, etc. In the adjoining modern town it was difficult to find a church
but in the end we found a small one. On again to Aleppo and south
through Homs back to Damascus. And then on to Jordan with the ruins of
ancient Petra.

The tour finished at a resort on the Dead Sea where I attempted to
find out how dead it was. Having covered my body except my eyes in
Dead Sea mud available in pots on the rocky beach, I walked down the
sloping beach into the water, attempted to start a crawl, and by allowing
the hyper-salty water to get into my eyes with a consequent flailing about
caused a siren to sound. Pulled out of the water by a watchful beach at-
tendant, I was put under a shower.

I had used 2006, which would be my last year in Anguillara, to make
a long overdue visit to my old love, Germany, and to write essays both
about that and about several other matters, including a retrospective one,
which would appear the following year 2007 in a new Athol book: About
Behaving Normally in Abnormal Circumstances. *Several of these*
follow below.

2007

ABOUT BEHAVING NORMALLY IN
ABNORMAL CIRCUMSTANCES★

WHEN I HAD taken flight again abroad in the 1990s, various novelties had occurred in Ireland and there had been an important ideological change. In 1965 Dervla Murphy had published *Full Tilt* in which she told of a journey by bicycle through Afghanistan to India. Supported by English and American publishers, she had gone on to become an internationally known travel-writer. Between the early 1970s and the 1990s, the Irish self-image as an essentially Catholic-Gaelic nation, inheritor of a long freedom struggle, dissolved. No generally accepted national self-image replaced it. War raged in the North. The Republic, along with Britain, joined the European Community. The increasing wealth, which by the 1990s made the Republic a rich country, underpinned both a cultural metamorphosis and the neoliberal preaching that encouraged it. It also enabled the Irish mass media to have far-flung correspondents. The most eminent of these, Conor O'Clery, wrote several books—published in Ireland because his journalism had made him well known—about the places where he had been posted. Conor Cruise O'Brien wrote about his experiences in the Congo and another book about the history of Israel. Aidan Higgins wrote about his sojourn in South Africa. Bob Quinn, using film language, had stretched the notion of 'Ireland-related' to include Morocco and Tatarstan—thereby suggesting that it might be a boundless notion. Raymond Crotty began publishing, with difficulty, his theory of world history.

However, these changes and occasional novelties left the norm unchanged that had limited the range of Irish realist writing in the 1960s. Scrutiny of *Books Ireland* from its foundation in 1976 to the 90s makes this evident: the magazine publishes, with brief notices, an almost comprehensive list of new books by Irish authors.

While Irish academics and writers produced scores of books about Irish matters, past and present, travel did not become a recognised genre of 'Irish writing'. Explorations of foreign societies

★ From *About Behaving Normally in Abnormal Circumstances*, Athol Books, Belfast, 2007.. This essay is a continuation of the essay on page 15.

undertaken not as adjuncts to journalism but as personal initiatives, original depictions of the contemporary world or narratives of national histories other than Irish, did not appear. The fact that still in these thirty years, after all the centuries, no Irish academic or writer produced a book about England or its history—to go no further—speaks for itself.

As a result, I became once again, by acting normally, in an only somewhat diminished degree an Irish freak. In 1990 there was to be a general election in Communist East Germany which was likely to lead to the dissolution of that state and to German reunification. Familiar with West Germany, but not with the Communist East, I wanted to take this last opportunity to see it. So I went there and wrote a book, *Dreams of Oranges*, about my experience and the death of socialism (it appeared some years later, in 1996). By chance, in 1993, I was offered an opportunity to spend a month in an apartment in Minsk. Wanting to see what life was like in a large provincial Soviet city—the formal end of the Soviet Union would have made little difference—I went there and wrote *A Month in Minsk* (which remained unpublished).

But full flight into deviant realms began when, retired from my job in Rathmines College of Commerce, I took a holiday in the American state of Washington. Those six weeks and a subsequent fifteen-month stay in Seattle gave me a new vision of the contemporary USA and the contemporary West as a whole (the 'Ameropean' West as I chose to call it) and of the progressive 'modern' period since around 1500. I began to query the standard narrative of European history. There was a lack of coherence between the story of the West's progressive 'modern' period since around 1500 and its contemporary condition as I was perceiving this to be. Thus I moved reconstructively into territory—the history of Europe—not previously charted by an Irish mind.

At the outset of this retrospective I mentioned another recurrent feature of my writing which emerged in the 1960s: a deviation from the standard Irish nationalist view of things. It emerged when, after nine years spent mostly abroad, I began to focus my attention on Irish affairs. I had been observing the human condition in various nations, and the nations themselves as functioning entities. I had become familiar with both, and it was with that familiarity present in my mind that I addressed myself to my own nation.

I did not then have the considered understanding of the Irish nationalist self-image that I have since acquired. I regarded our nationalism simply as a 'movement' that we had inherited from the Revolution, a movement with 'two national aims'. These were proclaimed intentions to revive the Irish language and to bring about a politically united Ireland. Throughout the 1960s, I listened, intermittently, to the public discourse. Even in learned circles, I heard no discussion of man. In particular I listened to what was being said, and not said, about the nation and its history, and about the circumstances which the two national aims were meant to correct. The accounts of these matters which were being given differed from what I saw with my own eyes and knew to be the case.

Looking at the Irish, I saw human beings, but the language that referred to them either suggested they were non-human or, when reference to their humanity was relevant, suggested by silence that they lacked this quality; were merely 'Irish' beings. Two instances struck me forcefully. There was a constant suggestion and assumption that, while widespread abandonment of Christianity had occurred in many European nations, Irish Catholics were inhumanly immune to such change; Catholicism was part of the Irish nature. Had not St Patrick wrestled with the Archangel Michael on the summit of Croagh Patrick and, having won, received from him the promise that the Irish would always remain true to the Faith? And there was the matter of the Revolution.

Reading the writings of the leaders of the Revolution, I found abundant evidence that they saw their enterprise as having, like the American or French revolutions, a human as well as a national dimension.★ Man, during the revolutionary years, was present in Ireland! But the now current public discourse was treating the Revolution as a merely Irish struggle for merely Irish objectives, and its leaders merely as Irishmen, not also as the human beings and conscious humanists I knew they were.

Regarding the circumstances surrounding the 'national aims', there was a thicket of eccentric language use which hid the realities

★ See 'The Humanism of 1916', "The Humanism of 1916" on page 69.

from view. 'Language revival' and 'reunification' were responses to two circumstances which nationalism saw as disorders. These were the fact that, while the overwhelming majority of the descendants of the Gaels spoke English, the Gaelic-speaking communities—collectively the Gaeltacht—had been shrinking or had disappeared; and the fact that a fifth of Ireland existed as a separate unit under British rule. The public discourse regarding these disorders stated or implied as follows. [While not as much as one pub had changed from English to Irish speech], 'the language revival was progressing'! The Republic of Ireland had no language minority, only a religious minority, the Protestant one, which, as if to stress its uniqueness, was referred to as 'the Minority', with a capital M. The Gaeltacht, far from being a minority was the majority-in-waiting, the Real Ireland that temporarily English-speaking Ireland was on the way to becoming. The Gaeltacht, moreover, while it continued to shrink, was continually, by a succession of schemes, being 'saved'. And speaking of minorities, neither did Ireland contain a national minority; from shore to shore its inhabitants were Irish to a man. The close on a million people in the North who celebrated their historic victories over the Irish, honoured the Union Jack, sang 'God Save the Queen' and called themselves British, suffered, so the story went, from a false consciousness. When Britain departed, that would dissolve. True, they differed from the other Irish, the nationalists, with whom they shared the North, but only in a 'sectarian' way. By implication, they adhered to a Protestant 'sect', the nationalists to a Catholic 'sect', when in fact they were Britain-adhering Protestants of various kinds and Ireland-adhering Catholics. Working on the basis of such descriptions of the relevant circumstances, the Irish nation hoped to achieve its two national aims.

Clearly, I had to do with a nation that, in the description of itself and its circumstances, used unreal language: language that misrepresented the phenomena in question. It was here that the passage from Daniel Corkery that I have used as an epigraph for this essay came to help me [see page 15]. I read it in 1962 in *Synge and Anglo-Irish Literature*. The Irish Revolution, Corkery made me realise, had been, and in its continuation was still, an attempt to repair the damage done to the nation by making it once more a 'normal nation'. A state, language and culture of its own, and a self-sustaining economy, were elements of such normality. But Corkery added 'a normal state of mind' and indicated its 'establishment among us' as a main aim of the revolutionary process. That fitted what I had observed: the abnormal, reality-missing language that the nation was using to describe itself and its circumstances resulted from the abnormal state of mind—out of touch with reality—which it had inherited from its abnormal history.

It follows from all this that, when I took to writing about Irish affairs, two factors influenced what I wrote and how I wrote it. Nothing else being possible for me, I described the Irish and their affairs in the real and linguistically normal terms in which I saw them. But at the same time, I wanted, by so writing, to contribute to situating the nation in reality, so that it might possess reality and be strengthened by that. This was both an instinctive patriotism and, after reading Corkery, part of my adherence to the Revolution. The net result was that I took to challenging the prevailing ways of representing the Irish and their circumstances by representing both in real terms.

I started with 'the Irish'. 'Will the Irish Stay Christian?' I entitled an article for the Dominican journal *Doctrine and Life* in May 1962. It began:

> There is no reason to suppose that the Irish Catholic people will continue indefinitely to be believing Christians. In Europe during the last 150 years the majority of people have abandoned Christian belief and practice; there is no reason why the same should not happen here. Sweden is often cited as an extreme example of modern paganism. But eighty years ago it was the scene of impassioned public controversy about the nature of Christ's Redemption and the proper ordering of the Communion service; wide sections of the people believed these matters to be of urgent concern.

The subtext was clearly: The notion of Irish, and specifically Irish Catholic immutability, is a delusion. Irish Catholics are human and therefore mutable.

For *The Capuchin Annual* of 1964 I wrote an essay entitled 'The Failure of the Irish Revolution—and its Success'. As an epigraph I chose a line from Padraig Pearse's poem 'The Rebel': 'I that have a soul greater than the soul of my people's masters'. The first lines were as follows:

> As I understand it, the revolution which took place in Ireland forty odd years ago was an attempt on the part of the Irish Catholic people to gain material and spiritual conditions of life more favourable to their fulfilment as human beings…On the highest level of need and of aspiration, the revolution was a rejection of the twentieth-century English gentleman in favour of a prototype of higher humaneness which would be more magnanimous and more in accordance with the twentieth-century Irish (Catholic) mode of being. It was a rebellion of the Irish best against the alleged English best and the point at issue was *how to be human*.'

In that same year, in October, I had a long article in *Doctrine and Life* entitled 'What I Miss in Sermons'. The message this time was for the core of the Irish Catholic self-consciousness, the Catholic clergy. Targeting the prevalent notion that our priests and monks were a race apart from men, it began:

> What do I miss in sermons? First, *a man talking*. I know what it sounds like and feels like when a man talks—I have heard it happen on the radio, I have friends who talk to me as men talk, I have even heard priests who talked as men talk when they were addressing gatherings of their Christian brothers and sisters.

This article was much appreciated by the clergy. It came to be referred to as the article that says 'A sermon is a man talking' and was reprinted in an American magazine.

In 'Cuireadh chun na Tríú Réabhlóide' (Invitation to the Third Revolution, *Comhar*, Nollaig 1965), in 'Irish Catholics and Freedom since 1916' (*Doctrine and Life*, January-March, 1966), and in my long, unsigned articles on Irish matters in *Herder Correspondence*, 1964-8, I continued to treat the Irish Revolution and Irish ecclesiastical themes in their human dimension. In other words, I dealt with them as the thought and action of human beings, who happened to be Christians, involved in modern and Irish circumstances. While so doing, I hoped I might induce my readers to see themselves in such terms, thereby anchoring themselves in reality, achieving normality, and acquiring the power and effectiveness that would give them in tackling their circumstances. It was not an entirely altruistic hope: I wanted the company of human beings; and they are that, really, only when they know they are.

However, for the successful tackling of our circumstances, we would require real perception of these also. One such circumstance was the fact that we were inheritors of the Revolution. That this did not only mean commitment to completing it by achieving the two national aims—a common view—but also meant complet-ing it in the spiritual and intellectual spheres, had been the theme of 'Cuireadh chun na Tríú Réabhlóide'. Now, a few years later, in 1969, the 'national aims' themselves, or rather, the circumstances that motivated them, presented themselves sharply to my attention. First, arising from my move for personal reasons to Irish-speaking South Conamara, I found myself up against the fragile condition of the Irish language. Then, because the North erupted violently, I felt called on to respond to the Northern Ireland problem.

Although my reaction in both instances was instinctive, I can see now that there was logic in the form it took, as if it were extracted from some manual. First, the shock tactic: 'The Emperor has no clothes.' So with regard to the 'language revival':

> We are today much further away than seventy years ago from achieving the minimum aim of the revival movement. Not only has the Gaeltacht diminished drastically in area and population: it has shrunk also with regard to 'social spread'. Many trades and oc-cupations which were then represented within the Gaeltacht are no longer represented there.

On 21 January 1969 I wrote that in an article, 'Revival or Not?', in an *Irish Times* supplement commemorating the fiftieth anniver-sary of the First Dáil. And similarly, with regard to the Northern problem, under the title 'A Plea for Realism', I pointed out that because the Ulster Protestants said they were British, they were ac-cordingly that.

The immediate aim of such writing was the dissolution of the unrealities of perception that remained lodged in Irish nationalism.

But because of my sympathy with the underlying purpose of that nationalism—the Revolution's purpose—the ultimate result was not to discredit Irish nationalism but to reformulate it in real and realisable terms.

Of course, trying in one's writing to depict reality is nothing new. Even trying with one's writing to replace an unreal representation with real representation is nothing unusual. I have tried to do precisely that in my *The Revision of European History*. Such a book, moreover, is written in opposition to previous treatments of the subject, and those who disagree with it will oppose it in their turn. So one man's passion to depict the real is always to some degree combat, and capable of provoking combat.

Irish people of the chattering classes feel a need to label in party or ideological terms anyone who says anything publicly. Their hope is that by so doing they will know how to feel about him or her and whether or not they should attend to what he or she is saying. In the light of the account of my writing which I have given here, it is obvious why such people have found it very difficult to find a fitting tag for me. In the effort, they have used many tags which ended up being contradictory. My writing, while following a consistent course, has simply not displayed consistent adherence to any contemporary Irish party or ideological line.

What kind of man, in terms of mental slant, has my writing shown? On the one hand, a human being curious to know what being human means, and how things have been and are with mankind in the West; on the other, an Irishman working in the spirit of the Irish Revolution, so that his nation might, like a normal nation, realise its humanity in the dual sense of knowing it for a fact and being it; and as part of that, rationally identify its circumstances and live successfully in the light of them. I think 'a humanist' would be a reasonable description of such a man.

Heidegger in his essay *On Humanism* defines the term as 'taking thought and care that man live humanly, and not inhumanly'. Some, referring not to my slant on life but to my occupation, have called me a 'philosopher'. Plato in his *Euthydemus* suggests that the two terms are effectively synonymous. Philosophy, he says there, is 'the use of knowledge for the benefit of man'. Call that 'investigation, perception and writing for the benefit of man'. And what can be more for man's benefit than his restoration to being where he has been separated from his being? A humanistic or a philosophical enterprise? Both at once.

But are 'humanist' and 'philosopher' acceptable ways of defining oneself in contemporary Ireland?

HOW THE STORY OF EUROPE COULD BE BETTER TOLD*

IN THE SIXTY years before World War I, when Europe was dominating and leading the world, historians in France, Germany and England gave the history of Europe up to their own time its definitive shape. It was a time when Protestants and Progressives were conducting the affairs of Europe. What was to become the standard History of Europe up to World War I was written by such men and to satisfy such men. It was a mythical narrative which showed European mental, moral and material progress after the end of the 'MiddleAge' and the beginning of the 'Modern Age'. The 'Middle Age' was a time of darkness, superstition, cruelty, and oppression. The 'Modern Age', beginning with the Renaissance and continuing through the Reformation, England's Glorious Revolution, the Scientific Revolution, the Enlightenment or Age of Reason, the French Revolution, the Rights of Man, and the Industrial Revolution was an age of growing liberation of minds and persons and of moral improvement. During these centuries, through the agency of successive European elites, the Good of today repeatedly triumphed over the Evil of yesterday. Truer understanding of life repeatedly replaced inherited illusion; respect for human beings and kindness replaced inhuman practices; legal changes, science, new technology and increasing wealth increased human power and made Europe leader, ruler and civiliser of the world.

This was what Herbert Butterfield, writing from an English perspective before World War II, called 'the Whig interpretation of history'. Clearly, the History of Europe told in this manner was a myth which, on the one hand, showed the Protestant and Progres-

---

* From *About Behaving etc.*, 2007.

sive elites as the culmination of European progress and, on the other, justified European imperialism. Adapting a phrase coined by Mao Tse-Tung, we might call this the Great Leaps Forward version of European history.

The Progressives who unified Italy after 1860 made it the history taught in Italian schools. (It contradicted in various respects Italy's previous understanding of its history, but the Italian Progressives wanted to unite Italian history with European.) In all European languages this Protestant-Progressive history entered the encyclopedias and the dictionaries and has remained there to this day. We find it reflected in everyday journalism: contemporary instances of cruelty or ignorance or backwardness are described as relapses to the 'Middle Ages'; 'modern' means good, enlightened, civilised, of benefit to man.

However, in the real world, World War I took place. To the historians of Europe who came after it, it looked like madness and enormous cruelty and the opposite of civilisation and reason. Then as they were adding it awkwardly to the standard history of Europe, Fascism and Nazism appeared and there was World War II. America, the most powerful part of Europe Overseas, became the determining force in European history. In theory, the Americans were the heirs *par excellence* of all that progress in true understanding, human rights and humane behaviour that had characterised the West for centuries. What were the historians of Europe to do? They were faced with the most murderous century in human history; and for the greater part it was the work of Europeans at home or of their descendants or relatives in America. How could they relate this to the story of the Great Leaps Forward?

They did so by suggesting that in the twentieth century it was discovered that the great advances of Good in European history had not entirely eliminated Evil. Evil had appeared again in great strength. But happily, in the two great wars of the century those Europeans, at home or overseas, who had profited morally by the previous great advances were victorious over Europeans who had not. Even the massacres of the century were divided between Good and Evil: Auschwitz and Belsen were evil, Hiroshima and Nagasaki were good. So the standard history was saved; Good was still triumphant.

With some irony, the English historian of Europe, Norman Davies, calls this 'The Allied Scheme of History'.

A true clear history that makes sense

The minimum we require when we read the history of a people or a civilisation—say, Egypt, Rome or Persia, China or Japan—is a story that is true and clear and that makes sense. Making sense is particularly important when it is a matter of the history of our own nation or our own civilisation. Sense then means that the story has an intelligible beginning and an intelligible development and that, when it approaches our own days, it accords with and explains why things are now as they are.

I intend to criticise the standard history of Europe and to suggest a manner of telling it which would possess those missing qualities. My purpose in so doing is not to urge change in how the story is told in the schoolbooks and the reference works, for such change is impossible. Since the nineteenth century many books by reputable historians have corrected and revised every period of the standard history, beginning with its ignorant caricature of the Middle Age. These studies have affected the teaching of every period of European history in the universities. But all that mass of piecemeal revision, and all that revised teaching in universities, has not resulted in the story as a whole being effectively changed.

The standard story, even including the two World Wars, has an attractive structure. It is entrenched in the encyclopedias and dictionaries, many publishing programmes depend on it, academic careers have been built on it, it is deeply entwined with the collective psychology and dominant ideology of the West. For all these reasons it will not be significantly changed. Only when European history comes to be written independently by Indian or Chinese historians will it be told in the normal, factual way in which history is usually told; for example, as we tell Chinese or Roman history.

So my purpose in sketching a better way of telling the history of Europe is very limited. It is the same modest purpose I had in mind when I spent two years writing a little book on the subject, *The Revision of European History*, published by Athol Books, Belfast, in 2003. That purpose is stated on the book's cover: 'to enable readers of the standard history wherever encountered to note the main distortions and make appropriate mental corrections'. My recommendations for a revised narrative are merely a means of providing the required criteria.

The 'Modern' Age

I begin with the absurdity at the end of the standard story. It does not make sense that Europeans from around 1500 became progressively wiser and morally better and then, after 1914, produced the most murderous century in human history. This can be remedied by doing two things. First, remove 'modern' as the description of this second age of Europe. The word has come to connote an indiscriminate moral approval. Second, narrate the history of Europe's second age on the basis only of the available evidence. There is sufficient evidence for the political, social and economic history of these centuries. There is no evidence that between 1500 and 1914 Europeans, or more precisely their elites, became morally better persons or improved their overall understanding of reality; in that regard there is evidence only that their knowledge of physical and mental reality advanced greatly.

Narrate, then, that, as in other evolving civilisations, a succession of worldviews were adopted by successive elites; that these included modifications of the prevailing ethical system; and that as a result of this and other factors there were certain legal, political and social developments. Narrate in particular, as the feature most characteristic of these centuries, how Europeans, by means of physical science, legal provisions and technological advance, achieved a mastery of nature and of their political and personal lives and the world generally, unequalled by any previous civilisation. As for the twentieth century, narrate it mainly in terms of its central feature: the final struggle to determine which of the most powerful western powers—Britain, Germany or the United States of America—would emerge on top.

Here a further improvement suggests itself. Because America emerged on top, and since World War II has formed with Canada and Western Europe what we might call an 'Ameropean' entity, tell the history of Europe after 1492 so as to reflect the growth of this transatlantic relationship. Represent 1492 as the start of Europe's, so to speak, Magna Graecia—its 'Europe Overseas'—so that it is clear to Europeans that when their ancestors settled and became active in other continents, but especially in America, they remained Europeans—as the Greeks of Magna Graecia remained Greeks and the Phoenicians of Carthage Phoenicians.

When the general narrative of the second age has been reformed in this manner, there remain only some 'big words' to correct. For example, there was no such event in *European* history as 'the Reformation', even if we understand that as shorthand for 'the Protestant Reformation'. Stating that there was is like stating that there was in *European* history an event called 'Socialism'; but we pretend no such thing. Using the word 'Protestant' to signify European Christians who broke with Rome, the historical fact is that in the course of the sixteenth century, in a number of countries, Protestant *reformations of various kinds* occurred. It was much as would later happen in the course of the nineteenth century, when in several countries various socialisms emerged. The heterogeneous plural is less dramatic, less like a trumpet blast of Protestant propaganda, but it is the truth. The big European event of the sixteenth century was 'The Division of the Church'.

It is also bad history to speak of 'the Enlightenment' as a historical event. Actually, until the late 1800s, there was no word for it in Italian. Then, the Italian dictionaries tell us, *l'Illuminismo* was invented to translate the French 'century of lights'. The corresponding English word, 'Enlightenment', suggests, as a historical fact, a collective spiritual experience such as mystics and pious Buddhists achieve. First used in 1865, it was a tendentious rendering of the sober German *die Aufklärung*, which means literally 'the Clarification', but according to Kant's definition, the attainment by individuals of independent personal thinking, the content of such thinking being unspecified. As the variety of names and concepts suggests, there is no agreement as to what the phenomenon in question was. In a book called *The Enlightenment* by the Englishman Norman Hampson, published in 1968, the honest author states:

The attitudes which one chooses to regard as typical of the Enlightenment constitute a free, subjective choice…Within limits the Enlightenment was what one thinks it was.

And in 2000 another Englishman, Roy Porter, prefaces his book on the Enlightenment in Britain with that last sentence: 'Within limits the Enlightenment was what one thinks it was.'

Surely the best way to deal with the intellectual history of 1680–1789 is to banish 'the Enlightenment' and its equivalents and call the period only as it is sometimes called 'the Age of Reason'. That records, in clear terms, the historical fact that, during this period, Reason and the effort to think and act rationally were central preoccupations of European intellectuals and rulers. I will deal later with another empty 'big word' in the standard story, 'the Renaissance'.

Pre-Columbian and Columbian

The history of Europe, as a distinct civilisation, began around the year 1000. The last barbarian incursion from the East, that of the Magyars, had been defeated by the German emperor in 955 in the battle of the Lech. The Viking incursions were coming to an end. In western Europe the space was secure for what turned out to be a successful attempt to found a civilisation. The prelude to it, which amounted to a first attempt, is not to be found where the standard History of Europe suggests: four centuries previously in the aftermath of Roman power in the West. It occurred in the Frankish kingdom, later empire, between 750 and the death of Charlemagne in 814. It was after that first attempt had failed that the second, successful effort got under way around the year 1000.

It was located in France, parts of Germany and the Italian communes, with France in the lead. It followed a course similar to that by which all civilisations had been founded. The control of land and its productive use were so organised as to give a regular surplus of food which enabled the growth of cities, the construction of large buildings and the development of trade. Rules were laid down for everything from clerical behaviour, warfare and reasoning to markets and the game of sexual love. Law was clarified and backed by the armed force of the rulers; justice was administered in the rulers' courts. The training of an intellectual elite was provided for, first in cathedral schools, then in the first universities, a European invention. Nourished by its inheritance from the Graeco-Roman past, the contemporary Arab civilisation and, centrally, by Christian theology and philosophy, a vigorous European intellectual life emerged. With the new security and growing wealth, the arts found a space in which to flourish: by the late twelfth century in France and Germany, and the late thirteenth in Italy.

Uniquely and absurdly among the civilisations of world history, this first age of Europe is called in the history books 'the Middle Age'. Myth is at work here too; in this case a myth created in the fifteenth century by Italian literati for their own chauvinistic purposes. Their intention was to designate as a mere in-between age, culturally speaking, all those centuries between the end of Great Rome and the Italy of their own time. Not until two centuries later was 'Middle Age' adopted by northern historians and literati as the name of a period in European history generally. In countless books since the nineteenth century, beginning with Ranke, who wrote 'The Middle Age has no reality whatsoever', historians have decried this term as historically useless while continuing to use it. No carpenter would do likewise with a bad tool.

Given that there is a fair amount of agreement that this first age of Europe ended around 1492 with the discovery of America by Columbus, we could aptly call it the Pre-Columbian Age. Since 'Pre-Columbian' is a term used by American historians for American history, that would fit well with what I have said above about the usefulness of coordinating the writing of European and American history from around 1500 to the present day. The second age of Europe, which we have freed from its tendentious 'modern' tag, could then be called appropriately the Columbian Age. Together, 'Pre-Columbian' and 'Columbian' would leave historians free to narrate the history of these ten European centuries freshly, without the straitjacket of forced conformity to a seventeenth-century myth that makes no sense for us.

The so-called Rebirth

The only important remaining obstacle to truth, clarity and sense is the so-called 'Renaissance', which the standard history represents as an abrupt discontinuity between the first age of Europe and the second. It is represented as occurring in Italy and, in an extended sense, throughout Europe, mainly in the years 1450–1550 although some place its start earlier. The Italians themselves first put *il Rinascimento* into their history books only in the 1860–70s. They called it the *Rinascimento* (Rebirth) to distinguish it verbally from *la rinascita delle arti e delle lettere* (the rebirth of arts and letters), the designation they had traditionally and accurately used for the cultural history of Italy *from 1250 onwards*. They now inserted *il Rinascimento* into their history because two Liberal-Progressive gentlemen, the Frenchman, Michelet and the Swiss, Burckhardt, had written books which proclaimed that in 1450–1550 a momentous Rebirth had occurred in Italy, and those books had acquired great fame in northern Europe.

Michelet was the first to use the term *la Renaissance* as an absolute, without adding the traditional qualification 'of letters' or 'of learning'. That had referred specifically to Classical studies, understood as letters and learning *par excellence*. *La Renaissance*, Michelet wrote, was 'the emergence of certainty and life, the discovery of man and the world'. Burckhardt made it also the birth of Modern Man, that is, of men like himself and Michelet and their acquaintances. The root of this fantasising can be found in the principal compilation of so-called 'Enlightenment' wisdom, the *Encyclopédie*, published in 1751; more precisely, in its introductory essay written by d'Alembert. There, referring to the fall of Constantinople in 1453 and the migration of Greek scholars to Italy, d'Alembert wrote the following piece of ignorant pseudo-history, using the historical present:

> The Greek empire is destroyed: its ruin sends coursing again into Europe *that little sum of knowledge that still remained in the world*. The invention of printing, the protection of the Medici and of Francis I, *reanimates minds; and light is reborn everywhere.*' *[Italics mine.]*

Obviously, if you believed that—and the 'century of lights' said so!—it was easy to believe and to write anything about the period 1450–1550 in Italy. A fairly accurate description of it would be 'The Recalling of Ancient Rome'.

I conclude with a summary of what really happened in Italy and Europe in those years. In the mid-1400s in Italy, after more

---

THE NEW HISTORY OF EUROPE

Ancient Rome	AGE OF TRANSITION	EUROPE (Western Civilisation)	*Post-European Postwestern Condition*
	284 Diocletian	955 Battle of the Lech	1945 Approval of Atomic Massacre	*New American Empire*

| | Late Antiquity /Prelude to Europe 751 Carolingian Monarchy | Pre-Columbian Age /Columbian Age 1492 Discovery of America Start of Europe Overseas | |

---

than two centuries of high culture second only to that of France, a period of exceptional and sustained creativity began. It was not a Rebirth or an interruption of any kind, but a splendid culmination of the Italian culture of those previous centuries. In part it was inspired by a greatly increased investigation of the Romano-Greek heritage and a corresponding celebration of it. Other high creative periods had already begun in Flanders and Portugal, and now, too, from mid-century, technical innovation and painting flourished in Germany. The Flemish, Italian and German movements exerted influence throughout Europe; but, except in technology, the Italian movement—which remember, included the oceanic voyages of Colombus, Vespucci and the two Caboti—had by far the greatest impact, so as to give Italy a cultural primacy in Europe. All four waves of innovation continued into the 1500s, with the Flemish one much reduced, the German strong to the 1530s, the Italian powerful to mid-century and continuing with somewhat diminished strength into the 1600s.

All these high creative periods were culminations in their various ways of the culture of Europe's Pre-Columbian Age. But they were also modifications of that culture. In the course of them—and here the Spanish explorations in America worked together with them—the second age of Europe began. The principal common characteristic which the high creative movements and the Spanish expansion exhibited was a greatly intensified desire to explore, to the ultimate, human earthly possibility and to master the world in all its aspects. That impulse, the roots of which lay in Europe's first age, was to become the most notable characteristic of its second or Columbian age, which ended as the Second American Revolution was relegating European civilisation to the past.

THE HEART OF GERMANY?★

IN FRANKFURT, I boarded an inter-city train headed for Leipzig, which two-and-a-half hours later deposited me in Weimar. It had been a journey through sunlit countryside, past villages and medium-sized towns. Weimar itself could be so described, but low on the scale; its population recently reached 64,000. Over the years I had seen much of Germany but never this town in Thuringia which, apart from having given its name to an unfortunate Republic, has been regarded since Goethe's and Schiller's time as the cultural heart of Germany. One reason I had missed it hitherto was that it was situated, with the rest of Thüringen—'Thuringia', too Latinate, misses the flavour—in the now defunct Communist state, the German Democratic Republic. From the station a bus took me two stops to the Goetheplatz which extends in front of the imposing Post Office. The inn I was to stay in for five nights was nearby. In the entrance a blackboard advertised 'Food as in Goethe's time. Four courses based on original recipes, Euro 18.'

Next morning, heading for the Marktplatz where a guided tour was to begin, I passed from the Goetheplatz to the Theaterplatz. There, on the right, on a high pedestal, were the twin statues of Goethe and Schiller; the former looking steadfastly forward and holding a laurel wreath, the latter gazing skywards with a hand reaching towards the wreath. (Later, I was told that in Weimar they say he is

★ From *About Behaving etc.*, 2007.

trying to grab it!) Behind them was the neoclassical Nationaltheater, where in 1919 the Constituent Assembly, removed from the street violence of Berlin, drafted the Weimar Constitution. On the left, the Bauhaus Museum reminded me that in that same year Walther Gropius, Kandinsky, Paul Klee, Moholy-Nagy and others launched a school here that revolutionised architecture and design. The town is mainly buildings of two to four storeys with steep roofs often marked by dormers, and facades in a harmonious variety of colours; basically an eighteenth-century princely *Residenz* town where nothing from the succeeding centuries obtrudes by modernity and the Industrial Revolution never happened. On the broad, tree-lined Schillerstrasse—the trees still bare in the days before Easter—a shop offers packets of 'Flower seeds from Goethe's garden'.

Our guide on the Marktplatz is a tall elderly man with chiselled features and a thick mop of white hair trimmed to the shape of an upturned bowl. He wears a black coat almost to his ankles. In the old times of which he begins to speak to us, Weimar was the Residenz town of the Dukes of Saxony-Weimar. The Duchy was one of the roughly three hundred large and small states—it belonged to the latter category—which made up Germany until Napoleonic times. The market square on which we stood was the centre of the old town. In the last months of World War II, American air raids had destroyed some of its buildings; our guide pointed out the parts of the square that had been rebuilt.

Outstanding because of its green and white Renaissance facade was the Cranachhaus, where the painter, Lucas Cranach the Elder, had spent the last year of his life. He owned a large workshop for painters, woodcut-makers and printers in Wittenberg, capital city of the German Reformation. He had been a staunch supporter of Luther and an effective propagandist for the new faith. Here in Weimar, in 1552, our guide informed us, he had begun a great painting of the Crucifixion (his son had finished it) which was an important representation of the doctrine of salvation by faith alone. In the group around the Cross, the Virgin Mary was absent, John the Baptist stood alongside Cranach and Luther. We could see it, Herr Nitsche told us—he wore a badge showing his name—in the Herderkirche or Town Church, which was also called St Peter's and Paul's.

The Herderkirche? I knew that, during the Goethe period, the philosopher Johann Gottfried Herder from distant East Prussia had spent some time in Weimar. I now learned that he had been senior pastor here for twenty-seven years. And there, on the Markt, beside The Black Bear, the oldest tavern, was the Hotel Elephant, where Hitler and other Nazi greats had liked to stay. Indeed, during his rise to power, Hitler made it and Weimar into a sort of headquarters for central Germany. He addressed crowds from the hotel balcony.

We moved to the nearby area of the palaces. At some distance was the great *schloss*, the *Residenz* itself, a massive, square four-storey building surrounding a courtyard, rebuilt and extended after a destructive fire in 1774. Nearer us, in various colours, were other lesser palaces and the lovely Anna Amalia Library building, damaged by a fire in September 2004 with the loss of many precious books. But they were only, Herr Nitsche said, a small part of the more than a million volumes which were stored in the main underground library, beneath our feet.

A park sloped down to the River Ilm. Continuing on the high ground we came in sight of Goethe's 'garden house' among trees on the other side of the park. It was the first place he had lived after his arrival in Weimar in 1775, twenty-six years old and author of the European best-seller, *The Sufferings of Young Werther*. We had passed Charlotte Stein's house, the seven-years-older married woman whom he loved, platonically it seems, until he tired, partly of her, partly of his government work in Weimar, and went to Italy for two years. Herr Nitsche, pointing out a bridge across the river, told us that, after Goethe returned, when he was out walking one day he had met a girl there. She was carrying a letter from her brother asking for employment by the ducal government. Her name was Christiane Vulpius and she was to become Goethe's housekeeper and mistress for nearly twenty years until, after she had borne him four children, he married her in 1806.

Turning away then from the river, our walk brought us uphill through the park and past Franz Liszt's house to the Old Cemetery where Goethe and Schiller lie buried in the temple-like burial chamber of the dukes. Returned to the town, we passed Goethe's big town house on the Frauenplan, Schiller's house on the Schillerstrasse and Anna Amalia's baroque 'widow palace' at the top of that broad street. Herr Nitsche left us on the Theaterplatz beneath the twin statues. For that evening, the Nationaltheater was offering a silent Fritz Lange film with orchestral accompaniment. From a corner of the square came the upsettingly sweet music of a barrel-organ, its grinder adding suitable percussion. On the Goetheplatz, on a squat round tower remaining from the old town walls and converted into a student club, I read, bilingually, 'Happy Easter celebrations—four floors, one event. *Oster*bunnys *und Gewinnspiel* inn.'

I was left to delve deeper on my own. I had discovered that Weimar was much more than I had bargained for, not just the town made famous by Goethe and Schiller, but a sort of central repository of German cultural history around that time. Herr Nitsche, when we were standing among the palace buildings, had told us about the nine years which Johann Sebastian Bach spent in the employment of Duke Wilhelm Ernst, from 1708 to 1717. Bach, whose aim in life was to make 'regular church music for the honour of God', fitted well with the devoutly Lutheran duke. When he came to Weimar, as court organist, he was twenty-three, and it was during the Weimar years that he became known throughout Germany, even if still in the shadow of Philipp Telemann. But he had a large family— six children, of whom four survived, were born in Weimar—with corresponding expenses, and was disappointed that Wilhelm Ernst would not promote him to *Kapellmeister* (orchestra director). Secretly he negotiated better financial terms and status with a neighbouring prince. His own duke, on discovering this, put Bach in jail in an attempt to bring him to heel, but after a month, having failed to move him, let him go 'with dishonour'.

I bought some tourist leaflets and, in Hoffmann's bookshop, 'founded 1710', an excellent book by Peter Merserburger, *Mythos Weimar* (*The Myth of Weimar: Between Spirit and Power*). They helped to light my way. Duchess Anna Amalia is in a sense the spiritual mother of the town, inasmuch as she founded its classical period. Daughter of the Duke of Brunswick and niece of Frederick the Great of Prussia, in 1755, aged sixteen, she married the eighteen-year-old heir of Weimar, Ernst August II, Constantin. Because he was a consumptive and likely to die soon, her dynastic task was clear.

Within a year she had fulfilled it by giving birth to Carl August. A year later, after the death of her frail husband, she had a second son. Then, successfully resisting all those who tried to impede it, she prevailed on the imperial government of the Reich in distant Vienna to declare her regent of the duchy and guardian of Carl August until he would come of age.

A firm ruler who led Weimar adroitly through the Seven Years' War, she was also a sprightly and highly educated young woman— she read Latin and Greek and spoke French. She set out to raise Weimar culturally to something like the richness she had grown up with in Brunswick. She promoted music and theatre and founded the public library that still bears her name. At the same time, taking special care with the education of Carl August, the duke-to-be, when he reached fifteen she hired Christoph Martin Wieland as his chief tutor. Wieland, a Francophile and sexy writer, influenced by Enlightenment ideas, was a senior figure in the revival of German literature that was under way. With his arrival, the emergence of what the Germans call 'classical Weimar' began.

Wieland published a monthly *Der Teutsche Merkur* which became, during the following decades, the definer of taste and merit in literature and in culture generally. He persuaded Anna Amalia to employ Karl Ludwig von Knebel as tutor for her younger son, Constantin. Von Knebel put Carl August in touch with Goethe, and the young duke, now in command, invited him to Weimar. He was to be based there for fifty years. Goethe, in turn, won Carl August's consent to appointing Herder as Lutheran Superintendent of the Duchy. It was this concentration of literature and intellect in Weimar which later brought Schiller looking for employment, with the result that he was appointed professor of history in the Duchy's University in nearby Jena.

What is reckoned as the climax of this 'classical' period began in the 1790s when Goethe and Schiller became friends and collaborators; it continued until Schiller's death in 1805. Duke Carl August was a loyal patron to his distinguished flock and he guided his state adroitly through the Napoleonic upheavals. Anna Amalia made her 'widow's palace' a centre of literary, learned and musical sociability spiced with fun. During this period the town of Weimar, sometimes referred to as *Athen-Ilm*, 'Athens on the Ilm', had a population of about six thousand. Yes, six thousand.

I was struck by the following sentence in Merseburger's book: 'In terms of cultural history, those three places, Wartburg, Weimar and Jena, must be seen as a triad standing for Protestantism, German philosophy and the highpoint of German literature; a literature which begins, historically, with Luther's Bible translation in the Wartburg'. The three places mentioned were all in the Duchy of Weimar as consolidated in the 1700s.

The Wartburg is the castle on a hilltop where Frederick the Wise, Elector of Saxony, provided refuge for Luther when the Emperor Charles V declared him an outlaw. While there, Luther translated the New Testament into German. Weimar and the rest of Thüringen were as early and staunchly Protestant as they were later to become early and staunchly Nazi. Luther had often preached from the pulpit of that same Town Church where Herder would later be pastor.

As for Jena, its university heard the first lectures on Kant, and in the 1790s Fichte, Schelling and Hegel taught there. I decided that, to see Weimar in its historical context, I would visit the Wartburg and Jena. The Wartburg meant going to Eisenach, the town beside it, back along the line to Frankfurt.

Early next morning, it was Good Friday, while waiting on the Goetheplatz for a bus to the station, I watched seven or eight uniformed men and women gathering in a group, the post horn of the Bundespost depicted on their backs. Each of them was grasping a trolley that carried two or three fat mailbags. As I watched, they dispersed in different directions, bearers of news. Among the wooden signs indicating the destinations of the buses, one said Buchenwald, the name of the concentration camp that had been situated near the town. My bus was punctual to the minute indicated in the timetable displayed at the stop.

A regional train brought me to Eisenach, which as it happens is Bach's birthplace. The landscape we passed through was misty; in the small towns there were some abandoned factories; a sign, I assumed, of the necessarily harsh restructuring of the East German economy which took place after Communism. On bus No. 10, I headed for the Wartburg, and already, as we moved away from the town centre, saw it skywards in the mist which formed a wraith on a high hill.

The bus leaves you at the start of a steep climb up steps of red sandstone. Many cars were parked nearby and a long line of people was mounting the steps. A drizzle had joined the mist, and the puddles it formed on the steps were blood-red—in keeping, it seemed to me, with the day it was. The Wartburg was built in the twelfth century. It is the best preserved Romanesque secular building north of the Alps. Grand Duke Carl Alexander of Weimar had it lavishly restored in the nineteenth century. Visits are by guided tours. As I joined the next waiting group, I wondered should I remove my cap, but looking around saw a couple of other men wearing headgear.

We had a very witty and erudite guide for the Wartburg castle, a real showman, who explained the function of each ancient room, drew our attention to beautifully carved pillars, and to the great oak beams above us which had borne the weight of six centuries. On many of the walls there were frescoes by the Romantic painter Moritz von Schwind. They illustrated events from the history of the landgraves of Thüringen; the life of St Elizabeth of Hungary who in 1207, as a child, was brought to the castle by Landgrave Hermann I as bride-to-be of his son, and who became famed for her care of the sick; and the 'Competition of the Singers' when the same landgrave assembled the six leading poets of the time to compete for a prize.

In a room called 'The Women's Room', St Elizabeth was again honoured, this time by pictures of her life and death in glazed mosaic which entirely cover the walls and pillars. These were donated by Kaiser Wilhelm II in the early 1900s. It struck me that this lavish honouring of St Elizabeth was a politic attempt by Protestant Germany to balance the markedly Protestant meaning of the Wartburg since Luther's time, by a tribute to the traditions of German Catholicism; or put differently, an attempt to integrate German Catholicism into the national myth. The Protestant emphasis had been reinforced in 1817 when an invitation went out from Jena to the Protestant universities of Germany to gather at the Wartburg in commemoration of the Reformation three hundred years before, and of the defeat of Napoleon at Leipzig. Their demand, when 450 students gathered there and burned the books of conservative writers, was for a unified and liberal-democratic Germany. In the castle's splendid and spacious Festive Hall, the black-red-gold flag which the students carried hung above the marble fireplace. There our entertaining guide left us to find our own way through the castle museum to Luther's study.

I had wanted to see this. There were two windows, plain wooden walls, a tiled stove, a chest of drawers, a chair, a whale's vertebra as footstool, and a table. A notice told us that this was not the original table which had disintegrated as a result of people chipping it for souvenirs, but a table from his father's house. Later, back at the station having lunch, I asked a man where Luther was born. 'His people', he said, 'were from Möhra, but he was born in Eisleben. He finished his schooling here in Eisenach. His father was an iron merchant. He could afford to send him to the best schools.' Local boy made good, I thought.

During the next two days I saw nearby much-bombed Jena where German Romantic literature was born, failed to see Buchenwald concentration camp because it turned out to be not the camp itself but a memorial site where it had been, and back in Weimar the Herderkirche with Cranach's great triptych that I referred to above, as well as Liszt's house and some early Jugendstil architecture. When I took the train back to Frankfurt I was thinking: 'What is there of German cultural history that Weimar and its surroundings has not seen?' I wrote 'in a ragged way, I have visited the heart of Germany'. But then I imagined a German Catholic saying, 'only of the Protestant part of it'. There seemed sense in that until an answering voice said, 'Since Luther, the heart of Germany is Protestant'. And again, there seemed sense in that. Hence the question mark I have placed after the title of this travel report.

BEYOND VASARI'S MYTH OF ORIGIN*

IT BEGAN WITH the exhibition in Siena in 2003-4. Actually, inasmuch as my subsequent quest was a revival of my passion for painting, it had begun long before that. Thirty years ago, in *Beyond Nationalism*, I wrote that I would have preferred to be a painter than a writer and that I had learned more about life from painting than from

---

* From *About Behaving etc.*, 2007.

books. But the nearest I had got professionally to painting was that happy time—happy also because it included my marriage and my firstborn—that I spent as an art critic in Dublin in the early 1960s.

News of the exhibition in Siena reached me where I was living, in Anguillara. It was entitled 'Duccio and the Origins of Sienese Painting'. I knew that Duccio had figured at the start not only of Sienese but of Italian painting and I was interested in the origins of the latter. By 'Italian painting' I mean characteristically Italian, in the naturalistic manner of ancient Rome, not Byzantinish or (as the Italians called it) 'Greek'. Such painting, was to be found mainly in Southern Italy which had been under Byzantium's control for a long period. I was not in the habit of travelling far to exhibitions. But the prospect of learning more about how Italian painting first emerged proved decisive. I went to. Siena, saw the exhibition, bought the weighty catalogue and, home again, began to read it selectively. I also read the special supplement published by *Il Corriere della Sera*. When I had followed up these cursory studies with other books borrowed from the local library, I wrote and dispatched an article to *The Irish Times,* which, for a reason I will come to, was not published. This was the article:

Siena Fires a Salvo in Old Dispute with Florence

The exhibition 'Duccio and the Origins of Sienese Art' held in Siena in 2003-4 tacitly fired another shot in the old dispute between Siena and Florence about which city has historical primacy in Italian painting. Duccio di Buoninsegna (1255-1319) was for most of his life a contemporary of the Florentine, Giotto. Mainly the exhibition presents, after years of restoration, those works of Duccio which have remained in Siena, along with a number of his paintings borrowed from galleries and collections.

The Duccio works represent, in Siena, a period when painting in Italy was engaged in a new departure. It was moving away from the previous Byzantine style—flat, formulaic and immobile—towards the depiction of corporeity, expression and movement, in space. The other centres of this movement were Rome and Florence. The Florentine, Giotto went furthest in naturalism. But the fact that he was subsequently celebrated as the 'founder of Italian painting'—and even of 'modern European painting'—and that this view of him has become traditional in Europe, requires moderating comment. Sixty years after Giotto's death a Florentine painter praised him for having 'translated painting from Greek [i.e., Byzantine] into Latin'.

Giotto was fortunate in that Florence also produced Dante, Boccaccio and Ghiberti, all of whom celebrated him as an illustrious compatriot. But while his work did influence many painters some time after him (he died in 1337), the mainstream of post-Byzantine in fact took a different course. There was not for the next ninety years, until Masaccio, a Florentine by adoption, any painter equally distinguished for his naturalism. It was only after Masaccio, in the 1430s, that Italian naturalism of the Florentine kind began to become the norm.

However, when in the middle of that century Florence won artistic ascendancy in Italy with painters who used an intensified, idealising, 'scientific' naturalism, they co-opted Giotto as their founding father. It was much, though the time gap since Giotto was greater, as if the French Impressionists had called Turner their founder. Then, a century later again, in 1550, Giorgio Vasari, a 'self-made' Florentine, confirmed that adoption by crowning Giotto as the originator of 'good', 'modern' and 'Italian' painting in his *Lives of Celebrated Artists*, which became a bible of art history in Italy and Europe.

Contrasting with this story is the fact that, after Giotto, the painting that was in vogue in Italy, rather than continuing his vision or his advanced naturalism, *was quite different from it in spirit and appearance*. It was 'Italian Gothic' derived from Duccio and his followers. Mannerist in the original Italian sense of 'stylish', it was a graceful, sinuous, decorative, colourful art which used a moderate naturalism, but which did not, like Giotto in most of his work, treat as a priority the true representation of visible shape and circumstance. Duccio, while not its actual inventor, *was the primary source of Italian painting of this kind*.

As had been the case with Giotto, he was influenced by the tentatively naturalising Byzantinism of the Florentine, Cimabue. The latter was in that sense the artistic father of both. Duccio, in developing in much of his painting a naturalism that almost equalled

Giotto's, remained tinged with Byzantinism. But he also—and this was to be fateful—incorporated Gothic elements that were familiar to him in Siena.

That Tuscan city, fifty-five miles southwest of Florence, and its commercial and political rival, was situated on the *via francigena*, the pilgrim high road from France, England and Germany to Rome. So the Gothic style reached it easily, in manuscript miniatures and in plastic art in various materials. The city's multitude of gold and enamel smiths used Gothic motifs inspired by French and English statuettes, chalices and jewellery.

These influences can be seen at work in Duccio's sinuous line, sumptuous colouring, delicate decoration and elegantly folded drapes. Simone Martini and the Lorenzetti brothers learned from him—some of their works are in the present exhibition. But whereas Duccio had been tentative in his adoption of the Gothic, they went on to seize and develop it. The charm and fantasy of their work led to the emergence of a Sienese Gothic school whose influence spread to other Italian regions and abroad. When Martini followed the Pope to Avignon in France, the papal court became a centre from which the new style radiated widely.

Thus, this Sienese art that derived from Duccio, rather than Giotto's work or the later Florentine naturalism that harked back to him, was the first characteristically 'Italian' painting. It was also the first Italian art to have an impact outside Italy. The upshot in the latter part of the century was the emergence of the manner of painting called International Gothic. A composite phenomenon, contributed to by Netherlandish, French, Bohemian, German and Catalan artists, it was the most favoured painting in western Europe and in Italy until the mid-1400s. International Gothic, like the con- temporary fictional literature, harked back romantically to the age of chivalry. It represented, before the Graeco-Roman naturalistic vogue, Europe's first historical revival movement.

About a month after I had dispatched that article to *The Irish Times*, I got a letter saying that they would not be publishing it because a re- view by John Banville of a book about Sienese painting was due to appear in the paper the following Saturday. I read Banville's review and found that the general argument of the book, by an Englishman,

Timothy Hyman, seemed to accord pretty well with what I had written on the subject. I also noticed that John seemed to concur with the book. So I posted him my article and he confirmed that my approach was similar to the book's and that he, personally, agreed with it. Given that I was not, as I assumed Timothy Hyman to be, a scholar in these matters, that was encouraging.

There were some questions to which, when I wrote the article, I had not found answers. In the article I had given Duccio and Siena, rather than Giotto and Florence, primacy in the launching of a characteristically Italian painting: Italian Gothic. But the manner of the emergence of naturalism in Italy was a question I wanted to clear up. Vasari had represented Cimabue, Giotto's teacher, as the first to introduce some, in his view, civilised naturalism into the 'clumsy Greek style', thereby initiating a new epoch in painting which Giotto confirmed and consolidated. The life-spans of the main characters were as follows:

Cimabue c. 1240–1302
Duccio c. 1260–1318
Giotto c. 1267–1337

The fat exhibition catalogue led off with an essay by Luciano Bellosi of Siena University on the painters who were working in Siena when Duccio came of age. Bellosi described them as *cimabueschi*. I assumed that this meant, in particular, painters influenced by Cimabue's tentative naturalism within the Byzantine mode. But what of the painters from whom Cimabue diverged? To measure the allegedly epoch-making nature of his and Giotto's work, *I needed to see contemporary examples of that other, straightforwardly Byzantine work in the region where they lived, or at least reproductions of it.*

Where in Tuscany, Umbria, etc.—i.e., in those parts of Italy where those innovating Italian painters lived—could one see it? I knew that plenty of Byzantine painting can be seen in the south of Italy where Byzantium had ruled for centuries. But where in Central Italy? That search is a long story which I will tell another time.

❖

THE SPECIAL POSITION OF THE JEWS:
BENEFITS AND ILL EFFECTS*

THE WORD 'SEMITE', according to the *Concise Oxford Dictionary*, means 'a member of any of the peoples supposed to be descended from Shem, son of Noah, including especially the Jews, Arabs, Assyrians, Babylonians and Phoenicians'. But the word 'anti-semitism' discriminates. It has to do only with the Jews, and means felt or expressed hostility to them. It is the antagonism to a human group which the hybrid Power that rules the West rates as the most abominable of such antagonisms. From San Francisco to Berlin, a day seldom passes but politicians or mass-media preachers remind us of its atrociousness, warn us against committing it, or express horror and indignation at some actual or alleged instance of it. The condemnatory chorus functions not only as a stern moral judgment but also as a punishment, inasmuch as it defames a public man among the right-thinking and can imperil or even end his career.

This singular stigmatising of hostility to Jews, as distinct from, say, Arabs, Catholics, Blacks, Germans or whatever, is not the fruit of moral reasoning. It derives from a political decision. It reflects the special status which the corporate Power that rules Amerope has conferred on the fifteen million Jews as a body and in particular on Israel, the Jewish state, where over a third of them live.

This special status, which has been created in the last half-century, is an approximate recurrence in our time of the special treatment accorded to the Jews in the Roman Empire and in its nominal refoundations, first in the Carolingian empire, later as the Holy Roman Empire. In the Roman case it took the form of what are usually referred to as the Jewish 'privileges', but might be more accurately called the Jewish exemptions. Practising Jews were exempt from the poll tax and from ritual sacrifice at the Emperor's altar. More generally, they could not be obliged to do anything which conflicted with their religion, such as work on the Sabbath, attend in pagan temples, or perform the occasional civic duty of tax-collection. In the two succession empires, the Carolingian and the Holy Roman, that ancient special status was transmuted into protection of the Jews by the Emperor personally; a protection often practised *in loco*

* From *About Behaving etc.*, 2007.

imperatoris by bishops, and which devolved, with the passage of time, on the German princes.

Those two elements, protection and exemption, recur in the special status accorded to Jews by Amerope. The vehemence with which the ban on anti-semitism is proclaimed, and the severity with which it is enforced, give to Jews a protection against defamation, criticism and aggression which exceeds that given to any other group. The exemptions apply to Israel. With regard to the latter, they derive from the diffused public doctrine about Israel to the effect that this small and relatively new state has a value far in excess of any other small state, however long established. Three important corollaries have followed from that. The maintenance in being of Israel is a duty incumbent on all right-thinking people. Israel's right to security far exceeds any right to security of the states and peoples surrounding it, most notably the Palestinians. When nuclear weapons were the prerogative of only a few great powers, the West allowed Israel to arm itself with such weapons and assisted it in so doing.

The exemptions which Israel enjoys follow from these premises. Israel is effectively exempt from international law, in particular with regard to Resolutions of the United Nations Security Council, and rules governing the conduct of warfare, and the exercise of military occupation. Israel also effectively enjoys exemption from such international principles of human rights as it chooses to ignore.

These exemptions are 'effective' rather than formal, inasmuch as Amerope has not openly declared that they exist, but intimates forcefully that they do, with the result that they in fact operate whenever Israel breaches the rules or principles in question. When it fails to comply with a Security Council Resolution that calls for its compliance, no punitive consequences follow. And quite otherwise than often happens when breaches of the laws of warfare or of military occupation, or offences against human rights, are perpetrated by ordinary states, when Israel is the perpetrator, there are no authoritative pronouncements that crimes have been committed, much less arraignments of those responsible before international courts.

The reason why Amerope intimates the Israeli exemptions tacitly, rather than declaring them formally, is the facilitation of the American power to strike correctively at will. Formal upholding of the theory that international law and human rights principles apply equally to all states enables the United States to exploit breaches of these in those weaker states which it has selected for intimidation or destruction.

In passing, a question suggests itself. From a western point of view those special freedoms of action (or inaction) permitted to Israel are exemptions. But taken together are they at the same time something else: a concession to the particular nature of Jewish political and military ethics? Something similar to that Roman package of exemptions which was in fact a concession to Jewish religious law and ethics?

Western political and military ethics, such as they are, are an end product of western Christian civilisation. In the shaping of that civilisation and its ethical systems, Jews, even if they wanted to, were not allowed to play an active part. Perhaps westerners assume too readily that not only western Jews collectively, but also non-western Jews worldwide, at some point subscribed, or now really subscribe, to those western and basically Christian values and ethics which they had no part in shaping.

Is it not possible that Jews, and in particular the Jews of Israel, find in the Jewish Bible, which we call the Old Testament, a quite different and non-western source for their basic values and, accordingly, their political and military ethics? In that book divine justification is provided for the ruthless massacre of neighbouring peoples by the army of Israel when it was victorious; a war ethics quite at variance with traditional or contemporary western ethics, whatever about western practice. Moreover, with regard to 'human rights', in the Jewish Bible there is no notion of the equal worth of all human beings from which the notion of 'rights' common to all mankind might grow.

It is not a question of whether rabbis in their teachings to the Jews of Israel have drawn on the Talmud's teachings about Jews and non-Jews. Of course they have. While Palestine was still a British mandate, Rabbi Abraham Isaac Kook, the first Ashkenazi chief rabbi of Palestine and a renowned scholar of the Halakhah or biblical law, said, 'The difference between a Jewish soul and the souls of non-Jews...is greater and deeper than the difference between a human soul and the souls of cattle.' In a booklet published in 1973 by the Central Region Command of the Israeli army, the Command's chief chaplain wrote:

> When our forces come across civilians during a war or in hot pursuit or in a raid, so long as there is no certainty that those civilians are incapable of harming our forces, then according to the Halakhah they may and even should be killed...Under no circumstances should an Arab be trusted, even if he makes an impression of being civilised...In war, when our forces storm the enemy, they are allowed and even enjoined by the Halakhah to kill even good civilians, that is, civilians who are ostensibly good.

Or again, in 2001, in a Passover sermon, Rabbi Ovadia Yosef, former chief Sephardi rabbi and a present member of the Israeli parliament, exclaimed: 'May the Holy Name visit retribution on the Arab heads, and cause their seed to be lost, and annihilate them!' and continued: 'It is forbidden to have pity on them. We must give them missiles with relish, annihilate them. Evil ones, damnable ones.'

The question is not whether prominent rabbis have taught or teach such things—it is logical that they should do so—but whether, and to what extent, such teachings influence the behaviour of the Israeli state, secret services and army. If in fact they have had considerable influence, this would go far to explain, and in Israeli terms justify, the extreme cruelty of their treatment of the Palestinians and, to a lesser degree, of the Lebanese. And that would also—to return to the thought that prompted this aside—render it inadequate and patronising to view the freedoms of action and inaction granted by Amerope to Israel merely as 'exemptions from the Ameropean system of values, law and ethics'. More accurately seen, the allowance of those freedoms of action and inaction to Israel would amount to a respectful recognition of a different system of values, law and ethics than that which Amerope nominally upholds.

However, leaving such speculation aside, it goes without saying that the special status granted to the Jews is well-meant, is intended to bring Jews only benefits, and does in fact bring them benefits. But it has also led to unintended ill effects. And indeed, if one compares the benefits and the ill effects which have accrued to the Jews as a result of their special status, one is forced to the surprising conclusion that the latter outweigh the former, certainly in the long term.

Undoubtedly beneficial are the direct results of the special status. Throughout Amerope anti-Jewish publications and statements have, with occasional, very marginal exceptions, been effectively suppressed. Wherever, particularly in the United States, Britain and France, bars existed to Jews becoming members of certain elite clubs and associations, or studying or teaching in certain elite educational institutions, such bars no longer exist. This has been of particular benefit to Jews in the United States, Britain and France, where such bars, tacit or explicit, were numerous and where half of the world's Jews live. All careers are now wide open to Jews, and where Jewish ability leads to notable Jewish success in one professional sphere or another, such success meets with pragmatic acceptance rather than the begrudging public complaint of former times. Although Jews form only 1.5% of the American population, *Forbes* magazine records that 25-30% of the wealthiest families are Jewish. Jewish money, sagaciously placed, gives Jews an entirely disproportionate influence on the politics and especially the foreign policy of the world's only superpower. Israel, as the Jewish state, has received regular and abundant subsidies and supplies of armaments from the US. These, together with the freedoms of action and inaction granted to that state, have enabled those six million Jews to become a power in the world out of all proportion to their numbers.

The immediate benefit of all these improvements in the Jewish condition has been a great increase in Jewish freedom and power. The crowning and ultimate benefit derives from Jewish awareness both of this freedom and power and of the fact that these are assured to them, unchallengeably, by their status as a specially protected category of human beings. That crowning benefit is a collective self-confidence and self-assertiveness such as Jews have not possessed since the time of Herod the Great, friend and protégé of the Roman Empire.

Unfortunately, however, both in Amerope and in Israel, in too many Jews for the general Jewish good this self-assertiveness has tended to deteriorate into intimidation, bullying and aggressiveness, And these Jews, by their very actions, are the Jews who get most noticed. Such deterioration was probably an inevitable result of the special status, given that this was granted only in the last half-century and that most Jews—and in particular most American Jews as well as the Israeli political and military classes—come from those lower strata of European and Russian Jewry on whom anti-Jewish discrimination most severely fell. When long-standing powerlessness attains power and privilege, there is a well-known tendency for these gains to deteriorate into abuse of them.

In Amerope this is particularly the case with American Jewish organisations. Not content with the special protection of the Jewish good name, and of Jewish interests, provided by the law and by the mass media, these organisations practise an aggressive militancy whenever there is an instance, even minimal, of criticism of Jews or of Israel, or something which might be so interpreted, or a visit or public appearance by a person deemed hostile to Jews, or a denial or diminution of the Jewish Holocaust, or anything which might be so interpreted. In such instances, in actions extending far beyond the United States, intimidation is set in motion by street demonstration, by thousands of concerted emails or telephone calls, or by boycott or legal challenge. The degree of organisation and mobilisation is impressive and is meant to impress. By the same token, the impression often given is of intolerance of free expression by non-Jews and of reaction out of all proportion to the matter in question.

With immensely more serious consequences, disproportionate reaction is Israel's norm. A disproportion smacking of arrogance and sadism has regularly characterised Israel's use of its military power in its responses to Palestinian resistance to its occupation of Palestinian land and to the virtual imprisonment of the Palestinian population by road-blocks, walls, fences and sea limits. The same is true of Israeli responses to the resistance by Lebanese guerrillas to Israeli occupation of Lebanese land and the capture and imprisonment of Lebanese. There has never been the slightest possibility that the Palestinian or Lebanese armed attacks would endanger the existence of Israel. In view of this, the Israeli punishment of Palestinians and Lebanese for resisting has amounted to grossly abusive use of the freedom from international sanction which Israel enjoys.

All too obvious has been Israeli delight in the employment of immensely superior military power for its own sake. Muscular pride of the 'Just look what we can do!' kind have shown through when Israeli forces bomb and shell Lebanon by air, land and sea simultaneously. Similarly, with the regular killing of Palestinian men, women and children by tank and rifle fire, by gunboat, and by rockets released from planes; a continual killing spree whose bag, to use the hunting term, amounts to about four times the number of Israelis killed by the Palestinian fighters. And that is not to mention the everyday bullying sadism of the Israeli soldiers: the capricious bulldozing of houses and ancestral olive groves; the phone call out of the blue informing a house-owner that he would be well-advised to leave his house because it is to be demolished in fifteen minutes; the random boring through interior walls in armed house-to-house searches; the wilful barring at a roadblock of a pregnant woman or a sick man, woman or child on the way to a hospital; the killing by fire from a naval ship of a fisherman who had strayed beyond the authorised area for fishing; the rearrangement of a local road-blocking system so that a journey by car from A to B which normally took ten minutes now requires two hours; the forcing of fifty male inhabitants of a Palestinian village to build a wall in the middle of the road and then to dismantle it again. It is a pattern of everyday behaviour, with the quasi-racial contempt included, which one might expect to hear told of a particularly Nazi-indoctrinated German army unit in occupied Poland during World War II. And add finally, to complete this snapshot of arrogant abuse of the special status, the grabbing of hill-top stretches of Palestinian land beyond Israel's legal boundaries and the building there of splendidly appointed Israeli colonies which mock the poverty of the Palestinian villages beneath.

Given that the Palestinians have the indisputably legitimate grievance of the dispossessed, the rational and self-serving Israeli policy would have been to treat them with respect and generosity, even in the face of provocation. The aim would have been to reduce their sense of wrong to a level where pragmatic good neighbourliness, such as exists with the ruling social strata of Jordan and Egypt, would have been possible. Instead, irrationally and tragically, the Israeli aim has been simply to subject, by inducing in the Palestinians a constant fear of death and destruction, so that the future relation-ship of the two peoples might be like that of Spartans and Helots, or of White and Blacks in the old American South or in the South Africa of apartheid.

The ill effects for Jews of these Jewish behaviours in Israel and vicinity and in Amerope belong to the category of predictable con-sequences and are therefore, unfortunately, fact. Israel's policy of in-ducing fear in its environment has ensured, and will continue to ensure, fear and insecurity as constant presences in the Jewish state. A far cry from the 'safe haven for Jews' which the early Zionists dreamt of, Israel's treatment of the Palestinians and its actions in Lebanon have made Israel hateful in the Arab world and in the wider Muslim world. And the Israelis being virtually the only Jews in those worlds, the result has been the emergence of a virulent and publicly expressed anti-semitism from Iran and Morocco to Indonesia; a vast area where previously no anti-Jewish antagonism existed. With bitter irony, this new phenomenon, casting its shadow over future centuries, dwarfs that historical European anti-semitism which oppressed Jews for hundreds of years .

In Amerope, and especially in Europe, the majority of people regard the special dispensation granted to Israel by the Power above them with amazement and dismay. Viewing Israel and its actions as they would any other state and its actions, they have felt towards the Jewish state a growing hostility that is tinged with contempt. On this view, Israel, on account of its long-standing behaviour, is rather than a value for mankind a blot on it, and constitutes a menace to the world's peace. Because the state in question is a much-vaunted democracy where the state represents the people, this aversion to Israel has an inherent consequence: it amounts to aversion towards more than a third of the world's Jews.

Fortunately, most westerners who share this hostility know to distinguish: they do not allow it to become an antagonism towards Jews in general. They are party to the collective moral decision of the West, in the wake of the horrifying fate of European Jews dur-ing World War II, that anti-Jewishness, even merely felt, would cease forever. That moral decision, combined with the fact that many westerners have Jewish acquaintances, friends or relations in whom they find no cause for complaint, successfully prevents most of these foes of Israel from extending their repugnance for one third to the other two thirds.

However, it is also the case that in the West in recent decades, and especially in Europe, a new anti-Jewishness has been emerging. Those factors just mentioned which work against an extension of anti-Israeli feeling to Jews in general do not always prevail. To some degree this is simply a matter of opponents of Israel not knowing Jews in the flesh. But by far its main cause is the intimidatory activity of the main Jewish organisations in America and Europe, and the message they deliver about Israel. Along with the annoyance sometimes amounting to disgust which these organisations cause by their petty-minded witch hunts, they offend many judicious non-Jews by supporting Israel's every action blindly; and they drive to fury by misrepresenting any criticism of Israel as hostility to Jews.

To put it another way, the honest attempt of westerners averse to Israel to keep that hostility distinct from their general feelings about Jews is too often defeated by the virtual inaudibility—perhaps so ordained by the Power—of the few Jewish groups and individual Jews who publicly oppose Israel's policies and atrocities. Thus, willy-nilly, the message delivered by default to westerners of good will is that 'we Jews who share your life and live among you do not share your standards of civility, but on the contrary support those who trample on your standards, if they are Jews.'

Granted, Jews have a perfect right to differ and to be 'different', as Jews have been known to be since time immemorial. Amerope, by according them a special status, implicitly recognises that right. But then it is a decision of the Jewish people as to how they use that status; and it injures them when it leads them to appear to base their difference on support for a state whose most notable external activity is to oppress and kill.

Having decided in 2006 that Anguillara had given me all I had wanted from it after my American discoveries and that I would return to Ireland the following year, I decided to visit Iran while I was still somewhat nearer to it. In January 2007 I flew there from Rome and in eight days en-

countered bustling Teheran, saw the architectural splendours of Shiraz and Isfahan, the tomb of the poet Hafez, the ruins of Persepolis. I just missed seeing the lane called Bobby Sands Street near the British Embassy in Teheran. I talked with about fifteen Iranians, but especially with my excellent guide and driver Ali.

In the autumn of that year I sold my house in Anguillara and returned to Ireland, sharing the apartment with Miriam in Maynooth, twenty-six kilometres from Dublin. Miriam drove to her school in Dublin and stayed three nights a week in Malahide with her aged mother.

I had an affectionate re-encounter with Mary who was still living in Salthill, Galway and, after her foreign travels and Jerusalem sojourn, back teaching in the 'Jes'. She had also been giving evening lectures on Hebrew scriptures in the Theology Department of the Galway-Mayo Institute of Technology. Lately she had not been in the best of health, troubled by her old lethargies.

I also caught up with what my 'children' were doing. Oisín was still working as project manager for the L and S construction company, sometimes in Liverpool. By now he understood, and enjoyed understanding, every building and every machine, and in regard to such matters was often the 'advice and repairs man' of the family, while sustaining his father spiritually by his ability to source good poitín. Cilian, a couple of years previously, had been so struck by the notion of the Story (or recalled its nature and function from his Maoinis childhood?) that he read books about the world's origin myths, travelled to Egypt and Greece, and retired for a time to his barge on the Grand Canal to read and think. Then with Natasha he founded a communications company, Stillwater, in central Dublin. For his part, he specialised in explaining to companies and start-ups from Shanghai to San Francisco the importance of telling their story. Benefiting from political connections which Natasha had acquired as a fundraiser for Fianna Fáil, he became an adviser to Taoiseach Brian Cowen. Natasha, for her part, trained people for interviews and public appearances and in how to acquire self-confidence. Daughter Sorcha and son-in-law Ron, whom I had visited in Malawi, having returned from far foreign fields, had bought a house in Maynooth where Sorcha's employer, Trócaire, had its headquarters and were living there with their two growing children and new arrival Zach.

As for Kate, she, too, had bought a house in Maynooth, left Liberty Films and was working as Irish-language officer in charge of Irish-language matters in University College Maynooth. From her latest visit to Turkey she had come back engaged to a Turkish young man, Sinan. Oisín, Ron and I 'interviewed' him, liked him, but sensed that he wanted to see more of the world before settling down, and in fact after six months the engagement ended. Kate left the Maynooth job, moved to Dublin, where in a section of Dublin city centre she called Sogo she and a girlfriend organised the Sogo Arts Festival to which she invited me to contribute a talk, 'On Thinking', which later found a place on YouTube. Unable to get funding for a repeat or an enlargement, Kate took refuge again in Turkey where, while taking clients for reiki therapy, she organised Irish festivals in several genres of the arts.

❖

2008

THE NEW ARRIVALS AMONG THE STATUES*

DURING MY YEARS in Italy Dublin's O'Connell Street was redesigned. That much I had noticed on a visit home a few years ago. The footpaths on both sides had been greatly widened, a broad walkway with new trees laid out in the centre, the spaces for the passage of motor traffic greatly reduced. In 2003 'The Spire' was erected at the central point of the street's length. It occupied the spot where Nelson's Pillar, honouring the famous British admiral, had stood for 158 years until it was blown up by the IRA in the late 1960s.

For years there had been debate about what should replace it. Because the spot was not only at the centre of Ireland's capital but also adjacent to the GPO which had played a central role in the 1916 Rising, there was an assumption that the replacement should have a national symbolic significance. A statue of Pearse or Connolly, or of both, or a monument in some way honouring Ireland's

* From *Ireland After the End of Western Civilisation*, Athol Books, 2009

freedom struggle, were the most frequent suggestions put forward and talked about. Then in 2002 the city council had sponsored a pointed pillar of glistening steel, 390 feet tall, designed by Ritchie Architects of London.

When I first saw it, I remarked that it would have been more suitable for the other Blackpool*—the popular English seaside resort—than for the centre of Ireland's capital city. But on reflection, I recognised that it was at least an honest statement of the Republic's state of mind after its prudent self-effacement during the Northern War and during the past-effacing enrichment of the Celtic Tiger boom. It stood for, represented, and said Nothing. In this respect it expressed the newly ascendant public orthodoxy which the Australian writer Vincent Buckley had noted in his book *Memory Ireland* in 1985 where he described Ireland as having effaced itself and come to represent precisely that: 'Nothing—a no-thing'.

Those changes notwithstanding, the basic layout and iconography of the street remains intact. Roughly at the centre of the west side stands the pillared GPO with the Tricolour flying above it. Forming a triangle with the GPO, the monument to O'Connell the Liberator stands at the south end, Parnell's monument at the other end. Beneath the portico of the GPO, behind a large glass rectangle at the centre of the façade, stands the bronze statue of the skirted warrior Cúchulainn. To hold himself erect in spite of his wounds he has bound himself to the stump of a tree. Spear in hand, he is leaning down to his left, his head drooped. A crow perched on his shoulder indicates that he has died and need no longer be feared by his enemies. On a slab beneath the statue, there is a quotation from the Easter Week Proclamation. It runs from 'We declare the right of the people of Ireland to the ownership of Ireland, and to the unfettered control of Irish destinies, to be sovereign and indefeasible' down to the seven signatories underneath. Reading them, one inevitably recalls Yeats' lines about 'spelling them out in a verse'. On the Liberator's monument 'O'CONNELL' suffices. A more or less permanent pigeon on his head besmirches more or less permanently his face. The tall granite pillar behind the statue of Parnell presents a golden harp and these words: 'No man has a right to say to his country thus

---

* In the original Irish, Dublin (Duibhlinn) means 'black pool'.

far shalt thou go and no further. We have never attempted to fix the "ne plus ultra" to the progress of Ireland's nationhood, and we never shall.'

Yesterday, walking along the street, it occurred to me that there is no statue of any twentieth-century figure apart from the labour leader Jim Larkin, who died in 1947. Not to mention the 1916 leaders, no de Valera, Collins, Douglas Hyde, Yeats or Lemass. After Larkin, the impulse to honour here by a statue or otherwise broke down.

As I was so thinking, I noticed something surprising on the street's central walkway, about a hundred paces north of The Spire. On a concrete plinth, behind a framed rectangle of glass, there was a lit-up human figure in walking motion. It was a slender figure, natural height, which for the lack of any evidence to the contrary seemed to represent a young man. The torso was composed of dots of yellow light; the head was a detached, featureless circle of light, bobbing in rhythm with its owner's walk. There were no feet. I guessed that, technically speaking, it was an LED or Light Emitting Diode. Closer inspection from where I was standing showed me that the entire rectangle was filled by regular rows of white dots. Those dots which were needed to represent the figure in motion became illuminated, or ceased to be lit up, as required. The figure was represented as dressed in a T-shirt and short pants; it had bare legs and short socks. Its walking motion was easy, lithe, suggesting general physical fitness and not a care in the world.

I crossed to the tree-lined central walkway. On the plinth beneath the framed rectangle I read 'Julian Opie: Julian walking 2007'. Then, lower again: 'Julian Opie: Walking on O'Connell St.' Mr Opie, I took it, was the maker of 'Julian walking'.

Spurred to further inspection of what the city fathers have been up to, I look beyond Father Mathew The Apostle of Temperance, in monk's robes, arms outstretched, towards the Parnell monument. And I see not far from Father Mathew what looks like another concrete plinth with superimposed framed glass rectangle. And sure enough, approaching it, I see what looks like a brother or sister of 'Julian walking'. A slight protrusion of bum along with a discreet protrusion on chest—nothing mumsy, these are free-as-the-air un-

attached singles—decides for 'sister'. Moreover, the writing underneath says 'Julian Opie: Sara walking 2007.' Gender balance naturally,
how could I think otherwise! Sara has the same detached bobbing
circle for a head. She is wearing a sleeveless top and slacks. Two pegs
protruding from the slacks serve as feet. Slender as Julian, she, too,
has that easy, swinging walk. The word 'lithe' springs again to mind.

Perhaps, I thought, unknown to me O'Connell Street has become populated by such figures. Setting out to inspect, I turn back
towards 'Julian walking' and The Spire, pass the latter, and sure
enough, there is another of them, opposite the Cúchulainn window of the GPO. It is 'Jack walking'. What seems to be a scarf bobs
in front of his neck; his upper garment is shorter than Julian's—is
it actually shorter or simply tucked into his trousers? It covers his
arms. His head, once again, is a separated, bobbing circle. Glancing at
the Cúchulainn window, I see that Jack's reflection is superimposed
on Cúchulainn. His illuminated upper body rises above the almost
horizontal line formed by the flat top of the tree stump and the dead
warrior's drooping upper body descending to head.

About sixty paces further towards Jim Larkin, gender balance
again maintained, 'Suzanne walking 2007'. Skirted this time, her
skirt swinging as she walks. Arms bare, the merest suggestion of
breast. Was her walk somewhat slower? It was hard to know as you
moved from one of them to another, mesmerised.

I progressed to Jim Larkin, who still stood there high, his arms
outstretched with hands upraised. His call, too, was still there: 'The
great appear great because we are on our knees. Let us rise.' On the
sides of his plinth, two quotations, from Patrick Kavanagh and Sean
O'Casey respectively, still celebrated his greatness. The view onward
to O'Connell, past Sir John Gray and William Smith O'Brien, was
clear of innovation.

How, I asked myself, as I went off about my business, was I to
understand the new arrivals? That in line with The Spire's non-ut-
terance of anything, they were intended to say nothing, struck me
first. But then, the placing of Jack in such a spot as to cancel, by his
reflection in the GPO window, the statue of Cúchulainn, was that
deliberate or merely accidental? Was it, or was it not, meant to 'say'
something? I could not decide.

Clearly, taking The Spire and the LEDs together, the city fathers had decided that O'Connell Street would no longer be used to honour notable dead Irishmen (or indeed Irishwomen) who had served their compatriots well. Notable objects would indeed be erected in line with the line of commemorative statues, but objects that, on the face of it, honoured nobody and said Nothing. About the reason for that, I could only guess. Was it that the city fathers believed that it was in general not a good thing to honour with monuments the meritorious dead, or merely that it was not good for Dublin in particular, or Ireland in general, to do this? Or perhaps, not good to do any more of it; that we had done enough of that? Without going and asking them, I could not know.

But if Sara, Julian, Jack and Suzanne said nothing and commemorated no one, what did they *represent?* All portrayals of human figures, since the most ancient cave drawings of hunters and gatherers, represented something; to begin with, human beings. Most obviously, these four human figures, in walking motion, represented young contemporary men and women. And by all appearances they were of the contemporary *genus* Singles. They did not in other words represent contemporary human beings as such, but the kind known as Singles. And there were further delimiting elements: they were slim, to all appearances healthy, and were wont to take exercise, either by doing what they were doing—walking—or otherwise, perhaps in gyms. They were also—an aspect, I suppose, of their 'contemporary' look—as near to unisex as representation of male and female could make them.

I said above, of one of them, 'without a care in the world', and it was true of all of them; they appeared so, and indeed it was part of what made them Singles. Did those detached, featureless, bobbing circles which represented their heads mean thoughtless as well as without care? It did seem so. And a final thing about them struck me: while not ugly, neither were they beautiful. Regardless of the artist's intention, the technique of representation he had used made that impossible. So it was excluded that, in the manner of some ancient Greek statues, they represented youthful physical beauty

But it struck me, at the same time, that they represented ideal human beings; ideal, I mean, in terms of the regime's canons of human excellence. And if, behind placing them there among those statues of Irishmen who had served Ireland by contributing to its freedom struggle (or in Cúchulainn's case by inspiring it), there was an illustrative intention, a minimal saying of Something, then it might lie in *just that*. 'All those leaders and heroes worked and struggled so that Irish men and women might be as these are: healthy, slender, unisex, well-exercised Singles without a care or a thought in the world.'

In early 2007, visiting St Patrick's Centre near Downpatrick, I suggested to its Director, Jim Campbell, that it was high time Ireland had a St Patrick's Way on the lines of the Camino de Santiago. In June of the same year I wrote an article for Ireland's Eye, Mullingar, *making the same suggestion and outlining a possible route. Jim Campbell passed on the idea to Seamus Crossan of Dundalk who was in the travel business, and lo and behold in March 2015 Mr Crossan launched St Patrick's Camino.*

In late 2008, after years in which Mary's lethargies had been diagnosed as due to anaemia or emphysema, a new doctor diagnosed the trouble correctly as lupus, an incurable disease in which the body's white blood cells destroy red ones; and additionally that she had pulmonary hypertension, so it would be necessary for her always to carry a supply of oxygen and occasionally to visit hospital for blood transfusions. She adapted bravely. Dear Mary! I visited her in Maynooth where she stayed occasionally with Sorcha in a special bedroom which Oisín had adapted for her. She was holding up well. We had a long chat. Natasha and Cilian, working in Dublin, alternated weekend visits to her in Galway when she was living there in her own house—oddly she was still able to drive her own car! Oisín's wife, Cathy, a public medical doctor in Galway, also lent a hand.

Over Christmas of 2008-9 Miriam and I flew to the Dominican Republic for a week of sea and sun. The Spanish-speaking Dominican Republic in the Caribbean fills most of the large island where Columbus made landfall. A memorable incident occurred at breakfast one morning in the hotel. Noting that there was no butter on the table to put on the bread, I went to the serving counter and asked for some burro. The two young men serving looked horrified, all the more when I repeated the word. I had unthinkingly used the Italian word for butter; they had understood it in its Spanish meaning of donkey. I was asking for donkey for my breakfast! The matter was cleared up only when Miriam joined us and asked 'But is burro the Spanish word for butter, isn't it mantequilla? The two young men's faces lit up with a smile and I got my butter and they had a good horror story to tell.

In the first half of 2009 we moved from Maynooth to an apartment in Dublin 4 on the southern edge of Sandymount. Without a regular income apart from a Rathmines pension of €860 a month, for day-to-day expenses and household contribution I was drawing on savings made up of the remains of €150,000 from my mother's will which sister Rosemary had engineered for me, a profit from the sale of my Portobello house and the proceeds of selling the Anguillara house. The Celtic Tiger years had just ended. The rent of the furnished was €1,350 monthly but had been €1,400 when we moved in.

In June of that year Natasha gave a family dinner for my 80th birthday in her lovely little house in Dublin's Ringsend. Miriam was there and met Mary for the first time. A mutual respect and liking began which grew with time. In October I attended Oisín's marriage in the Renvyle House Hotel, Conamara, to Cathy Higgins, a Mayowoman. With her family she added a Mayo dimension to our extended tribe.

2009

A PUBLIC RITUAL WELL PERFORMED*

YESTERDAY I WAS in Tullamore and Clara, both in Co. Offaly, witnessing the preparations for the celebratory homecoming of Brian Cowen, the new Taoiseach. In each case, because I wanted to avoid the huge crowds, I left before he arrived accompanied by his wife and children. Both in the county town where he lives, and in his native village, there was a great bustle of preparation and a joyous anticipation.

* From *Ireland after the End of Western Civilisation*, Athol Books, 2009.

It was the final act in a ritual of transition from one Taoiseach to the next, which has given me great pleasure to observe. It was both a public ritual well performed and a public acceptance of its legitimacy as a handing over of political power.

Over a month ago, on the steps of Government Buildings and surrounded by his Cabinet, the former Taoiseach Bertie Ahern announced his intention to resign. A month-long 'lap of honour', marked by public tributes to his performance as Taoiseach and by various symbolic events, included his address to the American Congress and concluded with his symbolic meeting on the Boyne with Northern Ireland's First Minister, Ian Paisley. They met there to open the Battle of the Boyne interpretative centre. In the meantime, the successor he had designated—very aptly bearing the Tánaiste (second-in-command) title—was elected president-in-waiting of the main ruling party, Fianna Fáil.

Came the date pre-announced by Ahern for his resignation and events succeeded each other rapidly: Ahern's visit to Áras an Uachtaráin to hand back his seal of office to the President; Cowen's confirmation by his party as its president; his election by the Dáil as Taoiseach, his visit in turn to Áras an Uachtaráin, his naming of his Cabinet, and the definitive seal on the new order of government secured by a second visit to the President. Finally, then, yesterday, like a Roman triumphator returning home, Cowen's festive return to his particular place in Ireland and his particular people there.

My pleasure in all of that has arisen partly from it being ritual well performed—a prescribed set of actions, carried out with punctiliousness and dignity, that bear meaning for a watching nation. But combined with that pleasure there was patriotic satisfaction: this was the Irish State displaying its existence and its legitimacy and having both reaffirmed by its citizens.

It was a consoling pleasure inasmuch as it made evident that at least that much of what the Irish Revolution intended survives healthily in form, if not in substance. Not that our state, as it is, is without practical as well as symbolic value: it played a vital, even if not always a wise role in the production of our recent and present wealth. But form it is rather than the substance which the Revolution intended for it.

2009-10

MAKING IRELAND UNLOVABLE★

An omission by Irish historians

I AM WRITING this to draw the attention of Irish historians to an Irish phenomenon of recent times which they have so far not researched and recorded. Because it is a phenomenon of a kind not normally to be expected in an independent, democratic European nation, it might continue to escape their attention. Its omission is equivalent to omitting from a telling of the recent history of Bulgaria an account of the impact and effect of Russian Marxist-Leninism on that nation between 1945 and 1990.

Our historians know well that, from the last two decades of the nineteenth century to 1916 and beyond, certain Irish organisations and individuals created a broadly supported Irish identity that the Irish increasingly loved; and that out of this growing love the Revolution sprang. They have recorded the names, and the love-inducing deeds, of the organisations and individuals in question. With regard to the relationship between the people and their nation the resulting renewed national identity had made Ireland in this respect like a normal European nation. That collective self-love was possible because, as a result of those creative actions, the Ireland of the day possessed again, for the first time in eight centuries, a coherent identity among the nations. Its past was as the nationalist historical narrative and the works of its writers told it. Anciently, it had owned its entire land in freedom; spoken and written its own language; was illustrious for its learning and art and for its saints and missionaries active in Britain and on the European continent. Objects and buildings (most of these now in ruins) in Ireland and on the Continent testified to that art, learning and history. Then for eight centuries the Irish were thwarted by an external intrusion against which they struggled repeatedly and under which they suffered much and in great part abandoned their native ways and language. Always since St Patrick a Christian people, they had remained even in the centuries of adversity and religious persecution staunchly Catholic. Characterised by a largely agricultural

---

★ From my website 2010, *www.desmondfennell.com.*

economy and rural ways and culture, from the nineteenth century onwards they increasingly repossessed things previously lost—their land, native language and native field sports. Increasingly, too, they were resolute in their struggle for political freedom; and their religious faith and morality were held onto. The 1916 Easter Rising and the ensuing Revolution brought them national freedom in most of the country. While those events were awakening thoughts of similar liberation elsewhere in the colonised world, thousands of Irish men and women formed a great missionary movement to Africa and Asia bringing along with Christianity schools, hospitals and anti-imperialist sentiment to those largely colonized countries.

The new, independent Irish state, and almost its entire mass media, promoted something close to this composite Irish identity. With the addition of heroes and events drawn from the Revolution and of the achievements of the Literary Revival, Ireland in this guise remained loved by the Irish, albeit with diminishing motivating force, until the 1950s.

Normally, a national identity is a collection of cherished mental images forming a framework within which, and with reference to which, the day-to-day business of the nation takes place. As with any national identity, that Irish one would have with time evolved and changed emphases. Indeed the economic and intellectual paralysis and heavy emigration which—along with a cultural flowering—characterised the 1950s suggested that an invigorating renewal of the nation's idea of itself, one that while carrying forward the regained identity would reflect new circumstances and generate them, was urgently due. In the 1960s new circumstances flowing from Seán Lemass's new departures, and from the innovations of the Second Vatican Council, suggested forms that such a revision might take place. Most of the nation now had its own sovereign republic. So in the normal course of events, that new, updated Irish identity would, like the one it had built on, be shaped mainly by realities and movements present in the nation. Useful cultural and social elements arriving from outside would be reworked and fitted in by Irish minds and action. But that, as it turned out, was not to be.

I come now to the phenomenon that has been neither researched nor narrated by our historians. From the early 1960s onwards, an increasingly successful effort was made, first by some elements of the national mass media centred in Dublin, then by the media as a whole and by certain politicians, to cancel piecemeal the established Irish identity. Their main instrument in this endeavour was the new left-liberal (subsequently called plain 'liberal') doctrine that was establishing itself in the USA with the support of the state, big business and part of the media. Spreading imperially into Western Europe, its initial centre of diffusion there was the city called for a time 'Swinging London'. A social idealism that was anti-religious, pro women rather than men, and opposed to the national idea in general except with regard to America, it redefined society as a collection of individuals pursuing happiness and justice and provided them with a new personal and interpersonal morality to assist in that pursuit. It was the Western counterpart of the Bolshevik collectivism then being implanted in the Soviet Union's satellites in Eastern Europe.

The message being delivered in Ireland by the native upholders of the new doctrine was essentially: 'What your parents and teachers taught you about Ireland and about life was wrong and must be replaced and corrected as our neo-imperial guides tell us.' As they preached, the everyday English language of the Republic became increasingly American, most markedly through the adoption of the neo-American politically correct or PC language. The lead was taken by *The Irish Times,* an ex-Unionist, Protestant newspaper, in financial difficulty as its circulation fell, which now saw salvation offered by this new, so-called 'modernising' evangel. From 1962, when Ireland's first television station was established in Dublin its mostly young Irish operatives with experienced foreign managers, tentatively followed the *Irish Times* line. By the 70s the other Dublin papers, indeed the country's media generally including national radio, had more or less been brought into line.

The flavour of the 1960s—a time in Dublin that I confess I enjoyed living through—can be well illustrated by two quotes from *Irish Times* second editorials of that decade. The first of them I quote is from 13 January 1966. I was struck, amid its general promise of glamour at hand, by the coded reference to 'coffee-skinned girls'. The Christian modesty and chastity of most Irish girls was a block

in the way of the consumerist programme. Current media advertisements that progressively unclothed women were a help towards removing it. But a hint that the colleens had dangerous foreign competition at hand in Dublin might jolt them to their senses.

> Young people want things in a hurry, and want to forget the past...
> The young man sees himself appearing in the pages of *Paris Match*
> or *Life* magazines...Without any trammel of the past, whether Prot-
> estant/Catholic or Separatist/ex-Unionist, the differentials are dis-
> appearing in our country. Our young people want to forget. Boys
> in Dublin gravitate to coffee-skinned girls...The past is not only
> being forgotten by the young, it is being buried with great relish
> and even with disdain.

The second quote from a second editorial of 21 October 1965
illustrates how the historical revisionism of some academics—in effect the ideological undermining and replacement of the revolutionary narrative—was popping its head up before the 1970s when
it became rampant.

> Young people of today are, in their own phrase, tough-minded...
> Young people coming up, no matter what allegiance their fathers
> had, can look at the evolution of other countries from the British
> Commonwealth and wonder honestly if 1916 was really necessary.
> They can ask if, with Home Rule on the statute books, we would
> not today have a united Ireland, with or without some tenuous links
> to the British Commonwealth.★

That was the *Times* aiming to shape the present and future with
a swipe at the past. Its most genial stroke in denigrating the past was
by coining the term 'the de Valera Era', with the connotation of
darkness and error during the previous decades.

The media, recognising their new unanimity of message took
to using the word 'media' not correctly as the plural it denotes, but
realistically as the singular it had become. Journalists, in their reports
on matters in the Republic, began to situate them not 'in the Republic' but rudely 'in this State', or simply 'here', lest any Irishman

★ Douglas Gageby, then Editor and a devotee of Wolfe Tone, told me that these two editorial pieces were not written by him.

feel a slight urge to stand up straight. The offensive, as it might well be called, was propagating the alien ideology with intellectual and practical consequences. Large and increasing sums of money kept it fitted out with all it needed. By 1985 it had so progressed that in his book *Memory Ireland*, published in that year, an observant visiting Australian, Vincent Buckley, wrote:

> [Ireland] has been asked to lose its national memory by a kind of policy, in which politicians of almost all parties, ecclesiastics of all religions, media operators, and revisionist historians co-operate to create (and let us hope they do not need to enforce, for if they need to, they will) a new sense of corporate identity. This sense contradicts the immediately preceding one (the one based on the rising of Easter 1916 and its aftermath), which proved first so exhilarating and then so wearying to its generations, some of whom had fought to realize it. Ireland is not a nation, once again or ever, so the new story runs, but two nations; maybe several; it does not have its characteristic religion—or if it does, it ought not; it does not have its characteristic language, as anyone can see or hear; it has no particular race or ethnic integrity. Ireland is nothing—a no-thing—an interesting nothing, to be sure, composed of colourful parts, a nothing mosaic. It is advertising prose and Muzak.

'Nothing' there was a pretty exact term. The idea of Ireland had become effectively *a few million people who together signify nothing in particular except supporters of an Irish football team when it is playing a foreign team; living in a sef-governing unit of the British Isles and using the term 'very Irish' as a sneer.* Having been able for a short period to speak, like a normal European nation, of 'our national values', they could no longer do so because they possessed none. Unlike the adjective 'British', which has a positive ring for Brits, 'Irish' was often given by the Irish media a negative connotation as in the mocking cant phrase, (used proudly by Charles Haughey), 'an Irish solution for an Irish problem'.

That same unelected and unchallengeable power of money, media and government combined, having reiterated its story for the following twenty-four years, has in recent months [of 2010] brought it to a chorused climax of assault: the 'interesting' nothing of twenty-five years ago has, we are told, become, a criminal, perversely stupid and disgusting one. This barrage by printed word and broadcast journalists' sound and image has been enacting the sort of overkill that was sometimes engaged in by aerial bomber fleets of the Allies towards the end of the Second World War when they re-bombed the rubble of a well-bombed city to drive victory home.

The climax of assault took off when the worldwide economic recession made itself felt, in local forms and for local reasons, in one of the world's richest countries. Spurred by that impulsion, it became an exposition of general rottenness of mind and morals in the affairs of the Irish Republic and in the all-Ireland Catholic Church. On page after page of Dublin's newspapers, among the reports of frequent murders and drug seizures—the suicides and self-harmings are not reported—headlines great and small have been accusing stupidity, cover-up, corruption. It appears the dim-witted Irish people have used an ill-conceived political system to elect stupid, selfish persons to govern them and no rescue is in sight. As for Irish Catholicism, the comforting, strengthening and guiding cultural garment of our nation since time immemorial, its self-discrediting in the child-abuse scandal is not to mean that its episcopate must purge itself, beg forgiveness and return humbly to supplying the only effective kind of motive for good behaviour, but that it must subtract itself from the nation, yielding full opportunity to normlessness.

The national broadcaster has been amazing civil citizens in their homes. On radio its main news programmes are largely not news but for the most part 'interviews' resembling police interrogations. (I discovered that one of my daughters calls 'Morning Ireland' the 'We Hate Ireland' programme, but I would not single it out.) The station's employed correctors of the nation shout and bark at summoned holders of public office, repeatedly interrupting their attempted answers, zealous only to establish 'blame' and to extract 'apologies'. On television the main 'talk-shows' with audiences, having planted in the audience selected angry men and women, call on each of them in succession to continue the barrage about the awfulness of life in the rich and well-fed Republic of Ireland.

I think I have made a sufficient case for a thorough exploration by Irish historians of how an offensive inspired by an American ideology that was begun by some of the Dublin media in the 1960s, and later engaged in by all of them with the backing of successive governments, reduced the established Irish identity to a blurred nothing, thereby rendering Ireland unlovable. I think I have made that case while merely nibbling at the theme, leaving untouched by far the greater part of the fifty-year offensive: the great onslaughts in the referendums of the 1980s to the early 2000s, and the story of how the Northern War, the misdeeds of Catholic clerics, and the banking crisis of 2008 onwards, were used by the assailants to finish the job.

The evidence of this fifty-year-old phenomenon, from its tentative beginnings in the 1960s to its present climax, is there in the archives of the American and Irish media for our historians to research. Their task and purpose would be to produce a structured account of its origins and development, together with an explanation of how its successive agents saw what they were doing. Obviously the reduction of a loved Irish identity to an unlovable nothing is of equal historical importance to the construction of that same identity which nourished the Irish Revolution and which our historians have amply recounted. But there is a danger that our historians might strangely continue to ignore it.

Deserving also of investigation is whether there was a background of political or other persuasion to the *The Irish Times's* decision to solve its financial problem by leading the consumerist neoliberal campaign, and to the   falling into line of the new TV station. Certainly at that time, at the height of the Cold War, America wanted an ideological conformity on consumerist-liberal lines of its West European satellites. It was the ideal ideological tool for producing in face of the Communist East a challenging display of prosperity which would in turn generate in revenue more money for armaments and the space race. And that display of consumerist neoliberalism in practice in the West would confront the Communist indoctrination of Eastern Europe.

❖

ON THINKING IN IRELAND*

IN MY REVIEW entitled 'The Irish Problem with Thought'** of Thomas Duddy's *A History of Irish Thought*,*** I reported something which the author recounts in his Preface. When he had mentioned to people in Ireland, and in London where the book was published, that he was working on it, he met with incomprehension or scepticism. Surely, people said, there wasn't such a thing as 'Irish thought', at least 'not in the sense in which there was English, French or German thought'.

This reaction is easily explained. In the first place, the words 'Irish' and 'thought' had seldom if ever been used together. Many educated people would know there had been a Scotus Eriugena, a Toland, a Berkeley and a Burke, but would not be aware—because there has been no such thing—of a more or less linked succession of well-known Irish thinkers through the centuries into the present day.

What is meant, of course, in this context by 'thinkers' is creative thinkers, offering new, arresting, argued views of one or other broad aspect of human, cosmic or supernatural reality. The second reason for that reaction to Duddy's book title is that the works of creative thought which Irishmen have produced in recent times have been absent from the image of Irish writing that is presented by the Irish mass media to Irish people and foreigners. Insofar as these media—print media, radio and television—publicise or discuss Irish creative writers, they confine themselves to writers of prose fiction, poetry and plays; that is to say, to fictive writing as distinct from creative writing about the real. And about Irish fictive writing they make a loud noise, so that the impression is given at home and abroad that this is the only significant kind of Irish writing that occurs. There is not even a magazine of ideas—not one—in which Irish thinkers might present themselves and their antecedents to readers at home and abroad by publishing new essays, debating with each other, discussing their antecedents, and having their books reviewed. Nor is

---

* Website 2010, *www.desmondfennell.com*

** In *Cutting to the Point: Essays and Objections 1994-2004,* Dublin, The Liffey Press, 2003.

*** Duddy, Routledge, London, 2003.

there any approximate equivalent on radio or television of such a magazine.

This overall, abnormal state of affairs, *unique in Western Europe*, has a result that can be exemplified with reference to some important works of Irish thought published in the last few years. The works were by Richard Kearney, James Mackey, Philip Pettit and William Desmond, in each instance in continuation of a long line of previous books. The educated reading public in Ireland is generally unaware that Kearney has recently published a trilogy named *Philosophy at Its Limits,* which comprises *On Stories (Thinking in Action)*; *Strangers, Gods and Monsters: Interpreting Otherness*; and *The God Who May Be: A Hermeneutics of Religion*. A similar general Irish ignorance applies to Mackey's two recent books, *Christianity and Creation: The Essence of the Christian Faith and its Future among Religions* and *Jesus of Nazareth: The Life, the Faith and the Future of the Prophet;* to Pettit's *A Theory of Freedom: From the Psychology to the Politics of Agency* and *Rules, Reasons, and Norms: Selected Essays;* and to Desmond's *Is There a Sabbath for Thought? Between Religion and Philosophy,* and *Art, Origins, Otherness: Between Philosophy and Art.*

These four writers, have spent the larger part of their careers abroad; in a variety of countries, mainly America and Britain. Three of them live permanently abroad. Having largely published in America and Britain, they are known to thoughtful readers there, but also elsewhere, partly through translations. However, any incidental awareness those readers might have of the Irish nationality of one or other or all of them, individually, would not outweigh the factors mentioned above which suggest that there is no substantial body of work, past or present, amounting to 'Irish thought'.

Apart from Scotus Eriugena, Toland, Berkeley and Burke, there have of course been other Irishmen through the centuries who produced sustained creative thought. Duddy's book was the first to search them out and give some account of them. His selection is shaped and limited by the fact that his point of view and criterion are that of a teacher of philosophy in a university (Galway); but he does find space for William Thompson and for some elements of Swift, Yeats, and even Oscar Wilde. No neglected genius is brought to light except perhaps Augustinus Hibernicus in the seventh century. Most of the thinkers treated are from the seventeenth century onwards and are predominantly Anglo-Irish Protestants. The final chapter entitled 'Irish Thought in the Twentieth Century' deals with Yeats, J. O. Wisdom, Maurice O'Connor Drury, Iris Murdoch, William Desmond and Philip Pettit. With the exception of Yeats, all those thinkers have in common that they spent—or have so far spent—most of their working life abroad and published all or most of their books abroad.

The omission of the late Raymond Crotty reflects the professional limits of Duddy's choice. But his inclusion would not alter the 'largely abroad' message which Duddy's twentieth-century selection, added to the similar characteristic of Kearney's and Mackey's work, conveys. In the Republic of Ireland a combination of factors discourages the formulation and expression of sustained independent thought. Not only does the public discourse conducted by the mass media ignore such writing, while discussing Irish fictive writing copiously. That discourse also celebrates the fictive writing hugely, with the implication that it is the only kind of Irish writing that deserves notice or celebration. When occasionally contemporary thinkers do figure in the Irish mass media, they are foreigners who have won fame elsewhere—more precisely in London and New York—whom we are invited to attend to.

The media's discriminatory celebration of fictive writing is reinforced by the cultural policies of the Irish State as implemented through the three agencies it has established to honour and fund Irish creative individuals. Aosdána, which is a self-electing institution, defines such individuals as 'artists'. Since its foundation in 1981, it has elected to its membership, which is limited to 250, practitioners of visual art, musical composition and literature. Of late it has added architects and choreographers. It pays annual stipends to those members who prove their financial need. Inasmuch as it caters nominally for what it calls 'literature', one might expect to find in its membership creative writers as various in kind as those who make up the canonical literatures of, say, England, France or Germany. Given that quite a number of these created merely new visions of human *reality*, they would not, if living in Ireland today, qualify for election to Aosdána. Aosdána, at its foundation, formally and eccentrically defined 'literature' as consisting of only the fictive kind, that is, prose fiction, plays and poetry. Thus while Aosdána admits photographers, it excludes philosophers, regardless of their literary merits.

In the matter of publication the Arts Council discriminates similarly. On the grounds that sales would likely be small, Irish publishers are reluctant to accept works of thought. To obviate this objection in the case of prose fiction, plays or poetry, the Arts Council subsidises the publication of such works. The only possibility of similar facilitation for works of thought arises when the thinker is an academic; his academic institution may subsidise his venture. But those thinkers who, like many of history's most influential thinkers, are not professors of philosophy lack even that recourse.

A third state-funded agency, Culture Ireland, is charged with promoting and subsidising Irish culture internationally. With the difference that it has no branches abroad, its nominal role is similar to that of the British Council, the Goethe-Institut or the Alliance Française. In the year 2008 it subsidised 282 Irish cultural events mainly Irish events abroad but also some international events at home in which Irish people participated. All these events fell under the headings of theatre and dance, film, music, visual art, literature and architecture. And the 'literature' in question was again solely of the fictive kind. In other words, the 282 events included none—not one—in which Culture Ireland subsidised an Irish thinker addressing a foreign audience about some aspect of reality, perennial, contemporary or past. Thus Irish culture is officially represented to the world as a culture lacking any notable thought.

What these discouragements, taken together, seem to amount to is the Irish establishment and its subordinate tiers working to confirm that very English notion, notably articulated by Matthew Arnold, of the ever so imaginative, thoughtless Celts: gifted entertainers of their pensive Saxon masters cogitating on how to run the world.

Certainly our past history plays a role in this. The Republic of Ireland was not born out of thin air. The objective discouragements which it presents to sustained, creative thought both grow out of, and reinforce, an inherited subjective discouragement present in many of its citizens. To see something, to see a circumstance differently from how your friends, neighbours and colleagues, differently from how the accepted experts in that field, at home and maybe also abroad, see it; and then to search for and find grounds and arguments to support the truth of your vision of it; and to write all that down and offer it to those around you as the reality and truth of that circumstance—this requires confidence in your ability and right to discover truth independently. But the legacy of centuries-long mental colonisation of the Catholic Irish—the great majority, the conquered 'natives'—by the English, by their colony in Ireland, and by the Catholic clergy, deprives many of us of that dual confidence.

On the one hand, the training of generations of our ancestors in the belief that it was only 'others'—the Anglo-Irish, the English, the priests—who had that ability and right has left an inherited ingrained mark in many. On the other, thousands of those so marked are active in the Republic's mass media, government, schools and seats of learning, and subliminally delivering a similar doctrine, with the 'others' now located outside Ireland. Accepted subconsciously, that confidence-destroying doctrine renews in the upcoming young the colonised mental inheritance. This goes far to explain why, when the Catholic Irish ultimately achieved the chance to call the shots, they created a republic that within its own territory discourages creative thought, and makes its sustained expression there a guerrilla enterprise. In view of the substantial sequence of creative and speculative thinkers which Duddy's book reveals among the Anglo-Irish from the seventeenth century into the twentieth, it is likely that in an Irish republic fashioned by the Anglo-Irish the case would have been different. But we have what we have.

This combination of discouragements has militated against the Irish achieving, in its intellectual aspect, the aim of the Irish Revolution: that they would become again a 'normal' nation—to cite Daniel Corkery's succinct description of that aim.* Normal, in the

---

* Daniel Corkery, *Synge and Anglo-Irish Literature: A Study*, Cork University Press, 1931, p.242. In an intellectual field adjacent to philosophy, the following detail illustrates the persisting absence in Ireland of adult normality. While there have been many histories of Ireland written by Englishmen, not one Irish historian has written a history of England, the nation that has most impinged on Irish history.

sense of being in every respect, like other free nations, a collective human adult, exercising autonomously all the faculties of a full-grown human being. Those faculties include the formulation, publication and digestion of argued independent thought. While the Catholic and post-Catholic Irish continue to frustrate the exercise of these faculties in Ireland, Irish life, conducted on the basis of unscrutinised borrowed thinking, falls short of adult life, and resembles that of minors guided by what adult elders elsewhere think.

But then, today, within that national life of minors figuratively speaking, what guidance do or can the actual, physical minors receive from the senior generation in the matter of avoiding thoughtless, undirected lives? As we witness, distressed, the swollen numbers of young suicides and the regular or occasionally spectacular nights of self-destructive youthful frenzy, a voice is sometimes heard saying: 'Now that in great measure our young people lack the guidance previously given by the Catholic Church operating through believing parents, teachers, clergy and religious, what a shame that we have not inherited a thought-out philosophy of life and ethical behaviour, with the result that we lack such a philosophy now!'

What is not added is: 'and do everything we can to prevent its production'. That is not added because, being so intrinsically a part of how our republic operates, it is not noticed. And, while not noticed or put in the way of remedy, Irish post-Catholic, physically adult, mental minors continue clueless in the face of their generated minors, and the undirectedness of that rising generation grows and spreads.

2

I know what I am talking about. Since my student days in Dublin I have been in a modest way, never reaching soaring heights, a creative thinker. I hesitate to say 'philosopher', but since the 1960s that description—in the broad sense of looking and thinking beneath and around the representations of things and writing accordingly—has been applied to me by others.

Neither metaphysical nor divine reality, but the worldly or historical kind, has been my field. It is the field in which Tom Barrington, Joe Lee, Raymond Crotty, Brendan Clifford, John Robb, Richard Kearney and Dónal Ó Brolcháin, to mention some, have been occasional or enduring Irish colleagues. Working always in the essay form (even when the book was a travel narrative) I have used, apart from books and pamphlets, Irish newspapers before the dumbing down; magazines of ideas (Irish when there were still such); and in recent years my website (*www.desmondfennell.com*).

A recurrent experience through the years has been private communications from young Irishmen which expressed interest in or gratitude for something I had written. Frequently I was told that I was providing a quality of insight not easy to come by in Ireland. I sensed a curiosity as to how I, another Irishman, came to be thinking and writing this way. Sometimes there were questions about, or disagreement with, something I had written. I answered the questions, dealt with the disagreements. I always replied. And then when each brief correspondence ended, I often thought about the young man in question, wondered was he trying to think out the world or some part of it for himself, trying to emulate my way of seeing and thinking but not wanting to take up more of my time by further correspondence. An effect of this was to make me aware that by thinking and writing as I was doing I was encouraging others to try to do likewise.

Arrived now at 80 years of age, and with no further challenge to think beckoning me, I want to add to that encouragement by example the encouragement of a brief tutorial. Naturally, it will amount to directive advice drawn from my experience of thinking in the 'worldly' or 'historical' field, as distinct from the fields in which strictly philosophical thought or the theological kind operates. And it will reflect my own particular way of tackling worldly themes, as distinct from other ways in which these might be and are tackled. But I believe that starting to think creatively, and continuing to do so, is a more or less similar process in all fields of reality. And I am aware that a given thinker's particular way of conducting his thought derives primarily from his particular temperament and will therefore inevitably not be reproduced exactly by another thinker.

First of all, to clear the ground between us as Irish persons, an anecdote. More than thirty years ago, in a community hall on Inishbofin, an island off the Conamara coast, I attended a play called *The Illaunaspie Triangle*. It was by the late Sydney Bernard Smith, a witty and erudite Scotsman who had lived many years in Ireland. In the play a being from outer space has landed in the form of a man on Illaunaspie, a small island off the Conamara coast. One of a number of emissaries from a star whose inhabitants are wise and far-seeing, he, like they, has been dispatched with an urgent message to the rulers of our planet. Going by the name of Patrice and speaking with an English accent, he thought he was landing in London. Having met an island man, Mickeleen, and realising his mistake, he strikes up a drinking acquaintance with Mickeleen in the local pub. Their conversations range widely, and a philosophical question arises. Patrice, in doubt as to the answer to it, says he had best consult his mentors on his star—he has a black box which enables him to communicate with them. Mickeleen remarks, '*But you know, true thoughts can be thought on Illaunaspie.*'

Bang! The words hit me so forcefully that I have remembered them to this day. I felt that Sydney—I knew him personally—was delivering a message to us, one that he thought we needed. He was after all a Scotsman, from a nation that has, or had, a tradition of strong independent thinking, and he had lived in Ireland many years. I have related that memory, as I said, to clear the ground between us as Irish persons by establishing my premises. I assume that the wider import of Mickeleen's remark is no news to you.

Note, then, to begin with, that the world, and your part of it, have always operated, and are now operating, on the basis of flawed assumptions about how things are; and that these assumptions mainly derive from the understandable acceptance by most people of the prevalent representations of how things are. These more or less untrue representations are prevalent because those who control by one means or another the general behaviour of people also control, in a general way, the representation of what is the case; and naturally, therefore, ensure that this primarily serves their control of people's behaviour rather than the truth.

This state of affairs has been notably useful in two ways. In large or small areas of our planet, it has often produced good public order: a fair degree of safety for adults and children in the streets and countryside, enabling work to proceed usefully and youth to reach old age. And given that the immediate purpose of creative thought is to reveal truth in one domain or another, that same state of affairs has always constituted, and now constitutes, the rich and challenging field in which creative thought operates.

When you engage in probing thought about present or past matters, you are attempting to replace with some truth the not true representations and the flawed assumptions which spring from them. To what ultimate purpose? People are endowed with the capacity to search for and to uncover truth; to see, at least broadly, how things really are. So with every piece of truth you discover and reveal, you are becoming more fully human, more a human adult, and helping those who read your work to do likewise: to be adults rather than minors.

Aristotle said that philosophy begins with wonder. Unaware of that, I called my first book, which was mainly concerned with travel in the very strange countries of the Far East, *Mainly in Wonder.* Certainly creative thought begins with an open-minded consideration of a circumstance and a search for words that describe it accurately. The 'circumstance' may be a set of circumstances amounting together to a composite circumstance. 'Open-minded' means with your mind emptied of anything you have heard about the matter— suspending your awareness of how the considered circumstance is generally or sometimes described or evaluated.★

How does this act of reflective wonder come to focus on a particular object? It may be that you choose that object because for some reason you feel a need and desire to know it well. Such was the case when I fixed on 'Asia'; and when subsequently I sought a commission from Hutchinson of London to write a book on Sweden. And again, after Sweden had disassembled my view of the contemporary western world and I wanted to reassemble a view of it, that need and desire embarked me on an inquiry into the modern history of the western world. You may perform the focusing because someone commissions you to do so, as when, after my Far Eastern journey, Douglas Gageby of *The Irish Times* commissioned me to go north and write six articles on 'The Northern Catholic' (thus

★ See the chapter 'Approach to Asia' in *Mainly in Wonder,* London: Hutchinson, 1959; also pp.13-18 in *The Turning Point: My Sweden Year and After,* Dublin: Sanas Press, 2000.

beginning in 1958 what would later turn out to be a long engagement with the Northern Ireland problem). Or you may notice a
prevalent misrepresentation of a circumstance, as I did with regard
to that very problem in 1969 or, many years later, with regard to
Seamus Heaney's quality as a poet—and wish to correct it. Or again,
a theme may be thrust on you by your moving to a place which
features publicly as, and is in fact, a problematic place. This happened
me when I moved to the Conamara Gaeltacht in the West of Ireland, a twosome of problematic places that impelled me onto a path
of creative thinking that reached far beyond them. Or mere chance
may bring about the fortunate fixation, as when (with a momentous
outcome) I went to visit a friend in a village in Washington State,
USA; or later, in Italy, travelled to an exhibition of the painter Duccio in Siena.

Obviously, in order to bring that seminal act of looking to its
first conclusion in language that is provisionally accurate, you must
draw on your prior store of sure knowledge. This means, if the circumstance is unique, on your prior knowledge of facts pertaining to
it; or, if it is a circumstance of a kind, on your prior knowledge of
other circumstances of that kind and of how they are described accurately. And you must do relevant research to increase your store of
sure knowledge. If you find that the language habitually used about
the matter in question shows a serious misunderstanding of it, you
have hit gold, you have a lot of work to do.

However, from personal experience I must add that you can also
'find yourself' launched into far-ranging thought and new vision
without having fixed your mind probingly on any particular circumstance. It can so happen that a stimulating combination of forces
in your environment makes you feel 'full' and in need of verbal
release, and that this release begins with jottings and then flows
on as far-reaching, visionary thinking. In the mid-1960s it was like
that for me when, simultaneously, the movement of Church renewal emanating from the Second Vatican Council, the build-up to
the celebration of the fiftieth anniversary of the Easter Rising, and
an exciting conflicted phase in Dublin painting, pressed in on me.
'Cuireadh chun na Tríú Réabhlóide' in *Comhar* magazine and 'Irish
Catholics and Freedom since 1916' in *Doctrine and Life* flowed from

that. Likewise, other essays in *Doctrine and Life*, in *Herder Correspondence*, and pieces on painting in *Hibernia*. If that sort of thing happens to you, well, you just go with it, let it rip.

You are not a polemicist. There is nothing wrong with taking to bits, critically and perhaps aggressively, a view or narrative presented or divulgated by an individual or a group with whom you seriously disagree. But you don't make a habit of it. After doing so, you have not coherently expressed your own thought-through and calm viewing of the matter in question, which is the work of the thinker. So being a thinker, you elaborate and ground your own divergent view insofar as is practicable without attacking any individual or group who believe or argue differently. And if that, for reasons of your argument, is impossible, then your dealing with their error will consist merely in pointing it out, without insulting or denigrating them. After all, your thought when published to the world will, if you are lucky enough not to meet with silence, encounter opponents; no point in making them venomous enemies.

It will occasionally happen that persons who dislike the thrust of what you have written misrepresent it in whole or in part, alleging that you have said something which you have not said. For example, this has happened to me more than once with regard to my pamphlet on Seamus Heaney. If you consider their misrepresentation sufficiently important to require correction, the best response is to ask them publicly to cite the sentence or passage where you have said what they allege. Their inability to do so will expose their misrepresentation.

The worst response you can encounter is public silence; either literally, or in the form of no coherent response. If your theme concerns specifically an Irish circumstance which is somehow topical, and your thought is both deviant and prominently published, you will encounter publicly a silence of that second kind. There will be condemnation and name-calling from upholders of the current orthodoxy—formerly Catholic-nationalist, now neoliberal. This response, while depriving you of useful feedback, has the benefit of advertising your thought, even if negatively. At the same time, privately, you will receive commendation and enquiry.

If your work is both deviant and of book length, has a relevance broader than merely Irish, and you are not an academic, you will find it impossible to discover an Irish commercial publisher willing to give you a contract. Only if you are an academic, and your institution is willing to subsidise publication, will you have some chance of success. You may have to do, as I have done on some occasions, pay the costs of printing and publication yourself, or alternatively, forego royalties. If you do manage to get such a work published in Ireland, be prepared: you will encounter public silence (with private responses). Those Irish who are in the habit of making public pronouncements, having heard no pronouncement on your novel thought from London or New York, will not know how to respond.

For this reason, if you have written a work of broader than Irish relevance and you remain in Ireland, you might attempt to get your work published in Britain. For a non-academic this will be a difficult undertaking because the British publishers and quality press are not programmed to expect thought from Ireland, let alone publish it. Having an academic post, with the possibility that British academic advisers to the British publisher will approve your work, would help. Alternatively to all this, you could use the Internet—a blog or a personal site—and hope for the best.

If you are by profession an academic, you do not of course, in your thinking, behave academically, in the sense of working out and presenting a variation, slight or striking, of the standard vision of your theme. You prove yourself a thinker by subverting the standard vision, not as your aim, but as a side-effect of your finding that no variation of it convinces you.

What you most hope for, of course, is to encounter by one means or another serious articulate opponents or, much better, painstaking critics pro and con. They would enable you to refine your thought. Even your best effort cannot capture the full truth of your theme; at most it will constitute a substantial advance towards the full truth. That, the full truth, is always something 'out there' which a competing fraternity of mutually correcting thinkers can approximate to.

You are not a moralist let alone a moraliser. Whether the terrain in which your mind is operating is contemporary or past, you will find it mined with moral characterisations and moral judgments expressed by a great variety of epithets. Not being yourself, as thinker, a partisan of any cause but that of factual truth, you ignore these and employ none of your own. Naturally, where there occurred, or is occurring, a breach of the moral or legal rules in force around an action, you say so as a fact of the matter. At the same time you know that no one ever did anything with the single intention of doing evil, but always to achieve a real or imagined good. So where clarifying a motivation, yours or another's, seems relevant, in the service of truth you mention in passing such intended goods. In sum, simply in order to practise no higher virtue than that of a thinker who keeps to his craft, you always heed St Paul's injunction in his letter to the Ephesians 'to speak the truth in love'.

What if you realise ultimately, or are persuaded of it by others, that your version of the truth is fundamentally wrong? You accept this as well as you can, knowing that you made your best effort in a good and worthwhile cause, and intend to try again, having learned much.

THE STAGGERED END OF EUROPEAN CIVILISATION*

> There were whispered arguments between our parents while we watched TV—arguments about changing the rules, we gathered, that applied to all of us, the dads and moms as well as the kids—Naomi Wolf in *Promiscuities* (1997) on San Francisco in 1970.

DURING THE PAST ninety odd years western civilisation has been coming to an end in three revolutions: the Russian and German revolutions, and the Second American Revolution which is still shaping life in the West today. Let me clarify three key terms.

First, *a civilisation*. A civilisation is essentially a grounded hierarchy of values and rules covering all of life and making sense to a people, which they and their rulers subscribe to over a long period. (Given that human beings can construct a civilisation, living together as one such is the normal way for human beings to live and living together otherwise, as the West is now progressively doing, is an abnormal collective condition.) The civilised community is motivated to keep

---

★ *Village* magazine, Dublin, Oct.-Nov. 2010; 2000 *The European Journal,* Rome, Year 11, No 2.

reproducing itself by the *sense* that it finds in its set of values and rules, its framework for life. Some of the rules are circumstantial and therefore changeable as time proceeds; others are essential, forming the civilisation's defining core.

European or western civilisation: Founded in western Europe in the twelfth century AD by Latin, Germanic and Celtic Christians, it later crossed the Atlantic and other seas and lasted into the twentieth century. Its set of essential rules of behaviour made sense to our ancestors for about 800 years.

A revolution: It begins with a group of people who adhere to a new ideology which they believe contains the formula for a good and just life. These believers take possession of a nation's central government and by unconstitutional means increase its power. Using that augmented power, they preach their ideology, proclaim new values and rules derived from it, empower those who support these, and disempower opponents. This process takes at least twenty years, maybe longer.

Until the first half of the twentieth century there existed a tacit agreement of European nations, at home and overseas, that all political and military action must respect—or after a transgression reassert—the essential rules of European civilisation. This tacit agreement applied also to revolutions: the new rules which a revolution enduringly established must not breach the essential European rules. The Irish Revolution and the Italian Fascist revolution operated within this framework.

But three revolutions, in three powerful countries, Russia, Germany and the USA, rejected the rules system of European civilisation. The revolutionaries, finding that European civilisation unjustly limited their power to create the good life they envisaged, made new rules that, while forbidding certain behaviours, justified states, groups and individuals doing things which European civilisation forbade. The Russian revolution maintained its post-European rules system for seventy years. The German revolution was beginning to establish its rules when it was overthrown. From the 1960s onwards the Second American revolution established its post-European rules system in its own country and, by proxy, in Western Europe. That rules system is still in force.

The Second American Revolution: The Second American Revolution began in 1933 during the Great Depression when Franklin D. Roosevelt became President. The American revolutionaries were left-liberals. Their liberalism required a big and powerful state shaping the lives of people for their good. Roosevelt brought them to power as advisors and colleagues because he was convinced that their demand for a Big (meaning very powerful) State, like the Soviet state, was the best means of tackling the Depression and creating a just society. His New Deal programme greatly increased the power of the State, the federal government. When the Supreme Court pronounced twelve New Deal measures unconstitutional, Roosevelt, in effect, got the new Constitution he needed by appointing left-liberal judges who found the measures constitutional. In 1940, in disregard of American precedent, Roosevelt was elected President for a third term, and later, while America was at war, he sought and won election for a fourth term.

The Big State which the left-liberals (calling themselves simply 'liberals') created reached its apogee with the manufacture of the atomic bomb, the use of this weapon against two Japanese cities, and the official justification of the resulting massacres. This justification of massacre signalled to the liberals that the state they had worked to create was likely to approve those elements of their programme that rejected other core rules of European civilisation.

The aim of their programme, given the Big State, was to bring about a perfect human condition. For that purpose, first, there must be an end to the tacit recognition of Christianity as America's 'national' religion, and to the consequent role of Christian morality as a determinant of behavioural rules. Second, categories of citizens who were legally or otherwise unequal must be raised or lowered to legal equality, so as to bring about a fraternity of individuals, equal in law and in their treatment by their fellows. Third, all citizens must have access to education and health services and be equipped with buying power. And finally, with due regard to the rights of others, the desires of individuals must be recognised as rights and realised as far and as equally as possible.

Implicit in that programme (subsequently to be transmitted to America's West European satellites) were Black civil rights and radical feminism; legal normalisation of homosexuals and of unmarried mothers and their offspring; political and financial empowerment of young people; maximal facilitation of the physically deficient; invalidation of intrinsic personal authority such as that possessed by clergy, males, parents, teachers and the aged; ample social welfare; unshackling of sex and of pornography; legalisation of abortion; and a blank cheque for science. Implicit, therefore, in their programme was a new collection of rules many of which would replace essential European rules, which were traditional in the USA and which they deemed oppressive or unjust.

The culmination of the revolution: Their chance to implement their programme fully came in the 1960s and early 70s when the US government and manufacturing industry needed to increase consumption, with its dual yield of revenue and profit. The government, committed to reaching the Moon, was waging the Cold War and the Vietnam war and producing many costly nuclear weapons. Manufacturing industry with the help of computers and automation was producing more goods than it could sell. First government, then also manufacturing industry, perceived in the unfulfilled parts of the liberal agenda the means of increasing consumption and the consequent money yield.

So from the late 1960s the American state began endorsing that agenda through Supreme Court rulings and by legislation. Under the liberal President, Lyndon Johnson, the revolution made its great breakthrough. The teachers and preachers of the post-European, neoliberal rules of correct behaviour came to function as a sort of secular state church or informal, doctrinally paramount 'Party'. Since their role had to do with defining correct thought, language and behaviour, to call it the liberal 'Correctorate' seems appropriate.★

FROM *AGGIORNAMENTO* TO RECOVERY★★

Although I was in Rome in the early 1960s only for a brief visit,

---

★ The spread of the values and rules system of American neo-, i.e, consumerist, liberalism to Western Europe is dealt with in my books *Ireland after the End of Western Civilisation*, Athol Books, 2009 and *Third Stroke Did It: The Staggered End of European Civilisation*, Publibook Ireland, 2014.

★★ *The Furrow*, Maynooth, Oct. 2010.

I was pretty close to the Second Vatican Council through working for the English-language edition of *Herder Correspondence*. Herder had good informants in Rome,was very much taken by the Council, and a supporter of its so-called 'progressive' wing.

In 1968 Geoffrey Chapman published a collection of articles from *Herder Correspondence* written and edited by me which dealt broadly with Irish Catholicism. Entitled *The Changing Face of Catholic Ireland*, it contained a long article 'Time of Decision' which I had written in 1964. With many facts and figures, it depicted Irish Catholicism as a church that 'by the standards of Late Tridentine Catholicism was flourishing, while containing a growing current of self-criticism and displaying a tentative opening to the new impulses from the Continent. In a Foreword to the book the leading German theologian Karl Rahner recognised the specialness of the Irish church—matched only perhaps in Spain and Poland—as effectively the church of an entire people in a world where the normal condition of the Church was that of a diaspora. He counselled the Irish to take from the new Continental impulses, which had arisen in that quite different situation, only what suited that special condition of their church.

I read very little of the Council theology or encyclicals. But I have continued to be a thoughtful member of the People of God and it is as such that I continue this article.

Back in Ireland after the Council had ended I paid attention mainly to the changes in Church practice. *Aggiornamento* had been the Council's principal slogan word and I took it to mean loosely 'renewal' or 'freshening up'. Noting the Mass in the vernacular, priests and nuns in secular dress, occasional use of plain bread rather than hosts for Communion, and greater involvement of the laity in active roles, I thought 'Incarnation': God's incarnation in the world is being advanced decisively by using the secular ever more to express the divine. Since I had encountered Dutch still-life painting of the seventeenth century, the Incarnation had become for me a central Christian theme. In those paintings I had seen how Dutch Protestant painters, deprived by the Reformation of saints and the Blessed Virgin for their paintings, had managed to transfer the holiness of such figures to bread, milk, fruit, and candlesticks and the interiors of Dutch merchant houses. Trying to further my Incarnational understanding of what the Council was about, I wrote to Cardinal Conway and the other bishops, urging a general assembly of the Irish Church based on elected delegates from the parishes. And I persuaded the priests and parishioners in my own half-parish of Cárna, Conamara, to set up an elected parish council.

By the 1970s the word *consumerism* and the reality it indicated were well established. Thinking in this context about changes the Council had brought about, I noticed that the abolition of prescribed fasting during Lent, of the fast from midnight before Communion, (a 'fast' of one hour had been substituted), and of abstinence from meat on Friday, seemed to signify the Church falling into line with the consumerist ethos. Fasting and abstinence were offences against consumerism. It seemed to me that Catholicism was now perhaps the only religion ever that did not have fasting as one of its regular devotional exercises. These thoughts began a gradual opening of my eyes to an aspect of the Council reforms that I had missed, and which seemed quite contrary to that sanctifying of the secular which had first struck me. It was more like the sacred yielding to, or conforming to a secular fashion.

Another thing moved me decisively to this view of the matter. Generally speaking, the consumerist-liberal ideology that had reached Europe from America in the 1960s, and that had entered the Dublin mass media via London, was presenting itself as a doctrine of liberation: sexual liberation, liberation of women, youth and homosexuals, liberation of everyone from self-restraint and frugal living. As it gained adherents and practitioners, this liberation movement had led many of the rising generation into a slavery of material and sexual consumption. I could not understand why the Church had not responded by expressly making liberation from that slavery through Jesus Christ into the core of its preaching in the West. Never in my experience did the word 'liberation' fall from the lips of priest, monk or bishop. The spoken and written preaching of the Gospel was not adapting to directly challenge, and compete with, the powerful and successful preaching of false liberations. Its displayed attitude towards this was a respectful passivity.

The meaning of aggiornamento:

All this sent me back to that slogan word of the Council: *aggiornamento*. As I said above, I had regarded its general import as an intention to refresh or renew; I had not attended to its literal meaning, which is 'bringing up to date', with the enormous ambiguity of what that means in real terms. With equal ambiguity the same idea had been occasionally rendered as 'making modern': Karl Rahner, in his foreword to my book, mentioned as taken-for-granted needs, 'a modern theology and a modern Church'.

In an updating operation, the 'date' which something is to be 'brought up to' is 'what is at present the case'. Making something modern means bringing it into line with 'what is at present "modish" or in vogue in the power centres'. If it is a matter—as it was in the 1960s with the Church—of updating or modernising intellectual, moral and regulatory matters, the most relevant part of 'what is now the case and in vogue' is the worldview that is at present predominant or advancing, together with the rules system derived from it.

In the 1960s, in the Soviet satellites of eastern Europe, that worldview with attendant rules system was Marxist-Leninism. In the West it was the advancing, equally Godless and utopian worldview of American left-liberalism, which with the support of states and business had become in effect consumerist neoliberalism. Open to all without distinction, it was a faith that offered its believers enlightenment; justification for rejecting many moral rules and social norms of European civilisation; equality of personal status and treatment; increasing buying power; glamour and sensual indulgence. Later it would be called in retrospect 'the ideology of the 60s', meaning mainly an exciting promise of a fresh start for mankind, a kinder way of living, and limitless possibility, that attracted many, especially young people, throughout the West. That was the main element of the up-to-dateness and modernity in relation to which the Church of the Second Vatican Council would try to update and modernise itself.

Conclusions: Council's weakening of Irish culture

Reflecting on this matter over the past thirty years, I have come to three conclusions. The first regards certain practical changes in the universal Church which emanated from Vatican II. I have in mind such changes as the removal of prescribed fasting and abstinence; the puritanical redesigning and consequent defamiliarising of many church interiors, including the removal of many statues; the downgrading of 'mindlessly repetitious' prayers such as the Rosary and litanies; the widespread cessation of Corpus Christi and May processions; the laicising of priests' everyday dress; the ending of the regulation that had women cover their heads in church; and so on. In the 1960s Irish Catholic practices supplied a large part of the distinctively Irish culture. So it was unfortunate that such imposed changes, of no obvious benefit to Irish Catholic faith or devotion, occurred in those years, weakening the Irish cultural edifice at a time when consumerist liberalism was beginning its assault on it.

Secondly, during Vatican II and subsequently, the Catholic Church in the West has been influenced by the western Myth of Progressive Modernity. (In what follows, when I say 'the Church' I am referring to the Church in the West.) That myth relates that, in the inexplicably privileged white West, the progress of years is accompanied by a progress of insight into the nature of man and the right way to order human society and behaviour. In the event of a clash of claims to possession of the newest and therefore truest insight—say, between socialism and the latest version of liberalism—the truest insight is determined by its having effective ascendancy in the West's power centres! That authenticates it as (the latest) intellectual *modernity*, i.e. as the truest insight into human reality and right order yet reached by the human mind. As such, it is something which by tacit accord of most western intellectuals imperatively demands respect and which it behoves them to conform their minds to. But clearly, the true insight that they thus aspire to is possessed by modernity only within the myth and for believers in the myth. In reality the fact that a certain new vision of human matters is in vogue in the West's power centres says nothing about its truth, merely suggests that it is useful to the power-holders.

The leading men involved in Vatican II and in the post-conciliar shaping of the Catholic Church belonged to the Catholic variety of western intellectual culture. More particularly they belonged to that segment of Catholic thought that was influenced by the West's Myth of Progressive Modernity. Accordingly they respected the intellectual modernity of the time—the 'ideology of the 60s' with consumerist liberalism at its core—as the truest insight into human matters yet reached by the *non-Christian* human mind. While it repelled them by being Godless and by proposing a morality that deviated radically from the European and Christian one, they respected it in two ways: by not opposing it outright (as the Church had opposed Communism) and by trying to learn from it as much as their Christian vision allowed.

An instance of this 'respect by not challenging outright' was the Church's failure to counter expressly with Christ's true liberation consumerist liberalism's claim to be a liberation movement. An aspect of this has been the failure to spell out with facts the falsity of the new liberals' claim of liberation in relation to various groups and categories. For example, women. During the last forty years that have been governed by neoliberal norms and rules, western women have found that the spaces and times in which they can walk safely alone have greatly diminished, and we have witnessed through the liberation of pornography and commercial advertising, mainly under the management of men, the most widespread presentation of women as sex objects in all of human history.

I believe, incidentally, that an important factor contributing to this respectful leaving of the contemporary world to the liberal Correctorate to describe and pronounce upon has been the post-conciliar regulation that the priest's homily during Mass must be based on the scriptural readings of the day. For most Catholics this preaching about incidents in the lives of Christ and the Apostles, spiritual advice given to early Christian communities, or exhortations by Jewish Prophets to the ancient Israelites, is the only Catholic preaching they hear.

The western Church's identification of consumerist liberalism in terms of the modernity myth, as the truest insight into human matters yet reached by the non-Christian human mind, caused a blindness with regard to its real nature. It prevented the Church recognising this late western ideology—as the Church in sub-Saharan Africa recognises Islam, or the Church in South America recognises evangelical Protestantism—as a powerful competing missionary faith; and as one, moreover, that has been particularly intent on capturing successive generations of young Catholics. And not recognising it as this—as what it was and is in the real world as distinct from the modernity myth—it did not respond accordingly.

As to the Church learning from its Godless rival, this occurred in a manner that was partly positive, partly mixed or negative. In respect of increasing the active role of women in the Church, it was positive. In respect of further learning from the central secular doctrine of the 1960s, the Church's learning from it was of mixed effect. That doctrine taught that people should be kind to others and to themselves. So rather than punishment for wrongdoing, re-habilitation was to be preferred; and self-punishment was a morbid practice. Learning from this the Church took a more humane view of unmarried mothers and homosexuals. It decided that imposed self-punishment by fasting and abstinence was not good and that punishment of sexually misbehaving clergy was not a good thing either. Recently we have been made aware how, much to their later cost, this latter change of mind influenced the Irish and other bish-ops in their handling of clerical paedophilia: rehabilitation by psy-chiatric treatment was preferred to punishment. I believe that the same prioritising of 'kindness' and rejection of punishment caused the virtual disappearance of Hell, as the posthumous punishment for grievous sin, from Catholic preaching.

An instance that I have noted, very particularly in Ireland, of a combined respect for, and active learning from, consumerist liberal-ism has been in relation to that ideology's desire to secularise public life; to remove any intrusion into it of religion. Some Irish bishops and Catholic spokespersons have decried this. But the fact is, first, that such secularisation has gone further in the Republic of Ireland than in any other Catholic part of Europe, say, Italy or Bavaria; and, second, that in the absence of any laws enforcing it, its principal agents have been Catholics. The widespread cessation of devotional processions in the streets was merely the first notable instance. Since then, Catholics working in many areas of Irish life have either de-cided to remove public displays of Catholic or broadly Christian devotion or presence, or to omit these where they would be appropriate. At the very least they have participated in such decisions. And most of this has occurred without any Catholic public protest of any note. In other words, Catholics, by their actions or inaction, have been the main agents of secularisation in the Republic of Ireland.

I am thinking of such as the following occurring over the past forty or fifty years: the removal from the national broadcaster's television screens of a picture of the Blessed Virgin when the evening Angelus is sounded, and of a Christian prayer last thing at night; the fact that, although RTÉ is obliged by statute to reflect Irish culture, the only serious TV programmes on Christian themes that are readily available to Irish viewers are on British channels, including Ulster Television; the removal of the RTÉ radio Mass on Sunday from the main wavelength to a secondary one; the failure of Irish Catholics to establish a Catholic radio station; the recent removal of a statue of Christ from the roof of the community hospital in Killarney; a big fall-off in towns and cities of the Irish Catholic custom of blessing oneself as one passes a church; the inclusion of many schools bearing the names of saints in amalgamated community schools which honour no saint; the fact that, with summer schools and local festivals long an established part of the Irish summer and autumn, there is not one dedicated to a local saint or with some other Christian theme; the cessation of the annual ceremonial blessing of the Aer Lingus fleet; the absence at Christmas of a Crib, as against the presence of two large shrines of Santa Claus and his reindeer, in the arrivals hall at Dublin airport; the shifting of the feasts of the Ascension and Corpus Christi from their traditional days mid-week (when people were regularly given time off work to attend Mass) to the following Sundays where no one notices them; the rearrangement of public holidays during the year with the result that the Whit Weekend has disappeared, and that the Republic marks with special holidays— apart from Christmas and Easter (which were holidays even in European Communist countries) and St Patrick's Day ranking as the diplomatically required 'National Day'—only extra days when the banks are closed; and finally, the silence of the Irish Catholic bishops in the face of two years of economic crisis affecting Government action and many citizens.

I am aware that such secularism may reflect an inherited uncertainty of Irish Catholics—unlike, say, Italian, Bavarian or Polish Catholics—about their right to display their existence publicly. It recalls how Irish Catholics, in the period when the Penal Laws were weakening but Emancipation had not yet happened, built their first new urban churches on side-streets or down lanes. But this recent hiding of themselves and their religion from public view has not been done out of caution lest they break some law, but voluntarily. There is a sad analogy with Peter's denying of Jesus when challenged in the high priest's court.

Recovery: its basis and circumstances

If in 1964 I was able to write truthfully in *Herder Correspondence* that the Irish Church was by the standards of Late Tridentine Catholicism a flourishing church, I could not today write that it is by any standards 'flourishing'. Not that it is in dire straits. The number of its more or less active members is still—because the national population was much smalller then—probably close to what it was in the 1920s or 1930s, and generally speaking they are considerably more affluent and better educated than their predecessors in those years. Advertisements for pilgrimages to Catholic shrines on the Continent suggest that these are still being undertaken by considerable numbers. Throughout Ireland many parishes are being led by devoted and enterprising priests with the greatly increased active support of lay people. The teaching of the Catholic religion is possible in the great majority of schools, and there are many Catholic schools, both primary and secondary, which provide the opportunity to transmit the Faith effectively to children and teenagers.

What the situation amounts to is that the Church in Ireland, as has previously happened throughout Europe, has ceased to be effectively the Church of an entire nation. Instead, it has become, as in the rest of Europe, a part of a diaspora of Catholic communities of communities existing throughout Europe and throughout the world. But that is how the universal Church has been in all of the world except Europe since the earliest times. Europe, remember, became an exception because in the Roman Empire in the fourth century the Church became the religious body favoured and supported by the state, and the new states of Europe followed that

Roman example. Now, since around the middle of the last century, European states have switched their patronage to consumerist liberalism and allowed it to use the national mass media as pulpits. Europe's new exceptionality is to be the only continent which is largely irreligious.

The time may have come when, numerically speaking, the principal presence of the Church in the world will be in some other continent. We do not know. In the meantime the task for us in Ireland is to make our community of Catholic communities a flourishing church within the Catholic diaspora.

In the Christmas period 2010-11 Cilian and I flew to Israel to visit Ron's parents. We were made very welcome in their house in a suburb of Tel Aviv. There was a grand dinner with parents, brother, two sisters and a brother-in-law, Eliran, Einat, Efrat, and Oshri—names that I had to write down afterwards with an (m) or (f) after each of them to remember and distinguish them genderwise! Everything but politics was discussed. Cilian and I went on to make Christmas visits to Jerusalem and, of course, Bethlehem.

2012

TELLING THE REVOLUTION AS IT REALLY WAS*

I BELIEVE THAT the Irish Revolution has not yet been narrated in its full and true reality. I want to make some suggestions about how this can and should be done. Such well-narrated historical processes as the Roman, French and Russian revolutions allow us to identify the common traits of a revolution as distinct from a *coup d'état* or similar change of regime. I believe that the Irish Revolution had all these traits, but that this has so far not been recognised by historians with the result that we have been given a shrunken and faulty account and lack a telling of the Revolution as it really was.

With an eye to those common traits of a revolution, I would describe a revolution in the following terms. A group of ideologues

* Expanded from article with this title in *History Ireland*, Dublin, Sept./Oct. 2012.

have a vision of a state of affairs in their political community that would be morally and materially superior to the existing one. They act to bring that better order about. Their actions have the following characteristics successively: Effort to Acquire the Sovereign Government Power; Acquisition and Augmentation of the Sovereign Government Power; Cultural Reform (involving Establishment of New Values and Rules and Moral Purification); Missionary Dissemination of the Revolution's Values; Completion of the Revolutionary Programme. (This last stage, as, for example, with collectivisation in the Russian Revolution, may take up to twenty or more years to occur.).

As I have suggested, the Irish Revolution followed that pattern. In order to narrate it so as to make that evident, the historian would need to do a number of ancillary things which can be enumerated as follows:

1. *Explain the situation in Ireland before the Revolution began.* In particular, among other things: that the population was divided into two ethnic-religious communities, the much larger one Catholics, the other Protestants, with the latter predominating in the North-east; the historical origins of these communities and the nature of their present relationship, including the fact that the Protestants generally were loyal to the British state, most fervently in the North-east, while the Catholics generally espoused an Irish nationalism that had two supreme values—the *Irish nation* (understood as consisting essentially of themselves while open to other adherents) which they wanted to acquire Liberal-democratic self-government, and *Catholicism* which they wanted to flourish. (A footnote here might state as follows: 'Neither the Catholics nor the Protestants constituted a sect, and neither described matters pertaining to itself or to the other by the term "sectarian", though some Irish historians after the mid-twentieth century acquired the inaccurate and unhistorical habit of doing so.') And, continuing the account of Ireland before the Revolution: that there was a secret society, the Irish Republican Brotherhood, ramifying among the Catholics, which held, and was pursuing, a single value and vision: an Irish Republic (meaning sovereign, Liberal-democratic state) comprising in fraternity all the inhabitants of Ireland, Catholic and Protestant, the latter having re-

placed their British allegiance with allegiance to Ireland; and finally, that there was a Gaelic-revivalist movement gathering force.

2. Narrate how the Effort to Acquire the Sovereign Government Power Began and Proceeded. How initially the Easter Rising of 1916, organised and led by the Irish Republican Brotherhood with majority input from the Irish Volunteers and some from the Irish Citizen Army, was intended to be a fairly well-armed rising of some thousands at various places throughout much of the country. How it turned out to be mainly limited to an action of over a thousand men and some women in Dublin accompanied by the proclamation of an Irish Republic. How the rebels fought and the British responded.

That the rebels were inspired by a combination of motives. How for most of the seven leaders, expressly, the obstacles to be overcome were the broken humanity of the Irish and the English rule that had caused it; and the achieved Republic the means of effecting that. That for Pearse, and more explicitly for Connolly three months before the Rising, that redemption of Irish humanity would be achieved through the effusion of blood in imitation of Christ on the Cross. (Here a footnote might say: 'A "redemption by blood", not a "blood sacrifice" '—a British term used to describe the deaths of British soldiers in the Great War which was later often and erroneously ascribed to the intentions of the leaders of the Rising.) That for the rank-and-file, Irish freedom, including a better life for workers and their Catholic religion on top, was the motivation. That a general religious inspiration was signalled for the Rising by the choice of Easter for its start and—anecdotally and illustratively— that on the Saturday before the Rising there were queues of young men for Confession in some Dublin Catholic churches and that during the Rising the Rosary was recited during lulls in the fighting in several of the battle stations.

And continuing, how after the Rising's military failure and the execution of sixteen leaders, public support for the rebels and their action grew. How the Sinn Féin Party gained support and with help from the Conscription Crisis won the 1918 election, leading to the First Dáil of the nominal Irish Republic. How in 1919 the War of Independence began and spread throughout the country involving the entire nation until the Truce in 1921. That the religious events of that and the following years would show that during the war many Irish men and women valued the strength and consolation that their Catholicism supplied, identified it with the national struggle and wanted to share its benefits with others. And finally, how the acceptance by a Dáil majority of self-government with British dominion status for four-fifths of Ireland; and the ensuing civil war constituted a halt lasting to the 1930s to the political progress of the Revolution towards sovereign self-governing power.

3. *Narrate the internal Augmentation of the Acquired Non-sovereign Power over four-fifths of Ireland.* (Useful for this would be Diarmaid Ferriter's *'Lovers of Liberty?' Local Government in Twentieth-Century Ireland.*)

4. *Narrate the Cultural Reform (involving Establishment of New Values and Rules and Moral Purification) in the Irish Free State.* That in Dublin in 1921 Frank Duff founded a Catholic organisation for lay apostolate, the Legion of Mary, which would soon be spreading around the world. That on behalf of Catholic morality and nationalist sentiment there was a campaign against British newspapers and that in 1923 film censorship was introduced, with book censorship following six years later. That reforms in education favoured the Irish language. That a notable feature of the Moral Purification was the campaign against prostitution in Dublin, where the Legion of Mary functioned as the Irish equivalent of the Interdepartmental Commission to Combat Prostitution in the Russian Revolution and, in the French Revolution, the procurator-general's office of the Jacobin Commune. That the Moral Purification of one kind or another purported to show (cf. the moral regeneration promoted by Augustus in the Roman Revolution) the moral superiority of the new regime over its predecessor.)

5. *Narrate the Missionary Dissemination of the Revolution's Values.* Namely, that while news of the Irish Revolution kindled anti-imperialist sentiment in the overseas colonised world, in the early 1920s two new female missionary orders joined with the Maynooth Mission to China (founded in 1916) to launch the second great missionary movement of Irish history, which would grow into the 1930s and beyond. That many of the men and women members of the new orders along with their lay helpers had taken part in

the War of Independence and that they brought, together with the Christian message, opposition to imperialism to colonised African and Asian peoples, with impact through missionary schools and hospitals on nascent independence movements. (Here a footnote might state: 'In view of the full treatment given to the first Irish missionary movement—that of the sixth to seventh centuries—in the standard history of Ireland, and of the inclusion of the British missionary activity of the eighteenth to twentieth centuries in standard British history, the virtual omission of this second Irish missionary movement, greater than the first, from the standard academic history of Ireland has been, to say the least, eccentric. An unfortunate result is that much human and written testimony to this major aspect of twentieth-century Irish history in Africa, Asia and elsewhere has been lost to Irish historical research'.)

6. *Narrate the Near-completion of the Revolutionary Programme in the 1930s.* (In his book *The Evolution of Irish Nationalist Politics* and elsewhere, Tom Garvin shows that the Irish Revolution belongs to the category of twentieth-century anti-colonial independence movements and shares the characteristics of such movements. Among these characteristics are that the movement divides, not along European left-right lines, but into two wings more or less accommodating to the metropolitan power; and that after independence is achieved, governing power in the ex-colony is exercised initially by the more accommodating wing and subsequently by the less accommodating one.) How applying this to the Irish case would show the Republican wing, tinged strongly with Catholic Nationalism, passing in the 1930s from parliamentary Opposition to exercise of Government and in that role almost completing the Revolution's political programme by attaining a sovereign Irish republic in all but name in four-fifths of Ireland. And finally, that the new Constitution, while acknowledging that the State owed 'public worship to God', formally recognised, along with the other religions, 'the special position of the Holy Catholic Apostolic and Roman Church as the guardian of the Faith professed by the great majority of the citizens.'

The above is the merest sketch, open to amendment in detail, of what I imagine as the Irish Revolution finally receiving in historical narrative its deserts as a revolution of the Irish nation.

In early 2014, climbing the stairs to my apartment, I fell forward, broke my right wrist and dislocated my right shoulder. There were a few days in St Vincent's Hospital, Dublin, which I left with my arm in a sling. When the sling was gone and the injuries more or less healed I found myself walking more carefully than before even on flat surfaces, not to mention at kerbs and on steps, and for the first time in my life feeling 'old'! In the former Donnybrook Military Hospital where I attended a few times, my physiotherapy instructor told me, 'Stride, don't shuffle', and I try to do so when out walking!

To mark my eighty-fifth birthday on June 29 Natasha organised a lunch in Dublin's Unicorn restaurant. She tried to reunite as much as possible the bunch of people including our two selves who over twenty-five years before had habitually lunched there on a Saturday. So I met again some people whom I had not seen for years as well as friends who had not been Saturday Unicorners. One of the old friends was Michael D. Higgins, now President of Ireland, whom I knew as a colleague from those 'Gael-tacht revolutionary' days and UCG days in Galway. Somehow we found ourselves seated and chatting in a corner while most of the guests were standing. It struck me that he was happy to be doing just that, he made no move to move, and it was I who had to excuse myself saying, 'I suppose I ought to mingle'. Cilian made an eloquent, moving speech covering my life from Maoinis on. I saw people's faces changing in tune with his eloquent words.

The following month Miriam and I were in Würzburg, Germany, on the way to meet up by train with Natasha in the Fennells' one-time tem-porary home-town of Freiburg. Unexpectedly Cilian joined us in Würzburg, not suspecting that his visit would miraculously coincide with the feastday of his patron saint, the Irish seventh-century missionary Kilian who is king in those parts and even has a bread firm, Kilianbrot, named after him. Mary and I when resident in Freiburg had brought the infant Cilian there. To his delight he was now able to attend the High Mass celebrated in his patron's honour in the local cathedral where the saint is entombed.

On another day we went all together to visit another tomb, that of the wandering medieval singer-poet Walther von der Vogelweide, a life-long favourite of mine, whose statue, as I previously mentioned, stands in the main square of Bozen, Miriam's and my Christmas headquarters in South Tyrol. Standing beside the tomb, we heard Walther's most famous poem, 'Unter der Linde', *sung by an attendant, costumed bard.*

For some months Natasha had been working on a book with Róisín Ingle of The Irish Times *and a group of other women who were also daughters and who met regularly. The subject was the mother-daughter relationship and it was to be called* The Daughterhood *and published in London by Simon and Schuster. That autumn it was launched in Dublin and, as they say, 'flew off the shelves'. It was to be launched subsequently in translation in Italy, Germany, Korea and some other countries .*

Kate returned from Turkey, it seemed definitively, with a girl baby Anu whom she had conceived in a brief affair with a young Breton man during a Christmas visit to Ireland and to whom she spoke only Irish. Her intention was to settle down (if such were possible for her!) in a still Irish-speaking part of Conamara.

2015-16: Concluding Thoughts and Occurrences

RECALLING DE TOCQUEVILLE

REMARKABLE IN AMEROPE has been people's acceptance of the micro-management of their feelings, language, lives and work by neoliberal Correctors in the media, countless government agencies, and in Europe by an unelected and mostly distant power in Brussels that showers them with regulations which their governments must enact as laws. Most docile of all perhaps, in the English-speaking parts of Amerope, has been their obedience to microregulation of how they must write and speak their English language: an obedi-

ence not to laws but to forceful hints from journalists and bureaucrats that this and this are now the done thing when you write or
speak, the Correctorate says so.

It calls to mind Alexis de Tocqueville's portrayal in 1840 in *Democracy in America* of a possible final form of Liberal democracy. An
indefinable 'Power' would rule the masses; not a tyrant nor a despot,
nothing of the historically known kind, but absolutely effective in
exacting obedience. To quote de Tocqueville:

> The first thing that strikes the observation is an innumerable mul-
> titude of men [he means 'people'] all equal and alike, incessantly
> trying to procure the petty and paltry pleasures with which they
> glut their lives. Above this race of men there stands an immense and
> tutelary power... That power is absolute, minute, regular, provident
> and mild. It would be like the authority of a parent, if, like that au-
> thority, its object was to prepare men for manhood; but it seeks on
> the contrary to keep them in perpetual childhood. It is well content
> that the people should have a good time, provided they think of
> nothing but having a good time... For their happiness such a gov-
> ernment willingly labours, but it chooses to be the sole agent and
> the only arbiter of that happiness; it provides for their security, fore-
> sees and supplies their necessities, facilitates their pleasures, manages
> their principal concerns, directs their industry, regulates the descent
> of property, and subdivides their inheritances: what remains, but to
> spare them all the care of thinking and all the trouble of living?...
>
> After having thus successively taken each member of the com-
> munity [each 'individual'] in its powerful grasp and fashioned him
> ['or her'] at will, the supreme power then extends its arm over the
> whole community. It covers the surface of society with a network
> of small complicated rules, minute and uniform, through which
> the most original minds and the most energetic characters cannot
> penetrate to rise above the crowd. The will of man is not shattered,
> but softened, bent, and guided; men are seldom forced by it to act,
> but they are constantly restrained from acting. Such a power does
> not destroy, but it prevents existence; it does not tyrannize, but it
> compresses, enervates, extinguishes, and stupefies a people, till each
> nation is reduced to nothing better than a flock of timid and indus-

trious animals, of which the government is the shepherd.

Perhaps, unknown to us, something like de Tocqueville's vision has come to pass and this is how neoliberal democracy is today—a sort of soft totalitarianism.

IS IRISH BECOMING LIKE LATIN?*

LATIN, A DEAD language, is taught in thousands of schools. A Latin online daily bulletin gives the world's news and carries ads. A radio station broadcasts the news weekly in Latin. Latin enthusiasts organise social gatherings. But despite all this, Latin remains a dead language. Is Irish is on the way to becoming like Latin?

For a minority language under pressure by a dominant language to have a chance of living into the future, it needs to have a sizeable self-renewing community speaking and writing it. With the former Gaeltacht districts now completing Ireland's shift from Irish to English, the Irish language has no such community.

Most of us don't want to speak Irish, but we like to have Irish in our lives. We cherish it, the surveys show, as a precious part of our national heritage. We are glad there are Gaelscoileanna, a Rádió na Gaeltachta and a TG4; that the destinations of buses are shown in Irish as well as English, and to hear that there is a magazine of news and comment in Irish on the internet. We would not like everything in Ireland to be in English only.

However, the aim and purpose of the Irish language movement since its origin over a hundred years ago has always gone beyond having state-funded teaching of Irish and other state-funded public uses of Irish to remind the nation that we have this heritage. Primarily the movement's aim has been to maintain and extend Irish as the language used by Irish people in their daily lives. So the fact that, at this late stage, no sizeable self-renewing community of Irish speakers exists betokens for the language movement a failure or, less dramatically, an emergency.

I suggest we treat it as an emergency and counter it as best we can by redefining the language movement as an effort to make Irish

---

* *Galway Advertiser*, Sept. 2015. I published an article on the same lines in Irish in *tuairisc.ie* online.

survive as a living language among the languages of Europe. That would mean creating out of the Irish-language resources available to us something as near as possible to a sizeable self-renewing community that speaks Irish well.

The most valuable achievement of the language movement hitherto is that there are now several thousand men and women throughout Ireland who speak and write Irish well; that is, as correctly, and with as wide a vocabulary, as the average educated user of any other European language. Collectively, therefore, these people in their speech and writing are a national treasure because they embody the Irish language alive today. Indeed, because of their wide diversity of circumstance and occupation, they embody it more fully than any Gaeltacht did.

Identify a thousand of these people and obtain their consent to be jointly responsible—together with others whom they would admit to their number through an annual examination up to a total of 8,000– for the survival of the Irish language as a living language. Have them agree on a name for the language community they would form; undertake to have Irish spoken in their households and hold general and regional conventions. They would choose a discreet badge that they would wear on their clothing to identify themselves to each other and to people generally.

That badge would become a mark of positive distinction. The annual entrance examination for new members would become a big national occasion. It would provide a prestigious goal for Gaelcholáistí and for the university courses in Irish. Apart from the holding of its conventions, this body of Irish-language perpetuators would carry out its remit simply by living, speaking and writing Irish and growing annually. Being enthusiasts for the language they would prove resourceful beyond their remit,

This is doable. It is the nearest thing possible to that sizeable, self-renewing community of people living together that we lack. I can think of no reason why it should not be done. If it is not done, Irish will be well on the way to becoming a dead language; a language spoken or written in classrooms, on radio and TV, or as the cúplaí focal of politicians and on the destination signs of buses. All this reminding us, symbolically, like a reproving ghost, of the language we could have kept alive.

A MORALITY THAT DOES NOT MAKE SENSE★

IT'S ABOUT BEING good, we were told, when teachers in the mass media urged us to endorse contraception, casual sex, abortion and same-sex marriage; to write Ms instead of Mrs or Miss, first-name everyone and avoid new evil *isms* with American names. Add these practices of compassion and equality, we were told, to the OK elements of the old European morality and you will be enlightened, liberal, progressive, in short, good people. Such was and is the new hybrid morality that we have been adopting since the 1970s when American left-liberalism spread its wings, imperially, across the West.

Those left-liberal idealists (they were to become neoliberals and to call themselves plain 'liberals') were animated, like their Russian communist counterparts, by moral disapproval of European civilisation and a vision of its just amendment and replacement. They were also countering with the support of small minorities of citizens—using the mass media, parliaments and supreme courts—the similarly godless and hybrid communist morality that was being imposed on Eastern Europe and evangelising westwards. They were a recrudescence of American Puritanism in secular form.

The American state and business corporations, mass media included, had noted the profit that could be made from these new rules of behaviour, thought and language. So the new 'liberal agenda' obtained their backing, and automatically that of the states and big business of Western Europe.

Thus this neoliberalism (the classical liberalism that partly shapes the Irish Constitution buried) supplied the ethic of the consumerist decades leading up to the Crash. That same alliance of social idealism with money-making by states and business is trying now, led by the mass media, to revive those halcyon days.

Human beings inherit from their millennia of experience an intuitive ability to assess the presence or absence of *sense* in the morality—the framework for life—that is prescribed for them by their

★ Written May 2016, published in *Ireland's Eye*, Mullingar, August 2016.

rulers. This is not a matter of assessing the justice or correctness of the morality. It is an assessment, rather, of the coherence of its rules with each other, and with human needs and the felt general nature of things. Such coherence is one necessary characteristic for the morality to make sense. Another is suggested by those historical societies that we call 'civilisations'.

That these civilisations perceived and felt sense in their respective moralities is attested by the fact that, unless destroyed by an outside force, they lasted for hundreds or more of years. And we note that in each instance—the morality's coherence being a given—it also had a venerated source, supernatural or human (seer, lawgiver, holy man or the ancestors).

So it seems reasonable to conclude that for a morality to make sense to people as a framework for life, it needs to have both coherence and a venerated source, supernatural or human. If it lacks these characteristics, it presents, rather than a framework that makes sense, senselessness.

The American neoliberal morality, while advancing over the past fifty years, has lacked those characteristics: basic coherence by being a hybrid of old and new; a venerated source, quite obviously. And the signs are that those to whom the corrective zeal of the neoliberal idealists has been principally directed—white Westerners—have been finding, consciously or subconsciously, the resulting life senseless. Most fundamentally, their desire to reproduce such a life has flagged. The white populations of Western Europe face steep falls in the next ten years. Among the ethnic groups in the US, the only fertility rate lower than that of white people is that of the Native Americans.

The plight of the Native Americans is instructive. It mirrors the well-known phenomenon of all so-called 'primitive tribes' after European colonisers had made them insert elements of European morality into their systems of moral rules derived from some venerated source. The result for the consequently hybrid system was the absence of such a source and an incoherence that by way of senselessness produced anomie or normlessness: spreading alcoholism, sexual licence, suicides and falling fertility.

Small wonder, then, that the West's senseless reigning morality

has had effects on Westerners similar to those which European co-
lonialism had on those 'primitive tribes'.

Witness the more sensitive of us, particularly if young, feeling a
pain of soul that issues in recurrent attempts to annihilate consciousness: temporarily by binge-drinking or drugs or—at a rising rate in
the past fifty years—permanently; the sharp-eyed types who, reading the senselessness as normlessness, have grown rich by supplying
the drugs; or, if bankers, by cutting corners; if statesmen, by spying
on citizens; if angry, by making murder, once a rare occurrence here
in Ireland, something that seems to happen every week or fortnight.

In two key respects, the consumerist-liberal morality has been
particularly bad for Western women. Since the 1970s the spaces and
times in which a woman can move safely alone have been diminishing. Only in the aftermaths of great wars have so many mothers had
to rear their children alone.

That a society of human beings faced with senselessness cannot last stands to reason. After a few decades disintegration sets in
and ultimately—as the fate of the Russian Communist experiment
shows—completes itself. When the West's turn comes, and signs of it
are there, it will be time for Ameropeans to get serious. Indeed, that
time is already here and advance thinking about what we will do
then is in order. This time round, no anti-human utopia, but—with
an eye to how China transits culturally from old to new—a new
civilisation. Our European ancestors began to build an enduring
one a thousand years ago.

*Last year, 2015, in November, Miriam was elected to the standing com-
mittee of her trade union, the Association of Secondary Schoolteachers of
Ireland (ASTI), and has since then been unfolding her political skills.*

*This year is the 100ᵗʰ anniversary of the 1916 Rising and I have been
pleased to see a generously large celebration by the State and the media
and by many local communities throughout the land. Cilian played a
notable part by organising and directing a TV show, 'Centenary' on RTÉ,
which the public widely enjoyed and acclaimed.*

On 18 June I attended with Miriam a discussion of 'The Return of

Nationalism' at the Dalkey Book Festival. The participants were two Indians, two Irish and a Scot, and it dealt mainly with Russia and certain countries of the European Union. At its end when interventions from the audience were invited I wanted to say, but did not say, something like this: 'It seems odd that there is this discussion of "the return of nationalism" in a country where there is no such return. Nearly fifty years ago, when the matter of our entering the European Economic Community arose and was put to referendum, our Prime Minister Jack Lynch told us: "Because Britain is joining we have no alternative but to join", thereby conveying that the long struggle for Irish independence had been ultimately in vain. The Irish government, acting on our behalf, does not assert Ireland's interests among the nations. Take a very present well-known instance: an Irish citizen, Ibrahim Halawa, has been imprisoned in Egypt for three years on a trumped-up charge and without appearance in court. The Irish government, well aware of this, has done nothing notable about it. The word "meek" was invented to describe Ireland's stance among the nations.'

On the night of 22 June in Galway, with Oisín, Cathy and Ron present and her favourite piece of music, Carmina Burana, *playing, dear Mary died. I am deeply sad, but also glad that a week ago, talking to her on the phone, I had said: 'Mary, you know that you remain for me that little girl of all those years ago to whom one day I said "I am in love with you, will you marry me?" And with your Yes, a long story began.' She laughed, throatily, and said, 'Yes, Desmond, a long story.' Three of the children of that story, Natasha, Cilian and Sorcha, organised the wake and funeral Mass in Galway. With Miriam driving, we went there for both. Brexit surprised us via television in the course of the night. Many people attended from near and far, including sister Rosemary from Oxford, two of my Glenelly cousins, several women from Maoinis and a female attaché from President Michael D. Today, 27 June, I went to the cremation ceremony in Dublin. I was disappointed that at the ceremonies in Galway and Dublin, with readings and brief speeches organised beforehand, the organisers had not allotted any role to me.*

In two days, Thursday 29 June, it will be my 87th birthday. After my

85th celebration in the Unicorn restaurant organised by Natasha, I got her to agree that in future there would be a special birthday celebration only every five years. So especially since it falls so near to Mary's death I expect a quiet day with Mel next Thursday.

Bhí saol maith agam go dtí seo, buíochas le Dia. Sláinte coirp fós agam agus m'intinn ag obair go maith. Gura fada beo mé le Mel, mo chlann agus mo cháirde! Tá mo scéal go dtí seo inste agam.

INDEX OF PEOPLE AND PLACES